2001 SUPPLEMENT

INFORMATION SYSTEMS

Policies and Procedures Manual

GEORGE JENKINS

PRENTICE HALL

Library of Congress Cataloging-in-Publication Data

Jenkins, George Henry.
    Information systems policies & procedures manual / George H. Jenkins. —2nd ed.
      p. cm.
    Includes index.
    ISBN 0-13-255845-9   ISBN 0-13-030673-8 (2001 Supplement)
    1. Management information systems.   2. Information resources management.
    I. Title.
    T58.6.J465 1997   97-29527
    004′.068′4—dc20   CIP

This publication is designed to provide accurate and authoritative information in regard to the subject matter covered. It is sold with the understanding that the publisher is not engaged in rendering legal, accounting, or other professional services. If legal advice or other expert assistance is required, the services of a competent professional person should be sought.

    —*From a Declaration of Principles jointly adopted by a committee of the American Bar Association and a committee of Publishers and Associations.*

Printed in the United States of America

10 9 8 7 6 5 4 3 2 1

ISBN 0-13-030673-8

ATTENTION: CORPORATIONS AND SCHOOLS

Prentice Hall books are available at quantity discounts with bulk purchase for educational, business, or sales promotional use. For information, please write to: Prentice Hall Special Sales, 240 Frisch Court, Paramus, NJ 07652. Please supply: title of book, ISBN, quantity, how the book will be used, date needed.

PRENTICE HALL
Paramus, NJ 07652

On the World Wide Web at http://www.phdirect.com

INTRODUCTION

The *Information Systems Policies and Procedures Manual, 2000 Cumulative Supplement* is a comprehensive update. Using this manual as an updated supplement guide, model, and frequent decision-making reference, an information systems policy and procedure program uniquely tailored to the needs of any organization can be devised. No two information systems operations could pass for twins, but they have elements in common: hardware, software, and personnel. This supplement defines these common threads that link all information systems operations, providing for a variety of situations; it is not a "one size fits all."

"Simplicity is the ultimate design." Often, an overabundance of forms is included in policies and procedures manuals, but this supplement guidebook attempts to provide a minimum. Frequently, a well-written memo or e-mail message can take the place of a form and reduce the complexity of an IT operation. The more complex an operation, the more fence-mending is required to keep it working. IS operations that have a formal systems and procedures manual in place are noticeably much better run.

The role of IT management is changing even more quickly than information technology itself. Today the IS operation is no longer found in some obscure corner of the corporate organization. Instead, it plays an interactive role in global systems. This manual will help with the formalization of policies and procedures that are needed for a formal program of documentation of the IS operation. This can be done with the savings of both time and effort by using the manual and this supplement, which identifies standard operations documentation needed but still allows for special needs.

End-user computer systems will grow with or without the guidance of corporate IS, but the two working together in concert will provide a synergistic dividend. This supplement updates the policies and procedures that can expedite this objective.

The research conducted for this book revealed many well-run information systems operations and some real disasters. The better ones had noticeably good management and practical documentation. Expensive consultants, fad innovations, and cutting-edge technology did not always produce the desired IT results.

The *Information Systems Policies and Procedures Manual, Cumulative Supplement* is not a product of the academic, theoretical dreamworld: it is a compilation of new supplemental information systems policies and procedures. It is an applications supplement that any seasoned information systems manager, working in a large or small IS operation, will find useful alongside the original manual.

In terms of setup, this supplement is numbered consecutively throughout. It is intended as a companion to the policies and procedures set forth in the main volume. Each section number is preceded by the letter S, indicating supplement. The comprehensive index included with this supplement catalogs all subjects in both main volume and supplement—entries found in this book will be preceded by the letter S.

A CD has been attached to the back of this manual. The CD contains the manual's forms and text, which can be downloaded and used by a PC.

ABOUT THE AUTHOR

Dr. Jenkins has spent 23 years as a professional IS practitioner. He began his career as an engineering programmer with General Electric, where he wrote an engineering end-user's policy and procedure manual; continued as a systems analyst with Xerox where he wrote an internal manual, *The Principles of Stock Keeping*; and worked as a DP operations manager with Columbia Record Club of CBS.

He was the Administrative Coordinator for Capital Record Club and Capital Record Club of Canada where he wrote a manual on how to write policies and procedures. He was also Director for Systems and DP operations for Nicolson File Company and an administrator for Wayne County General Hospital (University of Michigan teaching hospital).

His other accomplishments include: writing one of the first artificial intelligence programs (which designed electric motors for General Electric); designing, programming, and successfully installing the first exponential smoothing inventory control system; installing the second online real-time data collection system for production control, and converting the second-largest business unit record operation to computers.

Dr. Jenkins has had articles published in the *Journal of Systems Management* and the *Data Management* magazine, and is the author of *Data Processing Policies and Procedures Manual*. He has also earned his CDP, CDE, and CSP.

He is currently a Professor Emeritus of Systems Analysis with the University of Findlay where he developed a four-year degree program for systems analysis. He has had hundreds of systems graduates with the highest job placement record of any other discipline at the university.

Dr. Jenkins is currently involved with reengineering systems analysis research, teaching, writing, consulting, etc. He may be reached at: e-mail jen.acres@juno.com or FAX (419) 531-0725.

CO-AUTHOR

Michael Wallace has spent 19 years in the information systems field. He began his career after graduation from Lima Technical College as a mainframe operator for Super Food Services and then moved to a programming position at Reynolds+Reynolds.

He became a consultant after graduating Magna Cum Laude from Wright State University with a Bachelor of Science degree in Management Science. For eight years he was President of Q Consulting, a custom application development firm.

Mr. Wallace is currently Director of Project Services for Information Control Corporation, a mid-sized consulting firm specializing in client/server n-tier development, Internet application development, and mobile application development using handheld and wearable devices. The Project Services division provides "turn-key" solutions and offers an outsourcing alternative to our clients.

Mr. Wallace is a Microsoft Certified Professional, has served as Vice President of the Columbus Computer Society, and has served on the board of directors of the local DPMA chapter. He is presently a member of the Association of Internet Professionals, the Project Management Institute, and serves on the boards of various organizations.

Mr. Wallace can be reached by e-mail at michaelw@columbus.rr.com.

ACKNOWLEDGMENTS

Writing this book has been a challenge because of the technology explosion of IT. By the time one gets to the end of the book, technology changes are already being developed for the first supplement.

This book is dedicated to our wives. With them, Patricia Jenkins and Tami Wallace, it was all possible.

Our extended thanks to Susan M. McDermott, acquisitions editor at Prentice Hall, who foresaw the need for this supplement.

CONTENTS

Chapter 6 Ancillary Support Systems—S6-1

Chapter 8 IS Human Resource Retention—S8-1

Chapter 9 Internet and E-mail—S9-1

Chapter 10 Mobile Devices—S10-1

Chapter 1
COMPUTER HARDWARE ACQUISITIONS

1. POLICY

S1.1 COMPUTER ACQUISITIONS POLICY

The purpose of the computer acquisition policy is to formalize a uniform standard for computer hardware acquisitions throughout the organization. This policy mandates the endorsement and support by the CEO/head of the organization.

S1.1.1 Scope

The computer acquisition policy covers all computers, computer-related hardware, and supply items used by the organization. The organization is composed of units that are under the authority of the person that mandates the computer acquisition policy.

S1.1.2 Policy Objectives

This policy objective is to provide the guidelines for: proposing and recommending benchmarks, maintaining uniform standards, vendor contacting, vendor selection, vendor communications, and issuing purchase requisitions and purchase orders. This also covers receiving the hardware, testing, and approval for payment to the vendor. It will be the responsibility of the information systems unit generating the policy and procedure manual to provide this information and subsequent changes to all unit heads with in the organization. Unit heads that currently do not have any computer equipment shall also receive a copy of this chapter.

S1.1.3 Asset Management Policy

Information systems is responsible for maintaining and enforcing a company-wide computer hardware asset management program. The head of information systems will assign the computer software asset management responsibility to the information technology asset manager. An information systems hardware committee will be formed. The chairperson of the committee will be the information technology asset manager.

All user unit supervisors will comply fully with the policy. There will be procedures to enforce this policy. Any past acquisitions not on the current approved computer hardware list can still be authorized by the head of information systems. Current acquisitions are required to be on the list. In cases of special hardware needs, which are not on the Approved Computer Hardware List, a waiver may be granted by the head of information systems.

All computer hardware and related hardware of any kind are not permitted on the company's property that is not owned by the firm. Special permission can be granted by information technology management to vendors. Employee-owned computer hardware, related hardware, electronic devices, mobile phones, personal pagers, and magnetic devices are not allowed on company-owned property.

2. NEEDS ANALYSIS

S1.2 MAJOR SYSTEMS ACQUISITIONS

S1.2.1 Definition of Major Hardware Acquisitions

Any projects that affect more than one department and/or do not have any budgeted funds allocated for such a system are identified as major computer systems acquisitions by the head of information systems. User managers will send a memo to the head of the information systems unit and a copy to the person who the head of information systems reports to. This memo will address the needs for a major computer system acquisition. The memo can originate from one or more user management person(s) or the systems analysis unit's head.

The memo will cover the following issues:

- The firm's area(s) that will be affected by the new system.
- A defined need for the acquisition.

- Cost savings expected, and the expected life span of the proposed system.

- The maximum calendar time allowed for the expected system to be operational.

- A priority ranking will be provided for this project as compared to others under study or development.

S1.2.2 Analysis of New Systems Request

The head of information systems and his/her superior will review the requesting memo. Management will evaluate the merits of doing a preliminary systems needs study and the status of the total organization's budget situation. The information systems head will send a reply memo to the requesting manager. The information systems head will send a memo for the reason for the denial or approval for a feasibility study. If approved, a preliminary systems needs study (which is identified as a feasibility study) will be done. A memo to that effect will be sent to the head of systems analysis. The memo will ask for a feasibility study and provide the following information:

- When results of the study are to be expected.

- The people and monetary resources provided for the study.

- What user personnel are to be contacted.

- What level of confidentiality is expected of the preliminary systems needs study.

S1.2.3 Feasibility Study

An analysis of the users' areas can assist the feasibility study before it is under taken. The information would be helpful before attempting to contact the users for a formal study. Gather as much information about the units as possible before conducting a formal study of the units.

Contact the user personnel identified in the memo received for the assigned the project. Remembering the names of the unit's personnel and their respective titles would be helpful. Also, find out who controls the informal unit organization, who at times can be known as the power behind the throne. These people can influence the feasibility study, and even more so when and if a new system is in place. Any knowledge of corporate politics that the unit may be involve in can be helpful. The status of the corporate pecking order of the units will provide insight of the ability of the proposed computer system getting off the ground.

Examine current procedural documentation. Follow up with a study of the actual procedures followed by the employees of the units. The operating procedure study should include input and output documents. All existing files will be documented—these include hard copy and computer files. Computer files and their sources will be documented, including the following:

- Data files only on given computers.
- Data files on local area networks.
- Identify the local area network server's databases.
- Data used from other sources.

The current systems operation studied should provide the following information needed for a final systems design to be completed later:

- System flowcharts.
- Dataflow diagrams.
- Document flowcharts.
- Data dictionary
- Current procedure flowcharts.
- Any work sampling studies done.
- Current operations costs (i.e., direct costs and indirect costs).
- Generated reports and/or computer monitor displays.

An evaluation of the proposed system is made for its justification. The feasibility will be determined by several factors:

A. The operation feasibility

   Operation feasibility analysis determines if the solution will meet end-user requirements: does the solution fit into the end-user operational environment and meet the requirements of an acceptable time schedule? It ascertains meeting the user's human factors requirements and also fits into the organization's social work scene.

B. The technical feasibility

   Technical feasibility analysis determines if the solution is technically practical: is the technology available or soon to be available and can the end-user and the facilities accommodate the solution?

C. Economic feasibility

   Economic feasibility analysis determines if the solution meets measurements of cost effectiveness. It is justified by a cost/benefit analysis. There can be situations that may override economic feasibility. This is when government legislation, customer requirements, or union contracts mandate that it will be done.

When it is completed, the feasibility study will be sent to the head of information systems for his/her approval. When the head of information systems approves the feasibility study, he/she will write a cover memo. The memo will be attached to the report and sent to the his/her superior, and all user managers involved in the original needs request.

If the feasibility study is not approved, a copy will be returned to the authors of the study with recommendations noted on the document. A cover memo will be written and attached to the returned study reviewing why the study was being rejected and what is needed for it to be approved. The required changes and/or additions to the study will be done. If needed, a revised study will be resubmitted for the final approval of the head of information systems.

S1.2.4 Final Systems Design

The final approved system design will be one of the following:

- A turn-key system provided and operated by a third-party vendor.
- A turn-key system provided by a vendor.
- Company-acquired hardware with a third party providing the software.
- An in-house–produced software with a company-acquired computer hardware.
- An in-house–produced software with a company-acquired computer hardware with vendor assistance.

Whatever system design and installation will be designated by the head of information systems and his/her superior will designate the system design and installation to be implemented. Each of the noted installations has their own merit. It is up to the systems designer to rank his/her recommendations. Management approval is required for the final systems design and operation.

The priority placed by management will determine the priority of the project. The new major computer system will determine the resources and time-frame with which it will be installed. The systems designer that performed the feasibility study will (at a minimum) be available to assist the project's completion. The head of information systems and of the head of the systems unit determines the degree the project is supported by the current resources. A project manager will be appointed to manage the project's completion. Chapter 14, Project Management, of the main volume provides the project management procedures that will be followed.

S1.2.5 Systems Installation

Major computer systems acquisitions occur to either replace current operating systems or to obtain non-existing operation. There are advantages for both. Departments with current operating systems can provide knowledgeable workers who are familiar with the tasks and objectives that are to be attained. There will, however, be operations to unlearn that will provide varying degrees of problems.

A proposed new system operation (for a non-existing operation) does not have the problem of workers unlearning the old system skills. It actually has fewer options to select from for installing a new system. There are basically two types that are available within this group. One is a totally new integrated computer system—it presents the most challenge. Systems most often have to become operational all at once, and bugs must be worked out on the fly. The other type is a major computer system, which can be segmented. It allows for phasing in one segment at a time and debugging it before going on to the next segment. This system provides for far less problems.

New computer installations, which are not replacing a current operation, offer better learning environments. The employees do not have to unlearn an old system while learning a new computer system that does not yet have all the bugs worked out. They usually have a closer attachment to the new computer system. Scheduling employees for user training for brand new systems can be less of a problem.

Current systems in operation can be replaced with a new system in the following ways:

- Run both systems in parallel until the new system is operational.
- Install the new system in segments—do not go on to a new segment until the last segment is operational.
- Cut over to the new system as the old system is stopped at the same time.

Running parallel systems is the most costly but is the safest way to go. Cutting over to a new operation while stopping the old system is the least costly—if it works.

3. COMPUTER HARDWARE BUDGETS

S1.3 BUDGETED COMPUTER HARDWARE ACQUISITIONS

Computer budgeting can be done in several forms. Hardware budgets are allocated for the entire process of designing and placing the computer system into operations. This is a budgeted item that may cover one or more budget years. Other budgeted hardware acquisitions can be found in different budgeting forms. There are several options with which to acquire computer hardware. One or more may be employed by the organization.

S1.3.1 Information Systems Hardware Committee

The head of information systems will assign the computer hardware asset management responsibility to the information technology asset manager. An information systems hardware committee will be formed. The chairperson of the committee will be the information technology asset manager. The information systems head will appoint members from the programming, operations, and systems technology areas. A representative will be appointed by the purchasing manager. The committee will provide information required for the maintenance of the approved computer hardware list.

No less often than a monthly update of any added or deleted hardware will be made to the asset management hardware database. An asset management hardware status report will be issued monthly. The report will be made available to committee members one week before committee meeting. Minutes of each monthly and special meeting will be kept. Approved copies of the minutes will be sent by the to the committee members and the head of information systems.

Any hardware that is not on the current approved computer hardware list will be flagged. The approved computer hardware list is a screening device for current computer hardware acquisitions. The information will be current and available via online access or published listings. Past acquisitions not on the current approved computer hardware list can still be authorized by the head of information systems. Current acquisitions are required to be on the list. New computer hardware acquisitions may be placed on the list. The approved computer hardware list will be updated and distributed by the chairperson of the information systems hardware committee.

In cases of special one-time hardware needs, which are not on the approved computer hardware list, a waiver may be granted for the acquisition. A request will be sent to the chairperson of the information systems hardware committee. The chairperson will bring the request before the information systems hardware committee. The committee will reply to the request. The reply memo will be sent to the head of information systems for his/her final approval.

Approved memos will be signed by the head of information systems, and sent on to the person requesting the hardware. The IT hardware person will be sent a copy of the memo. Disapproved requests will be returned to the committee for their follow up action. These special hardware items will be added to the Asset Management Hardware database when placed into service.

S1.3.2 Corporate Lump-Sum Budget

Senior management will allocate a lump-sum budget based on information provided by the information systems head. The information systems head may assign the task to collect the information for the hardware needs to the information technology asset manager.

A. Defining needs

The starting point for the distribution of computer hardware would be a user unit head originating a memo requesting the equipment. The memo sent to the IT asset manager should contain the following information:

- The reason for the request.
- The date that it is needed.
- What, if any, other equipment it will be replacing, and the dispossession of the equipment the computer hardware will replace.
- Is the request to satisfy a temporary or permanent need? If the need is temporary, when will it be expected to be returned?

B. IT hardware loans

The IT hardware person will review the request in light of other approvals to the same unit. If it is not approved, a memo to that effect will be sent to the person asking for the hardware, and the reason for refusing the request. The memo may be in the form of a hard copy memo or e-mailed to the person. A copy of the memo will be stored with the request file for that unit. The copy may be in the form of hard copy or a file maintained in a computer database.

If the loan of equipment is available and approved, it will be issued from the reserve equipment stock. Organizations with a computer store will provide for the loan of the hardware. Whichever unit provides the equipment will maintain a follow-up file. Such further information as recording who signed for the equipment, the unit to which it is to be loaned, and the expected return date information must be filed by return date. The expected return dates will be followed up by the person making the loan. If the computer hardware is borrowed from another department the information technology asset manager will be informed of the loan.

C. Stocked hardware

If the information systems unit maintains a stock of computer hardware, the IT hardware person will issue the hardware from the stock supply. He/she will update the computer inventory stock file for the items taken from stock. The hardware may also be made available from the company computer store. The store's inventory record will be updated. The IT hardware person will post an approval and date and sign the memo. He/she will also record on the memo the proper item name and tag number of the hardware. The original copy the memo will be filed, a copy will be returned to requesting unit manager, and a copy will be sent to the information technology asset manager.

D. Hardware purchasing

Computer hardware that must be purchased is selected from an approved computer hardware list. The approved list is sanctioned by the information systems head. The head of information systems approves additions or deletions to the list. The list will contain the current or last purchase price of each item. Any significant price changes or pending change information will be sent to the information systems asset manager.

The IT asset manager will issue a purchase requisitions based on hardware stock needs or a memo from a user manager. If the needs of the user manager cannot be met, the user manager will be contacted by the IT asset manager. The user manager may appeal his/her needs to the information systems head. The information systems manager will make the final judgment. The requisition will be sent to the purchasing department. A copy will also be sent to the IT hardware person and the requesting unit manger. The purchasing department will issue a purchase order. A copy of the purchase order will be sent to the IT hardware person. The IT hardware person will compare and attach the purchase order to the purchase requisition and placed them in the open order file. If the two documents do not match up, the IT hardware person will contact the IT asset manager.

There may or may not be competitive bids for the item. The IT asset manager will determine the need for competitive bids, and provide information for any vendor contacting.

E. Accepting purchased hardware

The receiving department will contact the IT hardware person with the arrival of any computer hardware order by sending the packing slip that came with the shipment. The IT hardware person is responsible for confirming that the delivered hardware was what was ordered by the purchase requisition. The IT hardware person will authorize the delivery of the computer hardware if all is in order. If there is a problem with the delivery, purchasing or the vendor will be contacted. The individual who can best resolve the problem will be selected. The packing slip will be attached to the purchase requisition and purchase order and placed in a received file. A copy of the order invoice will be filed with the other papers in the received file.

All purchased and leased hardware will be tagged with a company identification tag. If the company does not have an asset property tagging procedure for identifying capital assets, the information technology asset manager will provide one. The procedure will have all received computer hardware tagged with an asset tag. The tag identification number will be written on the receiving report sent to the information technology asset manager. The IT hardware person will update his/her own received file records with the tag identification information.

He/she will notify the accounts payable department that the invoice for the received items can now be paid. The memo will contain the following information:

- The name and address of the vendor.
- The date the items arrived.
- The purchase order number for the invoice.
- A description of the items received.
- The expected dollar amount to be paid.
- Any early payment discount information.

S1.3.3 Itemized Computer Budgets

Organizations that itemize computer hardware budgets will require department heads to itemize each computer hardware item as part of their budgeting request.

A. Defining computer needs

The department head will provide a list of computer hardware, with expected costs for the items. This information is required for the itemized computer budget. As a preliminary step before submitting the budget request, the department head should contact the IT asset manager to confirm current prices and approval granted by the approved computer hardware list.

Departments with itemized computer budgets may want to change the hardware requirements of yet not expended items. The department head can appeal to the head of information systems. The information systems head may approve of changing the items within the itemized computer budget. This may be done as long as the total dollars allocated to the purchase of these items is not exceeded. The head of information systems will do it on a per item bases.

Computer hardware loans may be made to units with an itemized computer budget. A memo will be sent to the IT hardware person should contain the following information:

- The reason for the request.
- The date that it is needed.
- The date when it will be expected to be returned.

B. Computer hardware procurement

Departments that have itemized computer hardware budgets will procure their computer hardware through the IT hardware person. The loan of hardware will be requested by a memo from the department head. Purchases will require the writing of a purchase reacquisition by the department head. Both documents are sent to the IT hardware person.

1. IT hardware loan requests will be sent to the IT hardware person, who will review the request in light of other approvals to the same department. If it is disapproved, a memo to that effect will be sent to the person requesting the hardware, along with the reason for refusing the request. The memo may be in the form of a hard copy memo or e-mailed to the person. A copy of the memo will be stored with the request file for that unit. The copy may be in the form of hard copy or a file maintained in a computer data base.

   If the loan of equipment is available and approved, it will be issued from the reserve equipment stock. Organizations with a computer store may provide for the loan of the hardware. Whichever system is used a follow-up file will be maintained as to who signed for the equipment, the unit to which it is to be loaned, and the expected return date. The expected return dates will be followed up by the person making the loan. If the computer hardware is borrowed from another department, the asset manager will be informed of this loan.

2. For purchased computer hardware, the user department manager will complete a purchase requisition. He/she will send it to the IT hardware person. The IT hardware person will check with their records that are maintained for the unit's itemized budget and the approved computer hardware list. The records will be updated by item and cost. The hardware item may be a stocked item. If it is not a stocked item the next procedure to follow will be the purchasing of the hardware (see C. Purchasing hardware).

3. Stocked hardware will be made available from the information systems stock supply by the IT hardware person or from the computer store's reserve stock. The IT hardware person will update the computer inventory stock file for the items taken from stock and also approve and sign the purchase requisition. Both copies of the purchase requisition will have noted that the item was supplied from which stock, dated, and signed. The first copy will be filed and the second copy will be returned to requesting unit manager. The asset manager will be informed of the computer hardware transfer.

C. Purchasing hardware

For an item not available from stock, but which is on the approved computer hardware list, the IT hardware person will approve and sign the purchase requisition. He/she will forward the approved requisition to the purchasing department. The IT hardware person will contact the originator of the purchase requisition that the item has been ordered and if there is any problem.

D. Accepting purchased hardware

The receiving department will contact the IT hardware person with the arrival of any computer hardware order by sending the packing slip that came with the shipment. The IT hardware person is responsible for confirming that the delivered hardware was what was ordered by the purchase requisition. The IT hardware person will authorize the delivery of the computer if all is in order. If there is a problem with the delivery, purchasing or the vendor will be contacted. The one who can best resolve the problem will be selected. The packing slip will be attached to the purchase requisition and purchase order and placed in a received file. A copy of the order invoice will filed with the other papers in the received file.

All purchased and leased hardware will be tagged with a company identification tag. If the company does not have an asset property tagging procedure for identifying capital assets, the information technology asset manager will provide one. The procedure will have all received computer hardware tagged with an asset tag. The tag identification number will be written on the receiving report sent to the information technology asset manager. The IT hardware person will update his/her own received file records with the tag identification information.

He/she will notify the accounts payable department that the invoice for the received items can now be paid. The memo will contain the following information:

- The name and address of the vendor.
- The date the items arrived.
- The purchase order number for the invoice.
- A description of the items received.
- The expected dollar amount to be paid.
- Any early payment discount information.

S1.3.4 Departments' Lump-Sum Computer Budgets

Organizations that budget computer hardware for each department will have the department head apply for the computer hardware as part of their budgeting request. The department head will provide an expected budgeted amount for their computer hardware needs. The department head has the flexibility of adjusting his/her product mix with changing needs with in the department's budget year.

A. Defining computer needs

The department head will contact the IT asset manager to confirm current prices and permission granted by the approved computer hardware list for items planned. The item costs will be totaled, and this amount will be applied for in the budget year. The approved lump sum will start the computer acquisition hardware process. As items are ordered, the order sum of money will be reduced from the remaining lump sum budget. Contingency funds are seldom required because of falling computer hardware costs.

Computer hardware loans may be made to units with a lump sum computer budget. The memo sent to the IT hardware person should contain the following information:

- The reason for the request.
- The date that it is needed.
- The date when it will be expected to be returned.

B. Computer hardware procurement

Departments that have lump-sum computer hardware budgets will procure their computer hardware through the IT hardware person. The loan of hardware will be requested by a memo from the department head. Purchases will require a purchase reacquisition form from the department head. Both documents are sent to the IT hardware person.

1. IT hardware loan requests will be received by the IT hardware person who will review the request in light of other approvals to the same department. If loan is not approved, a memo to that effect will be sent to the person asking for the hardware, along with the reason for refusing the request. The memo may be in the form of a hard copy memo or e-mailed to the person. A copy of the memo will be stored with the request file for that unit. The copy may be in the form of hard copy or a file maintained in a computer database.

   If the loan of equipment is approved and available, it will be issued from the reserve equipment stock. Organizations with a computer store may provide for the loan of the hardware. Regardless of which system is used, a follow-up file will be maintained indicating who signed for the equipment, the unit to which it is to be loaned, and the expected return date. The expected return dates will be followed up by the person making the loan. If the computer hardware is borrowed from another department the IT asset manager will be informed of this loan.

2. For purchased computer hardware, the user department manager will complete a purchase requisition. He/she will send it to the IT hardware person. The IT hardware person will check with their records that are maintained for the unit's budget limits and the approved computer hardware list. The records will contain what the user department has received and what has been spent to date. When the budget limit exceeds 80% of a department's budget, a memo or e-mail message will be sent to the department head.

The hardware item may be a stocked item. If it is not, the next procedure step to follow will be the purchasing of the hardware (see C. Purchasing hardware).

3. Stocked hardware will be made available from the information systems stock supply by the IT hardware person or from the computer store's reserve stock. The IT hardware person will update the computer inventory stock file for the items taken from stock. The IT hardware person will approve and sign the purchase requisition. Both copies of the purchase requisition will have noted that the item was supplied from which stock, and then be dated and signed. The first copy will be filed, and the second copy will be returned to requesting unit manager. The IT asset manager will be informed of the computer hardware transfer.

C. Purchasing hardware

The IT hardware person will approve and sign the purchase requisition. He/she will forward the approved requisition to the purchasing department. The IT hardware person will return a copy of the purchase requisition to the originator of the purchase requisition. The returned copy will have the cost for the order and the remaining budget balance written on the copy. If there is a problem, the IT hardware person will contact the originator of the purchase requisition.

D. Accepting purchased hardware

The receiving department will contact the IT hardware person with the arrival of any computer hardware order by sending the packing slip that came with the shipment. The IT hardware person is responsible for confirming that the delivered hardware was what was ordered by the purchase requisition. The IT hardware person will authorize the delivery of the computer hardware if all is in order. If there is a problem with the delivery, purchasing or the vendor will be contacted. The one who can best resolve the problem will be selected. The packing slip will be attached to the purchase requisition and purchase order and placed in a received file. A copy of the order invoice will be filed with the other papers in the received file.

All purchased and leased hardware will be tagged with a company identification tag. If the company does not have an asset property tagging procedure for identifying capital assets, the information technology asset manager will provide one. The procedure will have all received computer hardware tagged with an asset tag. The tag identification number will be written on the receiving report sent to the information technology asset manager. The IT hardware person will update his/her own received file records with the tag identification information.

Any price variation to the order will require an adjustment with budgeted account balance. The IT hardware person will send a memo or e-mail to the user manager that ordered the computer hardware that the adjusted cost exceeded ten dollars.

He/she will notify the accounts payable department that the invoice for the received items can now be paid. The memo will contain the following information:

- The name and address of the vendor.
- The date the items arrived.
- The purchase order number for the invoice.
- A description of the items received.
- The expected dollar amount to be paid.
- Any early payment discount information.

S1.3.5 Leasing Hardware

Leasing computer hardware has gained popularity. It reduces tying up capital and the procrastination to replace aged hardware. It also reduces the accounting complexity by expensing the leased equipment and not having to depreciate it. Some vendors will lease, while others utilize a third-party lease program. Leasing can be had for:

- Corporate lump-sum budgets.
- Itemized computer budgets.
- Department lump-sum computer budgets.

Management's long-range budget planning will require a commitment to properly fund the leasing program as a permanent extended program. Management may want to reserve the right to purchase, at a nominal cost, the equipment at the expiration of the lease. This may be for part of a leased computer hardware package or the complete package. This allows for some financial flexibility. The company is not limited to any one source for leasing.

The head of IT or his/her appointed representative will be responsible for obtaining the best lease rate with each acquisition. This will include the monitoring of the performance of the hardware to ensure it complies with the vendor's warrantee. The performance may be defined by the lease contract. The lease contract will be approved by the company's legal representative before it can be signed by the firm's agent.

4. EXPENDABLE SUPPLY BUDGET

S1.4 EXPENDABLE COMPUTER SUPPLIES

Computer supply items cover all supplies used by computers, computer peripheral equipment, and other office support equipment. These items must meet the required standards established by an IT supply standards committee.

S1.4.1 IT Supply Standards Committee

The committee will be made up of IT operational, IT systems, and IT planning personnel. The purchasing department manager will appoint a representative to this committee. The committee will select supply items and the vendors to be on the approved purchasing supply list. These items and/or vendors may change at the discretion of the IT supply standards committee. The chair person for the committee will be appointed by the head of information systems. Representatives of the other IT units will be appointed by their respective unit heads. The committees will meet monthly and as needed.

The committee will address all internal correspondence and provide a reply from other correspondence. Vendors may contact the chair person of the committee to make a presentation to the committee. Other persons within the organization may refer their received correspondence to this committee to be addressed. The committee will reply to all correspondence referred to it by other departments. Minutes that will be taken at each meeting will be provided to all committee members. The minutes will be approved at the next meeting. The head of information systems will receive a copy of the approved committee minutes, and any top management person electing to receive it.

The committee will publish an approved purchasing supply list and provide copies to the supply department, computer store head, purchasing agents, and all unit supervisors. Any person not on the distribution list may request to receive copies of the approved purchasing supply list. Copies of the list are for company use and no part of the list is to be made available to anyone outside the firm.

S1.4.2 Maintaining Expendable Supplies

Maintaining an expendable supply policies and procedures for computer and computer support device's is the responsibility of the IT supply standards committee. This covers the following areas:

A. Maintaining quality standards for IT supply items

   The IT supply standards committee will set the supply product items standards, and is responsible for maintaining the consistency of the purchases.

B. Maintaining corporate purchasing polices

   The IT supply standards committee shall follow the policies set down by the company purchasing department and/or the material control department.

C. Expendable computer supply policies and procedures

   Policies will be recommended by the IT supply standards committee, which requires top management's final approval. The committee will approve of the procedures required for the provision, maintenance, and control of expendable computer supplies.

For vendor contracting policies, please refer to Chapter 15, Vendor Contracting, in the main volume. The vendors selected must meet quality standards first and price second.

> *Comment:*
> **There is a warehouse in one of the eastern states, full of paper documents that were purchased at a fantastic price that saved the company many thousands of dollars. It is still there and anyone could buy the entire stock for even a better price. The only thing is the paper will not feed through office copiers or computer printers.**

The IT supply standards committee will monitor the quality of all supplies on a continuous bases. User feedback is encouraged with all supply products. Committee members will spot check the use of the supply items with in its jurisdiction. Any problem will be studied to ensure that it is not a machine, operator, or environment problem before problem is brought to the attention of the vendor. The vendor's reaction to the problem will determine if that item will be purchased in the future from the same vendor. It is the sole responsibility of the IT supply standards committee as to which vendor the supply items are purchased from.

S1.4.3 Stocking Expendable Computer Supplies

The IT supply standards committee will be responsible for approving the policies and procedures for stocking expendable computer supplies before it is presented to the head of information systems. The superior of the information systems head will give the final approval for the policies. The information systems head will give the final approval for the procedures.

A project team approved by the information systems head and the IT supply standards committee will write procedures for the stocking operation. The IT systems unit committee representative will be the project team manager for this task. The following will be considered when pursuing this project:

A. Storage area

   A central location is recommended for the storage and control of the supply items.

B. More than one location

   If more than one storage location is required, one of the locations will be the major storage location. The major storage location will contain supply items that are seldom requested. It will also provide for a backup supply for some items. This stock may be items that if purchased in larger amounts will have quantity discounts.

C. Primary storage location

   If there is more than one stock location, the major storage location should have the largest number of stock transactions. Storage areas should be located to provide optimum distance from its users.

D. Security

   Storage locations will be well secured when not in use. They will be provided with the recommended optimum temperature and humidity at all times.

E. Inventory control system

   An inventory control system of all items may be maintained by a PC. Standard inventory control software packages are available on the market. The IT supply standards committee will be furnished a monthly usage report. The report will contain the following data:

- Monthly usage quantity and cost of item.
- The total expense of all items taken from stock.
- The monthly dollars each unit received from stock and the year to date dollars for all items received.
- The cumulative usage of each item and its cost to date.
- The percent of dollars of supply items received by unit of the total consumed. This will be by month and year to date.
- The budgeted dollars allocated by month compared to the actual used. The year to date of actual compared to budget dollars used.

S1.4.4 Budgeting Expendable Computer Supplies

Information from the inventory control system reports will be used by the IT supply standards committee to plan the budgeting needs. Any unit having an unexpected usage that affects the total budgeted dollars will be asked to explain their needs. This is so that more dollars may be requested for the next budget year.

Any excess of actual dollars used as compared to the budgeted inventory total dollars usage is reported, by memo or e-mail, to the head of information systems. When this problem is noticed, the head of information systems should be provided as much advance notice as possible.

The cost of maintaining the stocking of expendable computer supplies will be part of the information systems budget. The person responsible for the operation and control of this inventory will also report to the manager of corporate material control or to a person appointed by the head of information systems.

5. PROCUREMENT PROCESS

S1.5 Procurement Procedures

Company vendor policies are established by the company's purchasing department. The purchasing department provides a service for the entire company organization, just as the information systems unit provides service to the same organization. Working with the purchasing department, information systems is the user. Information systems should provide the same kind of cooperation with purchasing that it expects from its users. Purchasing will not necessarily be the only contact for vendors. This will depend on the type of purchased item.

Purchasing requisitions used by information systems will be the same kind used through out the organization. If there is no company purchase requisition form available, the systems unit will design a purchasing form. The head of information systems and purchasing will be required to approve the form. If the head of purchasing wants to use the form through out the organization, he/she may do so.

S1.5.1 Purchasing Expendable Computer Supplies

Computer supply items that do not require custom designing will be done by one or more purchasing department representatives. These representatives will be provided with a current copy of the approved purchasing supply list and any changes that will be forthcoming with the next issue of the list. This will provide for a more efficient operation. Purchasing's contact source will be known by information systems personnel and vendors. The purchasing department will, at times, be contacting the same vendor for purchasing other products that are not computer related.

A. Vendor payment discount

Purchasing may want to take advantage of early payment discount and can arrange for early payment. Information systems will have to adjust their expense records to reflect these cost savings.

B. Vendor special orders

Items that are custom ordered (e.g., preprinted forms) will require a purchase order sent to the vendor. In this case, the purchasing agent will be working with the unit representative submitting the purchase requisition and the vendor. The purchasing department will use its legal advisory source for any involved contracting for special supply items.

C. Credit card and requisition purchasing

The purchasing of expendable computer supplies can be provided by a variety of vendors today. Some of the vendors are not equipped to process purchase orders. Others that are will cost the company more money to issue a purchase order than what the item may cost. There is also a time factor. The purchase requisition procedure requires the following steps:

- Write a purchase requisition.
- Get a authorized signature for the purchase requisition.
- Send the purchase requisition to the purchasing department.
- Purchasing will check the purchase requisition for its approval. This can include checking if funds are available and the item is on the approved IT purchase list.
- Write a purchase order and send it to the vendor. In rush cases, purchasing will provide the person that wrote the purchase requisition the purchase order number for the requisition. This number then can be provided to the vender so the item can be sent or picked up. The purchase order will arrive at the vendor later. The vendor needs the purchase order number to bill the customer. Many order processing systems will issue an invoice for the customer and process a shipping order and packing list to send the item(s).
- Purchasing will send a copy of the purchase order to the accounts payable department and the receiving department.
- The item, when received by the receiving department, will be sent to the unit ordering the product. The receiving department will notify purchasing and accounts payable the item has been received.
- Accounts payable will issue a voucher check to the vendor if all the details are in order.

For credit card purchases, which replace the above purchase requisition procedures, the steps are:

- Contact vendor for item(s) wanted. There is a limit on each item not to exceed $50.00, and the total order not to exceed $300.00. Larger limits may be authorized for the head of the IT department.
- Approve the item received, OK, and sign the charge slip.
- Send the charge slip to the department head.
- The department head will file the charge slips. When the monthly statement is received from the credit card company, the charge slips will be compared with the posted charges. If there are any discrepancies, the person signing the charge slip will be contacted. If there is no charge slip for a listed charge, the credit card company and/or employee will be contacted to resolve the problem.
- The statement will be approved and the account coded (the account number to be charged for the payment), dated, and signed. The statement will be copied. The copy will be attached to the charge

slips and filed. The copies filed should be held for no less than three years. The original statement will be sent to accounts payable for payment.

There are credit card companies that will provide this kind of service, one being American Express, Small Business Services, P.O. Box 31502, Salt Lake City, UT 84131-9956. They will provide an American Express Gold Corporate Card. A list of authorized employees should receive the cards. This is a competitive business, and it is wise to shop around for the best service.

S1.5.2 Computer Hardware Purchasing

All purchase orders will be issued from purchase requisitions approved only by authorized information systems representatives. These purchase requisitions should be funneled to the same purchasing agents each time because of their familiarity with both the vendors and products. These purchases are for standard computer hardware items. If purchasing can arrange for early payment to take advantage of such payment discounts, they may do so. Information systems will have to adjust their expense records to reflect these cost savings.

A. Leasing

Purchasing may be helpful with arranging for equipment leasing. Leasing can be done through the vendor or even third-party leasing. The purchasing department should be familiar with leasing arrangements and can be helpful for finding the best leasing deal.

B. Other services

Special purchasing requisitions sent to purchasing may have attachments for more detailed information needed to contact vendors, select vendors for bidding, and provide vendors with information needed for the hardware purchase.

For repeat orders from approved vendors, purchasing can issue a purchase order number to information systems management for rush orders. This should be done on a limited bases.

C. Kinds of purchased hardware

Computer hardware is not limited to mainframe computers but can consist any of the following:

- Desk-top computers.
- Lap-top computers.

- Computer printers.
- Fax machines.
- Scanners.
- Copy machines.
- Combination scanner, printer, copy, and fax machine.
- Computer accessories and aids.
- Computer parts (e.g., mother boards and memory chips).
- Cabling connectors.
- Input/output devices.
- Power supplies.
- Pen scanners.
- Sound boards.
- Disk drives.
- Speakers and microphones.
- Modems.
- UPS (uninterrupted power supply).

Supply items for computer-related usage is not limited to the following:

- Removable disks.
- Laser printer toner.
- Laser printer toner for color printers.
- Jet ink for black and white printers.
- Jet ink for color printers.
- Paper for copiers and Fax machines.
- Paper for ink jet black and white printers.
- Paper for ink jet color printers.
- High quality paper for ink jet printers.
- Photographic quality paper for ink jet photo printers.
- Lap-top computer carrying cases.

D. Credit card and requisition purchasing

The purchasing of computer hardware can be provided by a variety of vendors today. Some of the vendors are not equipped to process purchase orders. Others that are will cost the company more money to issue a purchase order than what the item may cost. There is also a time factor. The purchase requisition procedure requires the following steps:

- Write a purchase requisition.
- Get a authorized signature for the purchase requisition.
- Send the purchase requisition to the purchasing department.
- Purchasing will check the purchase requisition for its approval. This can include checking if funds are available and the item is on the approved IT purchase list.
- Write a purchase order and send it to the vendor. In rush cases, purchasing will provide the person that wrote the purchase requisition the purchase order number for the requisition. This number then can be provided to the vender so the item can be sent or picked up. The purchase order will arrive at the vendor later. The vendor needs the purchase order number to bill the customer. Many order processing systems will issue an invoice for the customer and process a shipping order and packing list to send the item(s).
- Purchasing will send a copy of the purchase order to the accounts payable department and the receiving department.
- The item, when received by the receiving department, will be sent to the unit ordering the product. The receiving department will notify purchasing and accounts payable the item has been received.
- Accounts payable will issue a voucher check to the vendor if all the details are in order.

For credit card purchases, which replace the above purchase requisition procedures, the steps are:

- Contact vendor for item(s) wanted. There is a limit on each item not to exceed $100.00, and the total order not to exceed $300.00. Larger limits may be authorized for the head of the IT department.
- Approve the item received, OK, and sign the charge slip.
- Send the charge slip to the department head.
- The department head will file the charge slips. When the monthly statement is received from the credit card company, the charge slips will be compared with the posted charges. If there are any discrepancies, the person signing the charge slip will be contacted. If there is no charge slip for a listed charge, the credit card company and/or employee will be contacted to resolve the problem.
- The statement will be approved and the account coded (the ac-

count number to be charged for the payment), dated, and signed. The statement will be copied. The copy will be attached to the charge slips and filed. The copies filed should be held for no less than three years. The original statement will be sent to accounts payable for payment.

There are credit card companies that will provide this kind of service, one being American Express, Small Business Services, P.O. Box 31502, Salt Lake City, UT 84131-9956. They will provide an American Express Gold Corporate Card. A list of authorized employees should receive the cards. This is a competitive business, and it is wise to shop around for the best service.

S1.5.3 Vendor Contracting Procedures

Major systems acquisitions projects can involve more than one vendor. The purchasing department can be of assistance even before the project starts. Before contracts are signed, they should be reviewed by the legal representative of the company and a purchasing representative for their approval. Approved management personnel are the only persons from the information systems unit that may sign company contracts.

For major systems acquisitions, Chapter 15—Vendor Contracting—and Section 15.5—Selection Process—of the main volume should be reviewed. The project manager should send out several requests for bid proposals. Information as to the objective should be noted along with the system design, expected volumes, and completion date. Bid protocol will include the vendor contact person representing the company and the expected presentation date of their proposal.

With large-quantity hardware needs, the purchasing department will send selected vendors requests for bids. Purchasing will be given the technical specifications for the hardware, along with the date needed. The returned information will be studied by the information system hardware committee, who will make recommendations. The head of information systems will provide the final approval.

S1.5.4 Computer Hardware Disposal

The purchasing organization may be called on to assist with the disposal of unnecessary computer equipment. They may sell or donate it to a charity. The longer one waits to get rid of used equipment the harder it will be to be disposed. The IT asset manager and capital asset accounting unit should be contacted about the equipment disposal. They also should be contacted for any money collected or donation credit received for the hardware.

The removed hardware will be deleted from the computer hardware database. The IT hardware person will remove the tags before the hardware is disposed.

> *Comment:*
>
> **There are firms such as the Dana Corporation in Toledo, Ohio, which have their own used equipment store open to the public. All the software is removed from the computers before the hardware is sold.**

SUPPLEMENTAL ADDITIONS TO CHAPTER 1

S1.3.5 Leasing hardware

S1.5.1-C Credit card purchasing

S1.5.2-D Credit card purchasing

Chapter 2
COMPUTER SOFTWARE ACQUISITIONS

1. POLICY

S2.1 COMPUTER SOFTWARE ACQUISITIONS POLICY

The purpose of a computer software acquisition policy is to formalize a uniform standard for computer software acquisitions through out the organization. This policy mandates the endorsement and support by the CEO/head of the organization.

S2.1.1 Scope

The computer acquisition policy covers all computer software used by the organization. An organization can have more than one kind of computer software. The kinds of software will depend on its source. Each computer source will require its own software acquisition policy. The sources/kinds of the computer software include the following:

- Company-written software.
- Contract personnel-written software.
- Vendor written turn-key system software.
- Purchased operating systems.
- Purchased packaged software.
- Leased software.
- Bootlegged software.
- Pirated software.

S2.1.2 Policy Objectives

This policy objective is to provide the guidelines for having uniform: programming software, purchased operating systems, and programs. This also covers all proprietary software, including the development, writing, and contracting. The sole ownership of the program's source coding ratifies the programs as proprietary. The code is loaded to a compiler. It will generate the operating program. There will be policy standards for proposing and recommending bench marks, vendor selection, and contracting. Purchased software will be approved for payment after passing the testing criteria. The purchasing of operating program (object coded) software is limited to its defined purchase agreement specifications that come with packaged software.

S2.1.3 Software Policies

Each type of software will have its own software policy requirements. These are policies needed, in addition to the general policies, for all software.

A. Company-written proprietary software

All programming will be done in the approved programming language. All programs written using company software, hardware, and any other company-owned resources belong to the company. Programming documentation and operation manuals will follow established standards.

B. Contract-written proprietary software

All contracted programmers will employ the same programming standards and procedures as do company-employed programmers. Documentation, test data, and drafted work information will be the property of the company. The company is the sole owner of the source-coded programs.

C. Turn-key system contracting

This is a vendor-developed turn-key system, including development cost and the program's source coding, and belongs to the company. The company will have the copyright and/or patent rights to the developed turn-key system software. Top management can approve other contract arrangements. Any third-party add-on software used will be identified. The limitations of the use of the third-party software will be defined. Its warranties, restrictions, and operations will be fully identified.

D. Purchased packaged operating systems software

There will be standard uniform operating systems software. There will not be any more systems in operation than what is licensed for. The information systems software committee will identify the authorized system software version.

E. Purchased packaged program software

Only approved program software is permitted. There will be only the number of programs that are licensed in operation. The version of the software allowed will be identified by the information systems software committee. Modifications will be done at the vendors discretion. These modifications will be provided and identified by the version number.

F. Leased software

Some software is only marketed by lease arrangements. There will only be the number of programs in operation that are leased.

G. Bootlegged software

Bootlegged software will not be loaded on to any company computer. Repeated violations of this policy are grounds for dismissal.

H. Pirated software

Pirated software will not be loaded on any company computer. Violations of this policy are grounds for dismissal.

S2.1.4 Asset Management Policy

Information systems is responsible for maintaining and enforcing a company-wide computer software asset management program. The head of information systems will assign the computer software asset management responsibility to the information technology asset manager. An information systems software committee will be formed. The chairperson of the committee will be the information technology asset manager.

A monthly update of any added or deleted software programs will be made to the asset management software database. The database is an inventory of all software that is in the company's possession. It will also contain the inventory of all purchased third-party add-on software. From this data base information, an approved computer software list report will be produced as needed. Only selected software from the asset management software database will be furnished to the approved computer software list.

The approved computer software list is a screening device for current computer software acquisitions. The committee will be responsible for approving new software. The information systems software committee will maintain the approved computer software list. There will be procedures to enforce this policy. Any past acquisitions that are not on the current approved computer software list can be authorized by the information systems software committee.

A user waiver can be granted by the information systems software committee when special software purchases are needed. These special software items will be added to the asset management software database, but not placed on the approved computer software list. This special software is not required to be supported by information systems.

All user unit supervisors will comply fully with this policy. Software that is not identified by the asset management software database will be flagged for each computer that is not in compliance. Any software that does not meet contractual agreements will be removed from all computers employing the software. Bootlegged and pirated software is not authorized, and will be removed from any computer that is found by information systems. Employees copying and selling company-owned software will be dismissed. Any employee placing a software virus on any company system will be dismissed. All virus recovery cost will be charged to the former employee. Court action will be pursued when appropriate.

2. PROPRIETARY SOFTWARE

S2.2 PROPRIETARY-DEVELOPED SOFTWARE

Proprietary-developed software may be from more than one source. Required software that is not listed on the asset management software database file or available for purchase or lease may need to be developed. When the developed proprietary software becomes operational, this information will be put into the asset management software database file. The information systems software committee will make the decision if the software will be listed on the approved computer software list. The source of the software will be identified on the approved computer software list. This will allow potential users to contact the developers for information about the software. The company can have its proprietary software developed by more than one method.

S2.2.1 End-User-Developed Software

User-developed software will follow the firm's policy for software developed. Resources of the information systems area will be available as time is accessible from the information technology units. Monies may be budgeted to departments for such development. Some users can develop their own software. Depending on the area of operations, there can be different levels of skills available. Depending on the corporate culture, this activity by users can vary. At times it would not only be faster to accomplish the task, but even possibly at a lower cost. The average information systems unit is overwhelmed by backlogs. It would be helpful to have users reduce the load of the IT units. Department managers may even buy computers and vendor assistance if they are required to, hopefully not because of I3 disinterest.

> *Comment:*
>
> **I started to write software in the G.E. electric motor engineering unit years ago. All the software was user developed. I did something we called synthesized design programming, but years later it was given the name of artificial intelligence. No wonder it took 18 months to debug one program.**

> *Comment:*
>
> **Years ago I was installing a computerized production control system. The production control manager of some 37 years was very worried about his job because he didn't have computer programming skills. I asked him how long would it take to learn his job. He said it would take several years. Then I informed him that he could learn how to program in two weeks.**

A. The inception process

The end-user department head is required to approve user-developed software within their jurisdiction. The user's department head should receive a memo, from the person requesting it, defining the need for the unavailable software. The department head can also be the originator of the memo. The memo will be part of the project documentation. This is required before any effort is spent in the development of the software.

User-developed software will be done at the user's own expense. The information technology asset manager will be contacted before any effort is spent producing end-user–developed software. The user manager will be informed what software is available that may assist the project. Also, user management will be informed of what is available from the asset management software database. Not all company-used software is listed on the approved computer software list. Computer programs may be available that can be used as is or with some modification. Information is available about third-party add-on module software. This module software can be part of the program being developed and save programming time. When users are writing their software, they may find a need for third-party software. It is then that the IT asset manager should be contacted for assistance.

B. End-user resources

Consulting resources will be provided by the information systems organization as time is available. User management will determine what kind of assistance will be required. The amount of assistance available from the information systems organization, at the time needed, should be known before pursuing the project. The information systems unit may charge for this service, depending on the company policy for interdepartment service billing. If information systems does not have time available, they can provide vendor sources for user assistance. The payment for this service will be paid from the user's budget, unless other provisions have been made. The information technology asset manager will assist end-user management with vendor negotiations.

C. Developing end-user software

The user will employ an approved software compiler, for example Visual Basic (a Microsoft product). The user should contact the help desk with any problems with the compiler software. If the help desk person cannot be of assistance, he/she will provide a person to whom the problem may be referred. Writing user computer programs should follow the procedures for programming methods provided by IS. For more information see Chapter 4—Programming Procedures—*Information Systems Policies and Procedures Manual,* main volume.

> *Comment:*
>
> **A while back I was talking to a college instructor who had a data processing manager in his computer intro class. He asked the man why he was taking the class. The man said he had been the production and inventory control manager in an Ohio plant that was starting to computerize the operation. He and management felt it would be better to make him the IT user manager than to train an experienced computer person about their operation.**

D. End-user software documentation

A copy of the project, including source codes, software, and the supporting documentation will be sent to the chairperson of the information systems software committee. The committee will examine and test the computer software under the leadership of the IT programming representative on the committee. The approved software will require a memo written by the IT programming representative describing the value of the software. The memo will be sent to the head of information systems and the information technology asset manager. They will determine if the new software warrants being listed on the approved computer software list.

E. End-user project

When the decision is made to proceed with development of the software, it will become a user project. The project may be a simple one-person effort, but it will have its own identity and contain a project documentation folder. The project work time and any expenses incurred will be recorded and placed in the folder.

The software will use test data made available for program testing by the user. At no time will operation data files be used for testing. When such test data is needed, file or database information will be down loaded to the computer system that will use the data. At no time will the software testing be done online with any network operating system. Testing will be done at the company facilities using the company's resources. No test data or programs will be taken from the company site without the permission of the head of information systems or his/her designated representative.

F. End-user software completion

After testing is completed, all software documentation will be brought up to date. Test results will be part of the documentation. Any operation manuals needed for the operation of the software will be written and tested by users who do not have any knowledge about the new software. After extensive successful testing has been completed, the user may employ the software within their own operation. The manager of the user department will write an authorizing memo to permit the software to be used in his/her department. The memo will contain information as to how well the software met its objective. A copy of the memo will be placed in the documentation folder and a copy sent to the information technology asset manager. The IT asset manager will update the asset management software database from this information.

G. End-user software installation

Installation is placing into operation the user-tested software that either replaces existing programs or is completely new. When discontinued software is replaced by a new user system, the options include the following:

1. Phased

In a phased installation, the new system is installed in a modular fashion or phases. When one phase is identified as operational and accepted, the next part of the installation can begin.

2. Direct

Direct installation is a complete, one-time conversion or installation. The old system is replaced completely by the new. User operations personnel has to be totally involved with the instillation and operation of the new system software.

3. Parallel conversion

This type of user installation is most often used by companies. It is the safest and most preferred method of installing a new software system, but the most costly. If after comparing output results and the database status of both systems the results are compatible, the user installation is considered complete.

When one existing software is being replaced, new end-user software installation can occur as phased or direct installation. This kind of installation has the advantage of users not having to unlearn an old system. The end-users are familiar with the unit's objective and input problems—this is the advantage of installing a new user-programmed system.

H. User follow-up procedures

The user developer of the software will forward a copy of the project documentation folder and the software—both the source and object coded programs—to the chairperson of information systems software committee, who is also the IT asset manager. The copies will include both a hard copy of the program software and the operating program on disk. A copy of the operations manual, for user operation, will be sent with the copy of the documentation folder. The information systems software committee may elect to make the user-developed software available throughout the company by placing it on the approved computer software list. Approved software may be used by other company units. The approved computer software list will identify who developed and first used the software. The IT programming unit member, of the information systems software committee, will retain the software folder and the programs in a user-developed software file. The file will contain user-developed software found on the approved computer software list and software that is not on the list, but is in the asset management software database.

I. Other users' involvement

If the software will be used as part of a system employed by other users, approval will be required by the information systems software committee and the heads of IT programming and computer operations units. To insure that there will not be a problem with any integrated operating software or database, a copy of the software folder is sent to the head of the IT programming unit for their study. He/she will review the information with the head of IT computer operations. The programming unit's representative on the committee must confirm that the software meets the firm's information technology standards. Any IT unit head may request a duplicate copy of the software folder. With the approval of the IT programming unit head, the help desk will support the software.

J. Software maintenance

End-user–developed software will require maintenance at one time or another during its lifetime. The user who wrote the original programs should do the maintenance. If the person who wrote the original programs is no longer available, there are options to consider.

1. Selected maintenance person

   A selected maintenance person in the user department who has had programming experience should perform the maintenance. The experienced person should be familiar with the program language used for writing the original software programs.

2. IT programming unit maintenance

   Contact the IT programming unit head for his/her assistance. Depending on the involvement of the maintenance task, the state of the user program documentation and the availability of programmers will be considered before a decision can be made. If the IT programming unit will do the maintenance, the user department may be charged for the service—this depends on the company policy. If no one is available to perform the maintenance, assistance may be offered to a user department person assigned to do the maintenance.

3. Vendor-contracted maintenance

   Contract the maintenance with a vendor. The vendor can be paid by the hour or provide a estimated project cost. When considering the vendor route, the information technology asset manager will be contacted to assist with the procurement of a vendor maintenance contractor.

   After the software maintenance has been completed and tested, the user software documentation will be updated. Any user operations procedures effected by the maintenance will require updating the user operations manual. A copy of all documented changes will be sent to the information technology asset manager. A cover memo from the person who did the program maintenance will be sent with documentation. The memo will cover why and how the maintenance was done, and any other information that would assist with any maintenance needs in the future.

S2.2.2 Information Systems–Developed Software

The IT programming unit of the information systems department may develop software for users or its own needs. User department heads may request the software with a memo to the information systems head. The information systems head may have user management direct request to the IT programming unit head. The request will be reviewed in light of other requests and the current work load of the available programming staff. If the request is one that will not require a major new system, the information systems head will be notified along with the requesting user department head. A memo or e-mail message will provide what course of action the user manager may take. If the request has merit, the information systems head will refer the user manager to proceed with the procedure S2.2.2 A, New software development study. For further information see Chapter 4—Programming Procedures—from the main volume, *Information Systems Policies and Procedures Manual.*

When a major system project is to be undertaken, it will require its own budget—and can span more than one budget year. This kind of project can be for IT operations, one or more end-users, or both. This kind of major undertaking is covered in Chapter 3—Systems Analysis and Design—and Chapter 4—Programming Procedures—of the main volume, *Information Systems Policies and Procedures Manual.*

Software maintenance is approved by the IT programming head. If the maintenance requirements cannot be done in the timeframe the user wants, he/she will be referred to the head of information systems. Any IT head within the information systems organization can initiate a request for new software or the maintenance of a current program. This can be done by sending a memo or e-mail to the IT head of programming. The request can ask for the development of new software programs or the maintenance of current software programs.

A. New software development study

A study to be conducted for the development of new software requires a formal request by approved user management and/or IT unit heads. The request will provide the following information:

- When results of the study are to be expected.
- What software may be available that can be purchased and used as is or modified for this application. Whether the sources will be proprietary or whether they will have to be purchased or contracted for.
- When the project is to be completed and in operation.
- The amount of money allowed for the study.
- What user personnel are to be contacted.
- What the estimated cost will be to acquire the system and have it operational.
- If the software will require in-house development and what resource costs and calendar time will be needed.

After the requested information is returned and studied, the IT programming head will summarize the information in a memo and send it to the information systems head. The information systems head will decide what course of action the IT programming head will take with the project. The reply can be a memo or e-mail.

These procedures are for projects that do not have their own budget—resources are provided from existing budgets. Major system projects, with their required software development, will be provided with their own budgets when annual budgets are granted.

Completed software will meet the following requirements before placed in service and listed in the asset software database:

1. Have all programs tested with user-provided software test data.

2. Have all programming documentation completed and approved by the head of IT programming.

3. All operation manuals will be completed and approved by end-user management.

4. Backup and recovery procedures will be completed, documented and tested.

5. Any required user training is completed, within two weeks, before the software will be used.

6. The end-user management has signed that the software is now accepted for user operations.

B. Software maintenance

Updating current software being used by information system's IT operations or user application operations will require maintenance. A software maintenance request will be sent to the IT programming head and contain the following information:

- The completion date needed for the required program changes.

- What software programs will be modified.

- What the modifications will contain. Any I/O changes will have attached the current and new I/O layouts.

- The charge codes for the systems and reprogramming time spent on the changes.

- What end-user operations personnel will be contacted.

- What will be the estimated cost to modify the application programs?

After the requested information is returned and approved, the IT programming head will schedule the software maintenance. These procedures will be charged to the software maintenance budget. Software maintenance costs for user departments will be provided from existing user software maintenance budgets. If there is not a user budget for this within the IT programming unit, the time will be kept tracked for information that will be furnished to the information systems head on a monthly basis. Companies that have an internal cost accounting system may have the cost of user software maintenance charged to the user's department.

Completed software maintenance will meet the following requirements before being placed in service:

1. Have all programs tested with user-provided software test data.
2. Have all programming documentation completed.
3. All operation manuals will be updated and approved by the end-user management.
4. Backup and recovery procedures will be completed, documented, and tested.
5. Any required user training is completed within two weeks before the changes will be used.
6. The end-user management has signed that the software is now accepted for user operations.

S2.2.3 Contract Programming

Software development may be contracted for user or IT computer operations. Unless the company has already a blanket vendor contract for software development, competitive bids will be solicited from two or more software contracting vendors. The vendors will be provided with information for contract bid proposals. At a minimum, the request for bid proposals will contain the following information:

- Who the contact person will be for more information and for submitting their bid proposal.
- Will the contract call for maintenance or new programs?
- What type of application will be programmed? Examples would be billing, payroll, inventory control, etc.
- If maintenance programming is required, in what language is the software written?
- What language is desired for the new software to be written? If the vendor has an alternate one it would like to propose, what would be the benefits?

- Will the bids requested be for contract hour or a project? For projects bids, vendors who are interested will be provided with the detail information. It is advisable that the project be well defined before requesting project bids.
- The due date for bids.
- The expected start and finish dates.
- What are the skill levels of the people that will be working for the vendor?
- What is the dollar amount of their bid?

User managers will contact the information technology asset manager for assistance with the company protocol for such acquisitions. A large project with an unproven vendor is not advisable. Vendor confidence is built over time. The software programming vendor will need to have other clients to qualify as a vendor and not be the company's employee.

Comment:
An East Coast Senator, because of pressure of large consulting firms, made it questionable to allow a person to have a software programming business with only one client.

After the bids are received they will be reviewed. With the current demands for such skills the replies may not be encouraging. With budget money available, a contract or purchase requisition will be completed. If a contract is drawn, it should be reviewed by the firm's legal representative before the authorized person signs it.

Vendor programming can be done in one of two ways—hourly billed programming or by project contract.

A. Hourly contracting

The programming effort is paid by the hour. Enough money should be available to complete the task. It would be wise to have a contingency reserve set aside. For new program development, running out of money presents a far greater problem than a maintenance task. A partly completed program is more difficult to finish that someone else has started. The purchase requisition will identify whether the vendor will be paid for hours worked. Purchasing requisitions will identify how the vendor will bill, either lump sum or partial payments. If something other than a monthly check is issued, the arrangement should be made known to accounts payable.

1. Programming

   The programming can be done in-house or at the vendor's location. The programmers will submit a weekly report of hours worked by day. Each day, the work effort and persons contacted in regards to that days work effort will be recorded. If contact is not related to that day's work effort why is it being billed? A daily log will be kept for the detail supporting information for the weekly report. The log may be manually kept and will be the property of the company. It will be submitted weekly to the company's contact person. The vendor (for its own records) may want to make a copy of this log.

2. Company contact person

   The company's software vendor's contact person should examine each week's vendor billing information before approving payment. The daily detailed information will be examined weekly. As more time passes, it becomes harder to confirm detailed information. If need be, a contact may be made with the vendor to explain any questions that may arise. This action should not wait for too long. Vendors' memories are not any better than anyone elses.

Comment:

Time fades one's memory—the longer one waits, the less one can recall. What did you do last Wednesday at 2:30 P.M. and how long did it take?

---

3. Vendor payment

   Paying the vendor requires a purchase order. The purchase order may be in the form of a blanket purchase order, which allows the purchase order to be paid by accounts payable in installments as approved by the person signing the purchase requisition. The vendor will submit a bill to the company contact person for payment. The bill will be confirmed to be correct. Approval will be noted, dated, and signed, and then sent to accounts payable. A copy of the bill will be made for filing. The dollar amount left that was allotted for the task will be noted on the copy before it is filed. If it appears that the task will not be completed before the allotted funds run out, this should be reported to the contact person's superior.

B. Project contracts

Contract programming by project is for a well-defined programming project with detailed acceptance criteria. No vendor timekeeping is required. The project will have a calendar finish date.

1. Project tasks

The tasks within the contracted project will be plotted on a Gantt chart. The completion date of each task will be reported in writing, dated, and signed by the vendor. It will be sent to the information systems project contact person for the project. If it is a user project, the information will be provided to the user vendor contact person. A copy of the Gantt chart will be signed and dated for each completed week of the project. The chart will represent the work plotted for the work week, Monday through Friday, and will be provided to the designated company contact person who will receive it by the following Wednesday.

2. Project contract

A contract will be drawn for the project. It will define in detail what is to be accomplished. After the contract is approved by the legal representative of the firm, it will be signed by an authorized person. A purchase requisition with a copy of the contract attached will be sent to purchasing. Purchasing will send a purchase order to the vendor who will need the purchase order number for a billing reference. Input and output documents will detail the I/O information furnished the vendor. Printed program source and object codes will be provided no later than one week after it is shown as completed on the Gantt chart. Test data will be provided by the user for detail testing of all conditions that can be expected. Examples of output testing will be provided to the company contact person along with a printed copy of the actual test data used.

3. Penalty clause

The contract will contain a penalty clause. The clause will state the penalty for each work day the project is late in its completion. If the user would benefit from a early completion date, a bonus could be written into the contract for each work day it is finished early. The bonus would be added to the contract after all other things are agreed upon. This is to avoid any padding of days by the vendor.

4. Bill payment

An invoice/bill will be sent to the company project contact person. The company will have 30 days to confirm that all conditions of the contract have been met. Any work added to the project by the company will be paid by issuing a separate purchase requisition and following the same procedure as the original project contract. When the project is accepted as complete, accounts payable will be notified by sending the invoice/bill to them with a noted approval, date and approving authority signature. When the vendor is paid it will be with one check for the purchase orders. If there are any disputes with the vender that cannot be resolved, the legal representative of the firm will be contacted for further resolution.

S2.2.4 System Contracting

System contracting is for a major system effort with its own budget. This will be part of the annual budgeting procedure of the company. System contracting today is often for end-user system applications. The system can be an LAN system and/or span over the Internet with remote contacts. If the new system requires hardware acquisitions, the software will be the driving force of the project. The system with its intended software will determine what hardware is needed.

A. Computer acquisitions

Computer hardware acquisitions will follow the policies and procedures established in Chapter 1—Computer Hardware Acquisition. If older PC and file servers that are currently in use are used, the hardware will be more obsolete when the system and programming effort is complete.

B. Source of contract

A system development may be contracted for user or IT computer operations. Unless the company has already a blanket vendor contract for software development, competitive bids will be solicited from two or more vendors. The vendors will be provided with information for contract bid proposals. At a minimum, the request for system bid proposals will contain the following information:

- Who the contact person will be for more information needs and for submitting their bid proposal.

- What kind of application is the system? What parts of the firm will it involve?
- What language should the new software to be written in? If the vendor has an alternate one they would like to propose, what are the benefits?
- Will the systems maintenance be done by the vendor, the information systems unit, or an end-user department?
- Will the bids requested be for contract hour or a systems project? For systems projects bids, vendors who are interested will be provided with a detail proposed system documentation. It is advisable that the project be very well defined before requesting project bids.
- What current computer hardware will be used for the proposed system? What new hardware may be recommended?
- The due date for bids.
- The expected start and finish dates.
- What are the skill levels of the people that will be working for the vendor?
- What is the range of dollar amounts for the bid?

Bids are reviewed after they are received. With the current demand for people, the replies may not be encouraging. With budget money available, a contract or purchase requisition will be completed. If a contract is to be drawn, it will be reviewed by the firm's legal representative before the authorized person will sign it.

C. End-user systems

User management will contact the information technology asset manager for assistance with the company protocol for systems contracting. The IT asset manager will work with the user management. IT units may be contacted for their assistance.

D. More information

Vendors will want to study any current operations and require more information before a contract can be negotiated. The time required for this process depends on the complexity and size of the system involved. See the main volume, *Information Systems Policies and Procedures Manual*, Chapter 15—Vendor Contracting—and Section 5—Selection Process—for more information.

E. Vendor staff needs

The vendor's employees may require a desk and telephone. There will be a need for a conference room from time to time. When the vendor is shown the conference room, ask them if they will need any AV equipment. If the company requires ID tags, they should be provided to each vendor employee assigned to the systems project. The company's contact person will introduce the vendors to the people they will have need to speak with later. It would also be helpful to provide the vendor's people with a tour of the pertinent areas of the firm. The location of the rest rooms, vending machines, and eating areas will be pointed out. They should be informed of the smoking policy of the firm. Any parking restrictions should also be noted.

F. Vendor contracting

Vendor systems contracting can be done in one of two ways: billed hours or a contract sum for systems project. Each has its own benefits and disadvantages.

G. Hourly contracting

The programming effort is paid by the hour. To ensure that there will be enough money budgeted for the system project, the vendor should provide some sort of estimate. Let them know this is needed for the budget request, even though the billing will be done on an hourly rate. It would be wise to have a contingency reserve set aside. A systems project running out of money presents a problem that may not be resolved until more funds are found or until the next budget year.

1. Purchase requisition

The purchase requisition will identify what the vendor will bill for hours worked. Purchasing requisitions will identify how the vendor will be paid, either lump sum or monthly payments. If other than a monthly check issued, the arrangement should be made known with accounts payable.

2. Vendor record keeping

Vendor personnel will not always be working at the company site. Their work time will be recorded wherever they are. The systems analysts, programmers, and other vendor personnel will submit a weekly report of hours worked by day. Each one of the people working on the project can command different hourly pay scales. They will record their work effort and persons contacted with regard to that day's job effort. If contact is not related to that day's work effort, why is it being billed? A daily log will be kept for the detailed information of every vendor's employee whose service will be billed. This is the supporting information for the weekly billing report. The log may be manually kept and a copy provided to the company. It will be submitted weekly to the company's contact person. The vendor, for their own records, may want to make a copy of this log. It would be helpful if any telephone or e-mail references are made in the log.

3. Vendor work verification

The company's project contact person will examine each week's vendor billing information. It will be compared with the employee's logs before approving payment. The daily detailed information will be examined weekly. As more time passes, it becomes harder to confirm the detailed information. Any vendor contact should be made as soon as possible to explain any questions that may arise.

4. Paying vendor contractor

Paying the vendor will require a purchase order. The purchase order may be in the form of a blanket purchase order, which allows the purchase order to be paid by accounts payable in installments as approved by the person signing the purchase requisition. The vendor will submit a bill to the company contact person for payment after it is confirmed to be correct. Approval will be noted, dated, and signed, and then sent to accounts payable. A copy of the bill will be made for filing. The dollar amount left that was allotted for the task will be noted on the copy before it is filed. If it appears that the task will not be completed before the allotted funds run out, this should be reported to the contact person's superior.

H. Project contracts

Contract programming by project is for a well-defined programming project with detailed acceptance criteria. No vendor timekeeping is required. The project will have a calendar finish date.

1. Gantt charts

The tasks within the contracted project will be plotted on a Gantt chart. The completion date of each task will be reported in writing, dated, and signed by the vendor. It will be sent to the information systems project contact person. If it is a user project, the information will be provided to the end-user project contact person. A copy of the Gantt chart will be signed and dated for each completed week of the project. The chart will represent the work plotted for the work week, Monday through Friday, and will be provided to the designated company contact person who will receive it by the following Wednesday.

2. Project contract

A contract will be drawn for the project. It will define in detail what is to be accomplished. After the contract is approved by the legal representative of the firm it will be signed by an authorized person. A purchase requisition with a copy of the contract attached will be sent to purchasing, which then sends a purchase order to the vendor who needs the purchase order number for billing reference. Input and output documents will detail the I/O information furnished the vendor. Printed program source and object codes will be provided no later than one week after it is shown as complete on the Gantt chart. Test data will be provided by the user for detail testing of all conditions that can be expected. Examples of output testing will be provided to the company contact person along with a printed copy of the actual test data used.

3. Penalty clause

The contract will contain a penalty clause. The clause will state the penalty for each work day the project is late in its completion. If the user would benefit from a early completion date, a bonus could be written into the contract for each workday it is finished early. The bonus would be added to the contract after all other things are agreed upon. This is to avoid any padding of days by the vendor.

4. Vendor payment

An invoice/bill will be sent to the company project contact person. The company will have 30 days in which to confirm that all conditions of the contract have been met. Any added work to the project by the company will be paid by issuing a separate purchase requisition and following the same procedure as the original project contract. When the project is accepted as complete, accounts payable will be notified by sending the invoice/bill to them with a noted approval, date and approving authority signature. When the vendor is paid, it will be one check for the purchase orders. If there are any disputes with the vendor that cannot be resolved, the legal representative of the firm is contacted for further resolution.

3. PURCHASED SOFTWARE

S2.3 SOFTWARE PURCHASING AND CONTROL

This section covers the purchase and control of PC software. These are nonproprietary programs. The manufacturer of the software is the owner of the source and object programs. When the operating (object) program and instructions are packaged for sale, it is to be used by one computer. The purchaser of this software has limited claims to the software. Most often the software, registration card, and instructions are in a box sealed with a shrink-wrap material. To return the package without the shrink-wrap in place, if permitted, the vendor will require a restocking charge, which includes the re-shrink wrapping of the box. The program disks are often in a sealed envelope. The sealed envelope will most often contain the printed warranties and liabilities. Included is the warning that when the seal is broken it becomes your software and you agree to the terms of the license agreement. This is no longer a returnable product.

S2.3.1 Information Systems Software Committee

The information systems software committee is chaired by the information technology asset manager. Its major task is to keep abreast of new vendor-provided software that is acceptable. The committee will be made up of the heads of IT units, with the information technology asset manager as the chairperson. One or two users will also be on the committee.

No less often than a monthly update of any added or deleted software will be made to the asset management software database. The approved computer software list will be updated at the same meeting of the information systems software committee meeting. An asset management software database status report will be issued monthly. The report will be made available to committee members one week before a committee meeting. Minutes of each monthly and special meeting will be kept. Approved copies of the minutes will be sent to the committee members and the head of information systems.

S2.3.2 Asset Management Procedures

The information systems software committee will have duties other than what takes place at their meetings. All members will keep current with software developments in the IT profession and what proprietary software is being developed. If an IT operation is involved with any Beta testing, the status and results will be reported to the members of the committee.

Selected committee members will form a sub-committee to evaluate newly marketed software. This can be done by reading and evaluating published reports. Software that looks promising can be purchased and tested. The software will be listed on the asset management software database. Results will be reported to the whole committee.

There will be a selection procedure for buying new software. The procedure is for the information systems software committee. End-users will also be testing a sample of the software that they may want, which is not currently available to them through normal channels.

A. The acceptable software criteria requires that:

- The printed information and instructions that come with the software is understood by more than 90% of the intended users.
- The software is virus free.
- The documentation leaves no or few questions are to be answered by the manufacturer.
- The software has been tested by the information systems software committee and/or the IT programming unit. The testers are willing to give their signature of approval.
- The manufacturer provides a toll-free telephone number for customer support. If the telephone number is not toll free, what is the average waiting time for a technician to be available to help a customer with their software problem?
- What is the quality of user assistance offered by the manufacturer of the software?
- A user tutorial is part of the software package to assist the user with the operation of the software.
- Help references are built in to the software operation that is understandable by 90% of the people that will use the software.
- Not required, but helpful would be a teaching package for any user provided instruction. Also helpful, would be the availability of third party instruction books for the software.

B. Approved software

Approved software that has been sanctioned by the information systems software committee will be found on the approved computer software list. The software has been used, tested, and approved by the IT programming unit, and the information systems software committee. By being on the approved computer software list, it will be available to users or information systems staff. The only question is whether the software is to be charged to the information systems budget or a user budget. This question will be addressed by corporate policy.

C. Requesting software

The unit head requesting the software will send a memo or e-mail message to the information technology asset manager or their appointed representative. The memo will request the software be installed on identified computer or computers. This will be for software found on the approved computer software list. At times it may be made available from the asset management software database by the IT asset manager. The request will be for software not contained on the approved computer software list:

Comment:

Asset management has a greater problem with software than with hardware. Companies can have more dollars tied up in software than the value of their hardware. An in-house system may be developed or purchased to provide a tool for the information technology asset manager.

Developing such a system requires a lot of time by people that have little or no experience with this kind of project. The final cost will be far greater than buying asset management software. Also, the home-made software may contain bugs that may take a long time to find.

Janus Technologies Inc., makes an asset management software package called Argis. It is used for software and even hardware. It is reported to work with most types of computing platforms. It tracks asset ownership, so the information technology asset manager will know what he/she has that is home-made, purchased, leased, rented, or licensed. By now there should be other packages available.

1. Other software

   If software is not found on the list and is needed, the software may be looked for on the asset management software database. If the software is available and approved to be used it will be installed on the end-user microcomputer.

2. Special software needs

   There can be a special need for software not found on the approved computer software list or the asset management software database. The user's manager will send a request memo to the information systems software committee to ask that a waiver be granted for their special needs and a request to purchase the special software. When and if the software is purchased and received, the software information will be posted to the asset management software database. The end-user will be required to resolve any software problems with the vendor. If the software gains acceptance, it will be placed on the approved computer software list. The help desk will support the software.

S2.3.3 *Unauthorized Software*

Software that is not authorized will be of concern to the information technology asset manager and the information systems software committee. Employing unauthorized software can be a very expensive experience for the company. The information systems software committee is responsible for policing all company computers for any unauthorized software whether it is in use or not. Just having the software on the hard drive without its being used can provide a problem.

If the information systems software committee has never screened all the microcomputers and the task seems overwhelming, contact a few ven-

---

Comment:

It is estimated the software loss from piracy is 15 billion units worldwide. The loss is enough to have the Business Software Alliance launch a campaign to help employees report companies that use pirated software. They have installed a hotline to report the offenders by, of all people, including disgruntled former employees. Current employees can also qualify to call. The software pirated hotline number is 888-NO-PIRACY.

dors that specialize in this kind of work. Select the one that has worked with the same type of hardware/software environment. It will not be cheap, but it is cheaper than what could be the alternative. If the firm is small enough, around-the-clock scrutiny over a weekend and an examination of computers may reveal a lot. The asset management software database should furnish a list of what is authorized on each computer, including laptops. Have all the lap-top computers turned in for "upgrading" so they can also be checked.

Once the 100% clean sweep has been made, perform surprise checks in a random fashion. Each microcomputer and server should be checked no less than once a year. If the task is too large for the committee, hire contract personnel. It can be done during non-working hours, so as not to disturb the daily operation. All unauthorized software will be removed, and the asset management software database list will be confirmed as to its accuracy. Any serious violations will be reported to the information technology asset manager. If the problem is a serious one, the information technology asset manager will report the details to the information systems head.

S2.3.4 Antivirus Procedures

To start an antivirus procedure, no software will be brought into the firm that does not belong to the firm. Even authorized disks will be checked for viruses before they can be brought into the firm's work area. This includes newly purchased software, when it is received but not yet released to the users. The antivirus device will contain the latest version of virus protection. Down-loading of any internet information without specially granted permission is absolutely prohibited.

If any virus is detected on a computer, the machine will be disconnected from the network. The computer help desk will be notified as soon as possible by telephone. The e-mail service to the problem computer will be taken off-line along with the LAN service. All the things that lead up to the problem, the operators will have written down before the details are forgotten.

The next step is the recovery process, which will be done by a representative of information systems who works with microcomputers and their software. If it is a full-time job, it may be called a Micro-manager, or the microcomputer store manager may have this duty.

S2.3.5 Approved Computer Software List

The approved computer software list contains software that is approved for user acquisition, including approved software operating systems and company-developed software. To discourage the use of any unapproved software, help desk support will not be provided to any unauthorized computer/user. The list is primarily a screening device for new software acquisitions. Authorized software can still be running that is not on the approved computer software list, but will be found on the asset management software database. The asset management software database lists all software that is permitted to be in use and by whom.

There will be proprietary software that can be on the asset management software database (i.e., software developed by members of the firm and owned by the firm). Users who may have a problem with this software will contact the person(s) who developed the software. There will be a list of third-party add-on software the company has purchased and is on the management software database. This software has very limited use and is not supported by the help desk. If help is required, the IT programming unit should be contacted.

S2.3.6 Software Purchasing

All purchasing of new software will be done by the information technology asset manager with a purchase requisition. The requisition will note possible vendors for the software. Software is seldom purchased directly by the user manager. If it is purchased from the manufacturer, it will most likely be an upgrade. User management may acquire this software through its own or information systems' budget.

A. Unproven software

When purchasing software, avoid release 1.0 of the product. Any release of that kind can have bugs not yet found. In fact, it is safer to wait until the last number replaces the zero. Unless IT programming has been a Beta site for the software, try to avoid brand new software. This software may not be supported by the information systems help desk.

B. Software stock

Some requests for software can be made from proprietary stock of software. This will require contacting the information technology asset manger, who will arrange for it to be installed on the end-user's computer. Purchased software may also be available from the information technology asset manager or the company computer store. The computer store will have a small inventory of purchased software. The head of the company store will send a request to the information technology asset manager for any software restocking.

C. Help desk

The help desk will support purchased software as long as it is on the asset management software database. The asset management software database lists all software that is permitted to be used and by whom. This database would be the source with which users can be identified for help desk assistance. Also supported will be user-written software, with or without third-party–purchased add-on software if it is on the approved software list. One or more purchased third-party add-on products can be combined with an in-house written program. If the help desk has any problem with this kind software, the caller will be referred to the IT programming unit.

The IT programming unit will be the reference source for third-party–purchased add-on software. This software is not intended to be a computer program unto itself. It is intended to be used within a main program; therefore, it will not be the responsibility of the information systems software committee to provide any approved list for this kind of software. This kind of software purchase by the IT programming unit will be reported to the information technology asset manager. This information is required to update the asset management software database.

D. Credit card purchasing

The purchasing of PC software can be provided by a variety of vendors today. Some of the vendors are not equipped to process purchase orders. Others that are will cost the company more money to issue a purchase order than what the item may cost. There is also a time factor.

The following procedures will be followed for software credit card purchases:

- Software credit card purchases will be made for software only. If other items are to be ordered from the same vendor, they will be on another credit card charge.

- Contact vendor for software wanted. There is a limit on each item not to exceed $100.00, and the total order not to exceed $300.00. Larger limits may be authorized by the head of the IT department.

- The software will be tested for compliance as soon as it is received. At this time, the software should also be determined to be virus free.

- If the software is not acceptable, return it to the vendor with receipt requested from the shipper. After delivery has been confirmed, contact the vendor for a credit to the credit card account. If they do not provide a credit, contact the credit card company and inform them that the merchandise was defective and was returned.

- Approve software; OK and sign the charge slip.
- Send the charge slip to the department head.
- The department head will file the charge slips. When the monthly statement is received from the credit card company, the charge slips will be compared with the posted charges. If there are any discrepancies, the person signing the charge slip will be contacted. If there is no charge slip for a listed charge, the credit card company and/or employee will be contacted to resolve the problem.
- The statement will be approved and the account coded (the account number to be charged for the payment), dated, and signed. The statement will be copied. The copy will be attached to the charge slips and filed. The copies filed should be held for no less than three years. The original statement will be sent to accounts payable for payment.

There are credit card companies that will provide this kind of service, one being American Express, Small Business Services, P.O. Box 31502, Salt Lake City, UT 84131-9956. They will provide an American Express Gold Corporate Card. A list of authorized employees should receive the cards. The credit card industry is a very competitive business, and it is wise to shop around for the best service.

SUPPLEMENTAL ADDITIONS TO CHAPTER 2
S2.3.6-D Credit card purchasing

Chapter 3
MICROCOMPUTER OPERATIONS

1. POLICY

S3.1 MICROCOMPUTER OPERATION

The microcomputer operation policy covers all computers, computer-related hardware, and other devices that support information technology throughout the company organization. The organization consists of units that use information technology hardware that requires an authority to set standards and provide optimum use. Corporate policies for microcomputer/PC operations cover computers that are found on company office desks to the lap-top computer under the seat of an airplane. The dollar investment in microcomputers by firms today far exceeds mainframe computer investments. More companies today do not own a mainframe than ones that do. The polices cover ancillary information processing devices throughout the organization. This policy mandates the endorsement and support by the CEO/head of the organization.

Polices have to cover a vast variety of environments and applications. With the mainframe computer center, it was a much simpler task. There are many same concerns covering mainframe computers as there are with smaller machines. Both types have input, processing, storage, and output that is the concern of the company.

S3.1.1 Scope

The scope covers not only the operation of the main computer system, but different sizes, ownerships, distribution, applications, portability, and communications. All these items require policies. Because of the scope the policies cover, the vast area for policymaking has to be more generic.

The scope covers all company computers, attached hardware, and ancillary information processing devices no matter who is in possession of the equipment and its location. Because information processing is so widespread and interrelated, the equipment can cover: computers, printers, copiers, facsimiles, multifunction products, and communication devices. With the use of worldwide communications, policies and procedures must be in place.

S3.1.2 Policy Objectives

Policy objectives should be as flexible as allowed by top management to cover all the needs of computer and other equipment operations. Today there are equipment technologies that provide for a much broader policy objective. These policies now come under the umbrella of the information systems organization with its information technology units.

It will be the responsibility of information systems to mandate uniform standards of equipment to be acquired and operated. Requirements for user instruction manuals will also be provided. Supply selections will be coordinated by a representative of the information systems unit and a representative of purchasing. The end-user computer committee will advise them. The policy objective is to provide quality equipment and supplies at a minimum of cost.

S3.1.3 Microcomputer/PC Operations Policy

Information systems is responsible for maintaining and enforcing a company-wide operation program for computer hardware and ancillary information processing devices. The head of information systems will assign the responsibility to an IT unit to coordinate end-user microcomputer/PC and ancillary devices. An end-user computer committee will be formed. The committee will contain no more than seven or less than three end-users and a purchasing department representative. The representative of the IT unit should be the chairperson of the committee. The committee will follow management's policy and define it for company-wide policies and procedures.

All user unit supervisors will comply fully with the policies. There will be procedures to enforce these policies. Each unit head will be provided with a policy and procedure manual, which will also contain a recommended equipment list. The approved equipment list will be referred to for acquisitions. In cases of special hardware needs, a request memo will be sent to the committee chairperson. A waiver may be granted by the committee.

Employee-owned computers and other equipment of any kind are not allowed on the company's property. Special permission can be granted by information technology management to vendors. Employee-owned computer software, disks, electronic devices, mobile phones, pagers, and magnetic devices are not allowed on company property.

2. END-USER COMPUTER COMMITTEE

S3.2 END-USER COMPUTER COMMITTEE

A committee will provide policies and procedures to standardize and provide assistance and training for end-users of computers and ancillary devices. This committee should work with the hardware and software committees, chaired by the information technology asset manager. The hardware and software committee is formed more for the standardization and control of hardware and software. The end-user computer committee represents the users and their needs along with an expanded list of office equipment. The committee's main concerns are being a source of information for users, providing management with user needs, and policing operations to ensure that policies and procedures are being followed.

S3.2.1 Committee Organization

The committee will be made up of no more than seven or less than three end-user unit heads. The purchasing department will furnish a representative to the committee, as will the information systems unit. The chairperson will be the information systems representative. If the company has an office manager, he/she should be a committee person. If the company has a graphics unit, the head of that unit will be on the committee. The size of the committee will vary depending on the size and complexity of the company.

The committee will provide policies and procedures to standardize and provide assistance and training for end-users of computers and ancillary devices for the company. The actual name of the committee will not have to comply with the name provided in this document. The committee will meet once a month and call special meetings as needed. The committee will have notes taken of the meetings. A copy of the approved minutes will be provided to each committee member, the committee's file, the information systems head, the information technology asset manager, the information technology end-user computer technician unit, and the administrative VP.

S3.2.2 Secondary Committee(s)

If the company has other sites that are not in the same city, it will have a person, or chairperson, from each site reporting to the corporate committee. When the site is small enough, it will only have one person who will be appointed by the local plant or operations manager. This person will be doing the task for the corporate committee. This person will provide the committee with the location needs and the degree of compliance of the corporate policies and procedures. A copy of the information will also be provided to the local plant or operations manager. If the other site is large enough, it will have a committee to resolve local problems and needs. The committee will have three to nine members. The site's office manager, graphics unit, purchasing unit, and information systems units will each have a representative on the committee. The local plant or operations manager will appoint the committee chairperson.

The committee will provide policies and procedures to standardize and provide assistance and training for end-users of computers and ancillary devices at the local level. The actual name of the committee will not have to comply with the name provided in this manual. The committee will meet once a month and call special meetings as needed. The committee will have notes taken of the meetings. A copy of the approved minutes will be provided to each committee member, the committee's file, the local information systems head, the local information technology asset manager, primary company end-users' computer committee, and the local plant or operations manager.

3. USER IT SUPPORT

S3.3 END-USER TECHNICAL SUPPORT

End-user technical support is available in several forms. The information systems organization can provide some forms of support. Other end-user support is provided by different vendors. End-user support will be provided in one form or another for stand-alone computers and network microcomputer/PC systems.

Payment for these services will depend on company polices. The payment can come from one central source and/or department budgets. Whichever method is used, a record system will be maintained.

S3.3.1 Computer Technician

Computer technician is the title given to the IT person in the user support unit that helps with end-user computers and equipment problems. Some organizations use the title of PC manager for this job. In either case, the person in charge of this unit reports to the head of information systems. The end-user will contact this unit when there is no help desk or the help desk cannot solve a problem. The problem may be hardware, software, or a supply item.

A. Computer technician skill requirements

The computer technician will have general knowledge of the user's PC hardware and/or software uses, including supply items. The hardware and software are identified under their respected approved lists. For large, complex organizations there will be specialists for lesser-used equipment. Each computer technician will have given areas to cover within the company. These areas will have hardware and software similarities. The computer technician will be called if the computer operator thinks it is a problem that the help desk cannot walk them through. It could even be a problem where the computer technician said to call them the next time it happens. The computer technician will more often resolve end-user hardware problems than the help desk, while the help desk will more often solve the end-user's software operations problems. Help desk personnel and the computer technicians should get to know each other for a mutual benefit.

B. Computer technician resource requirements

The computer technician will be provided with a tool kit to cover the kind of hardware which he/she will need to resolve problems. This will be carried in an attaché case provided by the company. There will be a minimum of space for spare parts. Supply items that are often used should be stored close to the computer operation. Other items needed may be gotten by someone else, from the source, to save the technician's time. The computer technician will also be provided with a beeper. A portable cell phone will be provided the technician as needed.

C. Computer technician's responsibilities

The technician will maintain a daily activity log. The computer technician should perform the following computer tasks at the user's site:

- Replace faulty computer parts.
- Perform memory upgrades.
- Add additional ports to desk-top computers.
- Add an additional I/O device.
- Check connection cords.
- Run a virus check and remove the virus.
- Check the operation of the modem.
- Reformat a hard drive.
- Reload the operating system.
- Load new software and confirm that it is operational.
- Install hardware accessories.
- Perform routine diagnostics.
- Reboot the system.
- Remove any unauthorized software from the computer.
- Disconnect and/or remove unauthorized hardware. The hardware device will be turned over to the computer operator's superior.

At times there may be hardware problems that will require the user's computer or attached devices to be taken back to the repair shop. If the time the equipment will be away from its operating area becomes a problem, the computer technician will arrange for a loaner to be provided. The loan will be only for the duration that the user's equipment is not available for their use.

D. The computer technician's work log

While working with the computer, the technician should look for any bootlegged or pirated software. If any is found, the data about it will be recorded in the log. If any unauthorized hardware is attached to the desk-top computer it will be also recorded in the daily log sheet. The superior will acknowledge acceptance of the equipment by signing the computer technician's daily log sheet.

E. Weekly computer technician's report

The charge time will be portal to portal. The charge time will be summarized by user, user's unit, and other duties not charged to a user. An administration or other non-user charge time will be prorated to service calls. If the company has an interdepartment charge system the end-user's department will be charged for the service time for the maintenance. How these costs are handled will depend on the company's accounting practice.

The computer technician will write a short weekly report to the technical unit's head. The report will note any special hardware or software problems that have occurred during the week. Any operator problems that may be resolved will be recommended. Can the operator problems be remedied with operator training, new operation manuals, or equipment? If the operator problem deals with an ergonomics issue, state what the problem is in the report.

S3.3.2 Software Support

There will be software that is not on the current approved computer software list, but is in the asset management software database. Microcomputer/PC end-users that employ the software must have it approved for support before a computer technician can help with the problem. Some of the end-user's utilizing software will be assigned to a computer technician if the help desk cannot be of assistance. The end-user is encouraged to contact the IT unit when the help desk has been unable to solve the software problem. The technician will pull the software file folder for the programs and review the documentation before going to the end-user's workplace.

Computer technicians are not expected to solve all the end-user's problems that they are assigned. There will be special hardware and/or software technicians that are not generalists. They will work throughout the company sites that need their special skills. When the user or help desk contacts the IT unit for computer support, they will need to provide information to have the proper technician answer the service call.

Asset management software database has the inventory information of legally owned company software. All software on the approved computer software list will be on the asset management software database. Not all asset management software database programs will be found on the approved computer software list. Software problems for these programs will not all be resolved by the technician. The kind of software will determine its solution source.

A. End-user computer software

   The software for end-users is found on the approved computer software list. This software is supported by the help desk and the IT technical support unit.

B. IT computer software

   The software for the IT units are found on the approved computer software list. This software is supported by the IT programming unit.

C. IT unit's computer software

Other IT units that are using purchased packaged software may call on the IT technical support unit for assistance. If the software was developed by the IT programming unit, they should be contacted for support. This software is in the asset management software database, but seldom found on the approved computer software list.

D. Special computer software

All software is required to be on the asset management software database. This software can include several types of programs and may be supported by information systems. If the software is not found on the asset management software database it will not be supported. The question will be asked, how did the user come into possession of the software?

Some special computer software, not on the approved computer software list, but on the asset management software database can be identified as follows:

1. End-user software still in use

   End-users can use software that is no longer available but is still supported. The software may be no longer available on the market or about to be replaced. There is no need to replace the software at present. This software will be supported.

2. Mainframe computer operations software

   This software is used for mainframe operations and is not available to end-users of microcomputer/PC systems. This software is supported by IT operations programmers. The IT programming unit may help IT computer operations if it developed the program(s).

3. Software for special applications

   This software is purchased for specially approved application and/or hardware. The software will not be supported. The department that arranged to acquire the software is responsible for obtaining the needed support.

4. Software testing

   Purchased software for testing, for possible future use, will not be supported. The person who acquired the program(s) will seek his/her needed support from the vendor.

5. Turn-key software operations

   Contracts drawn for vendor developed turn-key operated systems will be supported by the vendor.

S3.3.3 Network Computer Technical Support

Networked microcomputer/PC systems and work group systems are more complex. Their hardware configurations are more intricate as well as their support needs. The network of computers depend on the system server. The system server computer may have a database. This all will require more support from the information systems' IT units than what the stand-alone computers require. There will be the need for support from the following IT units.

A. IT technical support unit

This unit support will be available for network or work group operations. The IT technical support unit can store more spare parts for the system at the user site. There should be a more knowledgeable person, such as a lead operator, with the system operation to resolve some day-to-day operation problems.

The technical support unit will also be required to provide communications support. This would be for an LAN (local area network) system. If there is a need for a gateway connection, it will be handled by that technician.

The technical support unit will work with the work group's lead operator with any training needs. If the technical support unit has a IT trainer, this person will provide assistance. If there is no IT training unit, the company training department or a training vendor can be used. The following types of assistance could help with training:

- Vendor tutorial software.
- Third-party video tapes.
- Programmed instruction package.
- Overhead transparencies.
- Slides.
- Audio instruction procedures.
- Operator instructional manuals.
- Troubleshooting program instructions.
- Lectures and demonstrations.
- Pretests for end-users.

B. IT Programming support

If the network or work group system was developed by the IT programming unit, it will be supported by them.

C. Database support

The information systems database unit will be fully involved with any database problems. The database unit representative can restrict access to database file information when he/she may think it would put the files in danger of being corrupted. Database support personnel would be available to help with any backup and recovery procedures.

S3.3.4 *Computer Ergonomics Support*

If the company has an environmental ergonomics unit, it should be available to provide service to the information systems units. If the service is not available, there are consulting firms available for this kind of support. Most ergonomic problems would not require a consultant. A person will be selected in the end-user technical support unit and trained. This person will provide support to IT units and end-users of computer devices. There are now college courses available along with short commercial programs on the subject of ergonomics. There are reading materials in the form of books and periodicals.

Comment:

There is a national organization with local chapters, which covers the area of ergonomics, called the Human Factors and Ergonomics Society. The address is P.O. Box 1369 Santa Monica, CA 90406-1369. Their Fax number is (310) 394-2410, and their phone number is (310) 394-1811.

Comment:

AliMed publishes an excellent ergonomics and occupational health catalog. The catalog also has information that is helpful to anyone working in this area. To contact them, write AliMed, 297 High Street, Dedham, MA 02026. Their Fax number is (800) 437-2966, their phone number is (800) 225-2610, and for information the extension is 6901. They also have training material available.

S3.3.5 Maintenance Contracting

All the hardware may not be maintained by a company's own IT personnel. Vendor equipment service contracting for some devices would be a better solution in some instances than in-house service. Some ancillary devices would be best maintained by contracting out the work. Some items that may be leased would also include service agreements. Contracts can be for an unlimited number of service calls or on a by-call basis. Contracts can provide for the spare parts or be charged as installed. Some vendors can offer an array of equipment that they can service. Service can be provided for normal working hours or around the clock.

There can be one or more service vendors. There are firms that will provide a full-service blanket for all or almost all hardware. Other firms may have service for one or more machines. It is something to consider when deciding the kind of service is best for the company.

If vendor bids are possible, request for bids letters will be sent. The bid proposals will be reviewed by the IS head or his/her representative and the end-user committee. The optimum vendor will be selected and receive the contract. The end-user charges for this service will be determined. If company policy dictates how the costs will be internally handled, there is no problem. If no such policy is in place, the end-user committee and information systems management will resolve the issue.

Before any maintenance contracts are signed, they will be reviewed by the legal representative of the company. After they are approved, they will be signed by the authorized management personnel. Purchasing will be contacted as to the arrangement they have for such contracts. The procedure that will be followed will be the corporate procedure for contracting services.

4. FREESTANDING MICROCOMPUTERS

S3.4 Freestanding Microcomputer/PC Operations

Freestanding microcomputers are not hardwired to any computer-networked system. They may contain a modem to assess other systems. The nature of their operation does not depend on other computers. The operators of such devices are expected to resolve some of the day to day tasks to maintain their hardware. These computers can be found any where within a company. The lap-top computers assigned to individuals may be allowed to be off the company's premises. These computers will be supported by the help desk and the IT end-user technical support unit of information systems.

S3.4.1 PC Procedures

Various PC operations may have differing degrees of autonomy, but the duties of the IT technical support unit and the help desk is to enforce the microcomputer/PC operation policies—this also includes the stand-alone PC procedures. The computer hardware and support devices will have a person responsible for the use of the equipment. The person will read all the printed rules, operator's manual, and the procedures for operating the hardware. He/she will know who to contact for the related problem. The PC operators will receive training for their related duties for the computer system operation. Additional training will be provided by the department management for the department's special needs. Professional training assistance will be solicited from the IT training unit or the corporate training department.

If the computer is operated by more than one person, a systems administrator will be needed for all the machines that have more than one operator. The unit manager will be responsible for assigning a person in his/her unit as the systems administrator for the multi-user equipment. The systems administrator will be assigned the duties that are normally assigned to a one-person operator for maintaining the system. The unit manager has the ultimate responsibilities for the computers that are assigned to his/her area.

There are standard operating procedures that apply to all PC operations. Those procedures are as follows:

A. Turning on the system

To turn on the computer system, the operator follows the manufacturer's prescribed procedures. If the computer does not receive its power from a UPS (uninterrupted power supply) source, do not turn on the machine if there may be a power failure. When a power failure is possible the equipment should be turned off. Turn on the surge protection switch if there is no UPS.

The operator checks to see that the monitor is displaying properly after the operating system has brought its display into view. If the system is not operating, the operator should reboot the computer. If the computer will not start, the operator will contact the help desk. If the help desk cannot walk the operator through the problem, the help desk operator will contact an IT computer technician.

B. Turning off the computer system

To turn off the computer system, the following steps are followed:

- Remove all external memory devices.
- Proceed with the exit from the operating system.
- Turn off the peripheral equipment.
- Turn off the computer.
- Turn off the surge protection switch and/or UPS.

C. Daily operation

There are items that the operator or systems administrator will do daily. These items may be done at the start or end of each work day. At times some of the items will require attention more than once a day. The following are checked daily:

- Paper supply is sufficient in the printer.
- Quality of printing meets standards.
- Quality of the monitor display is satisfactory.
- The computer equipment meets cleanliness levels.
- Mouse working properly.

D. Operation rules and procedures

Information systems' policies and procedures and special area rules will apply to the computer operation at all times. They are:

1. Food and beverages

   No food or beverages are to be placed on the hardware or data storage devices (disks, zip disks, CDs, etc.).

2. Smoking

   No smoking is permitted near the computer area.

3. Air-conditioned environment

   The computer work area environment is required to have clean air, recommended temperature, and specific humidity levels.

4. Telephone placement

   Telephones and magnetic devices will be kept away from the computer and disks. To be safe, a two-foot distance is recommended.

5. Surge protection

   All computer and peripheral devices will be plugged into a surge protection unit. Non-computer electric devices are not to be plugged into the surge protection or UPS outlets. The same wall plug used for computer equipment will not be used for non-computer devices. Only grounded electrical outlets are to be used for computer devices.

6. Illegal software copying

   The illegal copying of software is absolutely forbidden. This action is grounds for dismissal.

7. Removing hardware

   No computers or peripheral devices are allowed to be removed from the company premises. Any movement of equipment to another department or exchanging equipment will be reported to the information technology asset manager.

8. Personal computer restrictions

   No employee-owned computer hardware is allowed on the company grounds.

9. Disk restrictions

   No company-owned disk devices are permitted to be removed from company site(s). For company-owned use of lap-top computers with disks, see lap-top computer procedures. No personal disks are allowed to be brought onto company site(s).

10. Internet restrictions

   No use of internet for personal use is permitted.

11. Software restrictions

   No purchased or leased software may be copied unauthorized onto other company computers. This action is forbidden by company policy. The exchange of company-owned software should also be reported, so the asset management software database will be updated. All maintenance service calls that access the computer will check for unauthorized software. Unauthorized software will be removed during the service call.

12. Confidential data

   Any restricted or confidential data will be stored only on authorized computers and disk storage devices.

E. PC backup procedures

   All stand-alone PC operators will perform their own backup operations. Backup procedures should not violate any company information systems policies.

1. New software

   Newly purchased software is backed up in accordance with the software manufacturer's specifications. When a new type of software is received by the unit, that is not on the asset management software database, the end-user technical support unit will be contacted. The support unit will run a virus check on the new software before it is placed into a computer by the user. The software package will be handed to a computer technician with the seal unbroken. If only one copy can be made, it will be made by the end-user technical support unit. The backup copy is sent to the information technology asset manager. The information technology asset manager will receive a copy even if more than one copy is permitted.

   The original software copy will be returned to the end-user. After the software program is copied it is tested. If a problem is found, the vendor is contacted (if it was purchased by the unit). If it was not purchased by the unit, the person that wrote the purchase requisition will be contacted about the problem.

2. Hard-drive backup procedures

   Hard-drive backup procedures cover both software and data. Backup for stand-alone computers is not usually the same throughout the company. The operation the PC performs will dictate how often and in what manner the hard-drive backup be done. The IT database unit should be contacted for advice, to ensure that the proper precautions are taken. The following procedures are available:

   • At the end of each work day, all new data is copied onto disks or tape. Some operations will require copies of active transaction data and a backup copy disk be made.

   • A mirrored hard-drive copy be maintained on a second hard drive.

   • Copy the disk drive to tape more than once per day as needed.

   • Copy onto secondary disks only data that needs to be backed up.

   • If the device can be set to read-only after backup, set it to read-only.

> **Comment:**
>
> **While writing this book I had a disk crash. The disk had to be replaced. The repair person that came to help said "one should expect to have a crash, and not wonder *if* you may have a crash." The old disk went out with the trash, along with over three chapters that I failed to back up.**

F. Computer system crash

When there is a crash, the user turns off the system, writes down what occurred just prior to the crash, the time of the crash, and calls the help desk or the end-user technical support unit. Who is called will depend on the local procedure. If the computer has other users, a sign is posted on the computer stating that the system has crashed and it is not to be used.

G. Hardware problem

For hardware problems, the user refers to the operating manual. If the problem cannot be corrected, the problem and its effect on the hardware are noted. Hardware problems will be referred to the end-user technical support unit. If the computer has other users, a sign is posted on the computer stating that the system has crashed and it is not to be used. If a peripheral device is not working, a sign is placed on the inoperative device noting that it is out of order and whether or not the computer is usable without the device.

H. Software problem

Before contacting the help desk, write down the details of what happened. Make a list of the corrective measures that were tried. Before placing the call to the help desk, bring the program up to the point that the problem occurred.

S3.4.2 Lap-Top Computer Procedures

Various lap-top computer operations may have differing degrees of autonomy, but the duty of the IT technical support unit and the help desk is to enforce the lap-top computer operation policies and procedures. The lap-top computer hardware and support devices will have a person responsible for the use of the equipment. This person will read all the printed rules, operator's manual, and the procedures for operating the hardware. They will know who to contact for the related problem. The lap-top computer users will receive training for their related duties for the computer system operation. Additional training will be provided by the department management for the department's special needs. Professional training assistance will be solicited from the IT training unit or the corporate training department.

If the lap-top computer is operated by more than one person, there will be the need for a systems administrator for the machine. This person may seldom use the computer. Their duty is to keep track of who is using it and take care of its needs. There will be a sign-out and reservation procedure for the lap-top computer. All the policies and procedures will be followed by the multiple users. User failure to comply with the rules will forfeit their privilege to use the lap-top computer.

A lap-top computer assigned to a person will maintain the machine. The person signing for the lap-top computer and its accessories will be responsible for the equipment. They will be permitted to take the lap-top computer with them when they leave the company site. All the policies and procedures that govern the use of computers will still apply. They will be given an ID card with the brand name and serial number of the lap-top computer. The card will also contain the user's name, title, and assigned department.

Lap-top computer users will most likely also have a desk-top microcomputer or docking station. They will have to be very careful what information they exchange between the two machines. Software on one computer cannot freely be placed on their other computer without informing the information technology asset manager. Exchanging data between machines will require extra concern when the lap-top is taken from the company site. Sensitive data should not be on the hard drive if it can be stored on a disk. The disks and computer should not be carried together.

Lap-top and notebook computers are targeted by thieves to be stolen. Some even work in pairs to steal the machines. Sometimes the data stolen is much more of a concern to the company than the value of the computer. The insurance, if any, cannot cover the total loss to the company. Access codes can be used to start the system. They will be employed by all lap-top and notebook computers.

There are standard operating procedures that apply to all lap-top and notebook computer operations. The computer will be provided with a user procedure manual. Read the manual before first using the machine. Do not write anything in the manual that would help a thief, such as your password, telephone number, etc. The procedures to remember are as follows:

A. Transporting the system

When on a trip, keep disks and manuals apart from the computer. Never leave your computer case unattended.

B. Turning on and off the computer

Follow the instructions in the manual.

C. Daily operation

For prolonged use or when charging the batteries, make sure the power source provides the correct voltage and ground required. When using public phones in some parts of the world, someone else may receive a copy of the e-mail you send and receive.

D. Operation rules and procedures

Information systems' policies and procedures and special area rules will apply to the computer operation at all times. They are:

1. Food and beverages

No food or beverages are to be placed on or the hardware or data storage device (disks, zip disks, CD disks, etc.)

2. Smoking

Avoid smoking near the computer.

3. Air-conditioned environment

The computer work area environment is required to have clean air and recommended room temperatures.

4. Telephone placement

Telephones and magnetic devices will be kept away from the computer and disks. To be safe, a two-foot distance is recommended. When recording voice input to a word processing program, use a lapel microphone attached to a voice-activated tape recorder.

5. Authorized software

Only company-authorized computer software will be used.

6. Illegal software copying

The illegal copying of software is absolutely forbidden.

7. Personal computer restrictions

No personal computers will be down-loaded or up-loaded to the company computer. No personal disks will be placed into a company computer. No company disks will be placed into any personal computer.

8. Internet restrictions

The internet will be used with guarded caution.

9. Backup procedures

Valuable data should be backed up onto a secondary storage device. Word processing should have automatic backup at close intervals.

E. Computer system crash

When there is a crash, turn off the computer and remove any disk. Write down what occurred just prior to the crash. Take the computer and the information to your office and call the technical support unit.

F. Operating problems

Make some notes as to what happened and call the help desk for assistance.

S3.4.3 Security and Environment

Desk-top microcomputers should be located in a safe environment. This also applies to lap-top and notebook computers within a company environment and when taken from a company site. The physical location of the computer equipment is part of security. The location environment is a major part of security and operating conditions of computers.

A. Physical location

The room the computers are kept in should be locked when not in use. In the event the room cannot be locked, serious consideration should be given to the use of a cable-lock to deter removal of any desk-top computer hardware. Lap-top and notebook computers should be in a safe place at all times. Access to the room the computers are located will be secured when not in use. If it is in a remote area of the company, it will have a access alarm system. Only authorized persons should gain entry to a area with computers during off hours.

Comment:

I had an adult student that was a computer major and worked a full-time job. He was a night janitor in a local high school. When we got on the subject of computer security, he provided some interesting information. At night he would use the school principal's computer. He had access to all the employees' salaries and their evaluations.

The first computer rooms were air conditioned because of the heat from the radio tubes. With chips today being so compact, that heat can still be a problem. The internal fans keep the system cool enough to work on factory floors. However, a cool dry room is best for people and computer operations. The main computer center rooms have had controlled access for years. The concern was for the security of the data and software. Today much of the data and software has been moved out of the customarily well-secured area.

Microcomputers are now not as guarded as the mainframes were. Not only is the concern for the security of the same data, but now there is the concern for the hardware. With freestanding microcomputers found in many company areas, there is a concern for each of the computer sites as well as the transmission of data between the sites. In some ways the modern technology makes information systems more at risk, but it also provides the tools to guard the technology.

1. Room access

    Access to the room is the first line of computer security. The access is granted to people that have a need to be there, even at non-working hours. When the number of people that have access is reduced, the safer the hardware may be. A record of when access was made and by whom may be required.

2. Mobile computers

    Lap-top and notebook computers will not be in a company environment at all times. The person responsible for the computer will try to provide it with a suitable and safe environment. When traveling by air, it should be carry-on luggage while in transit. All removable disks and computer manuals will not be in the computer case.

3. Special transporting of computers

    In the event that microcomputers are transported for a special event that does not permit a carry-on status, written permission must be requested from the head of information systems or his/her agent. Approval will be granted in writing. A special procedure will be provided for this event. The software (either in part or all) should be hand carried.

B. Software security

The loss of software and data can do much more damage to a company than just the loss of the hardware. The precautions to safeguard hardware are not enough to protect the software. The access to software comes in many forms. Therefore to protect the software, several different devices are required. The following items will be reviewed and considered for software protection:

1. Computer access

   - Microcomputer access locks.

   - Password access.

   - Built-in date/time windows for access.

   - Lockable covering devices.

2. Safeguarding secondary storage data

   - Fireproof safes.

   - Off-site backup storage.

   - Alarm system to monitor for smoke and room temperature. The information would be sent to the firm's security force or it can be contracted to a service company. If this system is used, it would be advisable to add an intruder alarm. The alarm would also help protect the computer hardware.

   - Encrypted data storage.

3. Data transmission

   - Caller ID devices.

   - Encrypted data transmission.

   - Password ID.

Comment:

Due to popular demand, more security devices are coming on the market. One recent innovation is by CyberAngel. It is marketed by Computer Sentry Software, Inc., 381 River Drive, Suite 130, Franklin, TN 37064. Their telephone number is (800) 501-4344, FAX (615) 790-9051. It calls the company through the lap-top computer's internal modem and determines the physical location, after which it will lock the modem so no access can be made. Available features include password, encryption engine, and hot-key protection. For more information about their low-cost protection, contact CyberAngel at http://www.sentryinc.com.

5. WORK GROUP COMPUTERS

S3.5 WORK GROUP MICROCOMPUTER/PC PROCEDURES

A work group system will be an autonomous file server computer operation. The group will have a common goal that brings them together. The employees would be working together, with or without a work group computer system. Work group computer systems can vary, in configuration and process, from one area to another within the same company. The work group microcomputer/PC system will comply with the company's information systems policies.

S3.5.1 Work Group Computer Coordinator

The work group computer coordinator's duties and responsibilities vary from location to location to provide flexibility to best serve the company and the work group. The actual title of the work group computer coordinator may also vary depending from one company site to another.

A. Coordinator's responsibilities

The following areas of the coordinator's responsibilities are:

- Process purchase requests for hardware and software.
- Assist with budgeting for anticipated hardware and software.
- Be the unit's help desk.
- Be the unit's trainer.
- Enforce corporate computer hardware and software policies.
- Maintain a supply of spare parts, computer supply items, and loaner equipment.
- Ensure that database backups are done at scheduled times.
- Maintain the computer network server.
- Publish a work group newsletter.
- Maintain a work group electronic bulletin board.

B. Consulting coordinator

The work group computer coordinator is also the work group's consulting coordinator. He/she coordinates the computer needs of the work group with the following:

- IT units of the information systems organization.
- The information technology asset manager.
- The information systems software committee.

- Purchasing.
- Vendors.

The work group computer coordinator is the work group's unit consultant. This covers the work group's hardware, software, and the LAN system. If there is a need to have a gateway to access other data, he/she will consult the work group and define their needs with the database manager. The hardware and software consulting will cover the work group system needs, along with the unit's employee computer needs. This can cover special hardware and software needs that workers in the unit may have.

C. Work group log

The work group computer coordinator will maintain a daily log, which is the data source for monthly reports of his/her activities. The report goes to the department head that the work group computer system serves.

The daily log will be an audit trail of the work group computer coordinator's time. It will list times for the following items:

- Consulting management.
- Consulting end-users.
- User training.
- Software troubleshooting.
- Hardware troubleshooting.
- Vendor communications.
- Travel time.
- Administrative duties.
- Miscellaneous items.
- Processing purchase requests for hardware and software.
- Publishing the work group newsletter and maintaining a work group electronic bulletin board.
- Developing new systems.
- Continuing education and reading time required to stay current with new technology.

S3.5.2 Work Group Daily Operating Procedures

There are standard operating procedures that apply to all users of the system. The procedures will be written by the work group computer coordinator and be available at each monitor station. The procedures are as follows:

A. Turning on the work group system

Approved lead operators will start up the computer system. They will follow the procedure provided for the system start up. The lead operator will check that the file server computer for the system is working properly. All the peripheral units will be turned on.

The lead operator will go to their workstation and turn on their computer. He/she will log on to the work group's computer system. After being logged on, the lead operator will run a prescribed routine to confirm the system is operational. If there are any problems the lead operator cannot correct he/she will contact the work group computer coordinator. If the coordinator is not available, he/she will contact the help desk.

B. Turning off the work group system

The lead operator will shut down the computer system. They will follow the procedure provided for the system shut down. The lead operator will check that the file server computer disk information is saved as a backup before the system is shut down. The backup disks or tapes are locked in the fireproof safe. All the peripheral units will now be turned off before the computer is shut down.

C. Daily operations

As part of the daily operations, a log is maintained by the lead operators. When the system was brought up and when it was turned off will be signed and the time entered. Problems that occurred during the daily operations will be written in the log and the time it occurred.

The system is checked daily by the lead operator for the following items:

- There is a good supply of paper in the printer.
- The printing quality is good. If it is not, correct it.
- Any housekeeping that is needed is done.

S3.5.3 Operation Policies and Procedures

These are for all individuals in the work group using the work group's computer equipment. The rules apply to the network server computer as well as the machines that are wired to it. The network server can have printers attached directly to them or be placed any where in the network group area along with other peripheral equipment. These policies are:

- No food or beverages are to be placed on or near the hardware or storage devices.
- No smoking is permitted near the computer.
- A clean, cool, and normal humidity environment is required.
- Telephones and magnetic devices will be kept about two feet from the computers and data storage devices.
- The network server computer will be attached to a UPS device. The other computers will be provided with UPS devices as needed. All computers and peripheral equipment will be plugged in to surge protected outlets. Other equipment that is not part of the network will not be plugged into an UPS or surge protection device. The UPS and surge protection devices will be plugged into grounded electric outlets. The outlets that are used for the network computer system will not be used by other devices.
- No personal hardware or software is allowed on company property.
- No illegal copying of software is permitted.
- No hardware or software is permitted to be taken off company property without written permission of the department head.

S3.5.4 Work Group Microcomputer/PC Security

Work group microcomputer/PC systems should have the degree of security that is required for the nature of their activity. The work group computer coordinator has the responsibility for safekeeping the hardware, soft-

Comment:
A couple of years ago I had placed a video tape on a small pile of papers so I could use a high-power video/audio tape eraser to wipe it clean. Later, when I removed the papers, I found under them an unopened sealed envelope that contained some newly purchased software, which was now completely erased.

ware and data. This responsibility should be supported by the physical location and the security devices provided by the company.

A. Physical location

The area the work group computer system is in will be locked when not in use. Only authorized personnel will have keys to the area. If the area is not visible by company security, it will have an intruder alarm system. The area will also have a smoke and temperature alarm system. The floor close to the file server computer should be able to support a fireproof safe. There should be some lights left on continually 24 hours a day.

B. System access security

There will be a hardware access security to the work group computer system. It will be used when the system is not in operation. When workstation computers are not in operation they will be locked. This will consist of the following:

• Lockable work stations.

• Access code required to use a workstation.

• Workstation access code changed when needed or twice a year.

• Lockable file server computer that will be bolted to the table.

• Access code required to use the file server computer, which will not be accessible after three failed attempts to access the machine. To start the computer will now require the work group computer coordinator.

• Removable data and software disks will be stored in the fire-proof safe. The safe will be locked at all times.

• Keys to the safe and file server computer will only be given to the lead operators and the work group computer coordinator.

S3.5.5 Software Acquisition

Software may be developed in house or may be acquired from an outside source. In-house–developed software will be done by the IT programming unit. The work group computer coordinator position will be assigned to a person in the department that will use the computer system. This person will be the unit's representative while the system is being developed for the department. The work group computer coordinator will not be a full-time position at first. This person will assist the software developer to collect the needed information to develop the system. While the system is being developed, the work group computer coordinator will be gaining knowledge about the system.

The cost of this project will come from funds budgeted for which department the system is being developed. The budget will also provide funds for the purchase or lease of the hardware. The budget dollars may come from more than one budget year.

The work group system is not limited to in-house development. It can also be provided by contract programmer(s), or as a turn-key system. If the system is not developed in house, the work group computer coordinator will still be needed. He/she will still serve in the same capacity as he/she would have if the stystem had been developed in house.

There can be other forms of software acquisition. They may be done through the efforts of the work group computer coordinator.

A. Purchased software

Some use may be made of software sold on the open market. This requires the minimum of effort on the part of the user to have it running on the work group microcomputer system. One such software that will required to be purchased is the operating system program. This software will be purchased with the development of the system. If the end system is a turn-key system it will also require an operating system program.

There are marketed programs that maybe added as needed by the work group operation. If the workstation microcomputers do not contain disk drives, and one person in the work group needs the program, it will be loaded to the work group's file server computer. The person that needs the program will receive it from the file server computer.

B. New written programs

After the system becomes operational there will be needs for some special programs written for the system. These programs may be written by the IT programming unit, contract programmer, turn-key vendor, or the work group computer coordinator.

S3.5.6 Work Group Newsletter

The newsletter may be published monthly or even quarterly. It should provide news about the department and the computer system. It should announce:

- Forthcoming training programs.
- Who completed what programs.
- New hardware or software availability.
- New work group system policies and procedures.
- New work group job opportunities.

The ideal size for a newsletter is printed on a 11″ by 17″ paper. It then can be folded into a $8^1/_2$″ by 11″ document. It will be saddle stapled to hold it together. If this cannot be done, a stapled $8^1/_2$″ by 11″ paper will suffice. A desk-top publishing program or even a high-end word processing program can generate a newsletter. Graphics and photos will enhance the appearance of the newsletter. This information can also be provided by an Intranet website.

6. SOFTWARE SUPPORT

S3.6 END-USER SOFTWARE SUPPORT

There is a need for end-user software support for PC operations. This service may be available from an on-site help desk or an outsourced help desk service. There can be one or more sources of software support available to the end-users. The IT management will provide for this software support service. The service will be monitored to ensure that the support provided meets user's needs and is provided at an optimum cost. For each software support operation, the service cost may be part of the IT budget or charged back to end-users' budgets.

S3.6.1 IT Software Support Operation

The design of software support will be the responsibility of the IT software support unit, within the IT computer operations department. This unit may be one or more persons who will also monitor the ongoing software support operations. This is to ensure that the software support package will be altered as needed. The person responsible for this operation will have the title of IT software support coordinator and will report to the IT computer operations manager. The IT software support unit's budget will be part of the IT computer operations budget.

A. IT software support responsibilities

The IT software support coordinator may require assistance. This help may be in the form of temporary assistance or permanent full- and part-time people. The IT software support coordinator may have additional duties assigned by the IT operations manager if his/her load is not sufficient to justify a full-time position.

The IT software support unit will be responsible for:

- The analysis of what services are available that will address microcomputer user needs.

- Providing project leadership for packaging software support programs for microcomputer end-users. The project leader will be provided assistance, as needed, from IT operations, in-house help desk managers, end-user management, the IT training unit, purchasing, and the firm's legal counsel.

- Policing software use. All software should be authorized purchases or approved in-house developed.

- New software planning.

- Approving and controlling all microcomputer Beta programs.

- Coordinating and providing assistance with installing help desk software support tools.

- Providing and/or coordinating help desk training.

- Coordinating new end-user, PC, and software training. The training source may be a purchased third-party package, in-house–developed package, or a vendor software support package.

- Publishing and distributing a software support newsletter. The newsletter will be published monthly, or as needed. It will be sent to the IT computer operations manager, all in-house help desk software engineers, the IT training unit, and microcomputer end-users. The newsletter will contain pending changes to software, hardware, and help desk staffing information. This information can also be provided by an Intranet website.

B. Help desk services

If the software support service is to be provided by a in-house help desk unit, the charge-back procedures, if required, will be developed by the IT software support unit. The accounting department will be involved with the internal budget funds charges and credits. A monthly charge report will be provided to each end-user manager and the IT software support coordinator.

C. Vendor software support services

For vendor software support services, the IT software coordinator will receive statements from the vendors for payment. If any of the statements are sent to accounts payable by vendors, they will not be paid but will be forwarded to the IT software support coordinator. The IT software support coordinator will review each vendor statement for payment. If there is a billing problem, the IT software support coordinator will contact the vendor to correct the issue. If needed, the vendor will send a revised statement to the IT software support coordinator. Statements to be paid will be hand stamped. See Exhibit S3.6.1-1 for a sample of the stamp. The following will be posted to the provided areas on the stamp:

- The current date.
- Date to be paid.
- Purchase order number.
- Control number, the sequence number of the authorization to be paid. This number will identify the number of the authorizations approved to date. This will not be needed if there is only one statement a year to be paid.
- Signature of the authorized person.

APPROVED TO PAY

CURRENT DATE_____   PAY DATE_____

PO NUMBER_____ CONTROL NUMBER_____

APPROVED BY_____

Exhibit S3.6.1-1

A copy of the approved statement, after being stamped and posted, will be filed by vendor in the IT software support coordinator's work area. The original document will be forwarded to accounts payable for payment.

D. Monthly service report

The IT software support coordinator will issue a monthly service report to the IT computer operations manager that will contain the costs of software support. These are costs from the vendor software support and the in-house help desk support. The report will list, by line, the unit(s) receiving the software support, the charges incurred for the month by the unit(s) and the budgeted amount, and year-to-date amounts for actual and budgeted. Vendors will be listed first, followed by in-house listings. A copy of each month's report will be filed at the IT software support coordinator's desk.

The IT software support coordinator will issue a monthly usage memo. The memo will be sent to each end-user manager, listing the unit's software support and help desk support usage status. Any abnormal conditions will be noted in the memo.

S3.6.2 Designing a Software Support Package

The process for developing and maintaining a software support operation will depend on several variables. The variables will have different priorities depending on cost and necessity. The following items will be considered and evaluated for the design of the end-user software support program:

- The end-users and their computer skill level.
- The complexity of the software operation.
- Purchased or in-house–developed software.
- The quality of the software operations procedures manual and the level of understanding by the end-users.
- The end-user acceptance level of the software.
- The benefits the end-user expects from the help desk support.

Based on the above collected information, the IT software support coordinator will be responsible for the analysis of what services are available that can address these needs. The service may be a vendor software support service or an in-house help desk. Current vendor software support services or in-house help desk services being used may also be considered to undertake the new need. Costs will be attached to each possible source of service. The IT software support coordinator will be responsible for computing the optimum service cost. A budget request will be made based on the cost expected and a project contingency. A memo will be sent to the IT operations manager detailing the reason for the selection, the cost expected, and the implementation date required. The detail information used in the computation will be attached to the memo.

The IT operations manager will assess the need and determine the approval of the service. If the service is approved by the IT operations manager, he/she will determine who will be responsible for the payment. If IT is to pay for the service and funds are available in the current IT budget, the IT operations manager will request an approval from the head of IT. The approval can be in the form of a memo or e-mail. When the IT operations manager receives notice of approval, if needed, he/she will issue a purchase requisition for the service. A copy of the requisition will be sent to the IT software support coordinator. The IT computer operations manager will send a memo or e-mail to the IT software support coordinator and the affected help desk software support manager, if the service is to be provided by an in-house IT help desk.

If the service is to be paid by the end-user's department, the manager of the end-user's department will be contacted by the IT operations manager for a meeting to discuss the issue. The IT help desk coordinator will also attend the meeting. The help desk process will be started if the end-user manager has the funds available and approves the plan. If the service is to be outsourced, the IT coordinator will complete a purchase requisition, file a copy, and forward it to the end-user manager for his/her signature. The end-user manager will sign the purchase requisition and forward it to purchasing. Purchasing will e-mail the purchase order number to the end-user manager and the IT software support coordinator. The IT software support coordinator will be the vendor contact person for the company.

S3.6.3 Defining Support Structure

Defining support structure is predicated on need of the microcomputer end-users. This need covers both the current and future needs. Proactive software support requires forecasting the end-users' future needs, along with product planning resources to serve the software support provider. The software support will not necessarily all come from one source. The source of different needs of support will come from sources that best serve the given need in the most optimum level of cost for service. The software provider may be the in-house help desk or a vendor-provided software support.

A. New product planning

The IT software support coordinator's new product planning covers new hardware and software availability, Beta software, training technology, developing software support vendors, and how to integrate these items. Effective software support planning requires a mixture of project management skills, IT technical systems analysis skills, and training needs assessments. The IT software support coordinator will be the person responsible for new projects that require new product planning. Supporting the project, as needed, will be other IT software support members and help desk software support engineers. Vendors with their new technology may be enlisted to be involved with the project team. The product that is new to IT services and end-users will be considered as new, even if it has been available from outsourcing vendors for some time.

1. New product planning

New product planning projects have a sequence of events to deliver a solution. The sequence of events is:

- Look at where the end-user and/or help desk is now with currently used hardware and what the requirements are. This first step may be originated by the help desk service or the end-user with a current need.

- The IT software support coordinator will assign the next task to a member of the software support team or do it himself/herself. The task may be simple enough to be performed by one person or may require additional help. The person responsible for developing a plan will set in motion the project effort required. Any additional help will be assigned to the project.

- An analysis of the current operation will be done. The requirements needed to provide the service level wanted will be defined.

- Research will be conducted and software support vendors contacted for the information needed. From this effort, a plan will be defined.

- The final plan will be presented in the form of a proposal, with the benefits described and the expected costs broken down. Alternate plans, if pursued, will be attached to the proposal and the rational for the selection.

- The proposal will require management support and funding; this can be IT management and/or end-user management approval.

- The plan, if approved, will be implemented. If it is not approved, the collected information and proposal will be filed for future reference.

- A post-implementation audit will be conducted by the IT software support coordinator when the new procedure has been operational for one month. This information will be provided to the IT computer operations manager, the end-user manager, and the help desk manager or software support vendor.

2. Planning factors

The plan may require that the following information be contained in the proposal:

- An overall schedule of the process to become operational. Milestone dates will be provided for each segment of the process leading up to the successful operation of the new system.

- An overall assessment of the current help desk software support system, if there is one. What impact the proposed help desk software support system will have on the end-user and the investment cost.

- The hardware and software requirements.

- Training needs of the people involved. Provisions for individual training of new people, because of turnover or expansion. The expected learning curve of the trainees.

- The creditability of the software support vendors involved. Their track record with current or former customers. If need be, the credit department should be able to provide a D and B status of the software vendor.

- If the new procedure is replacing a current one, what can be utilized from the present help desk software support operations.

- How the process will be implemented. The contingencies available during the time the new help desk software support system is being brought up to full performance levels. The contingencies can be any of the following:

  a. All the help desk software engineers assigned will be available. This is not the time to have a software engineer on vacation.

b. The software support vendor will have a contact person available during the time the help desk is in service.

c. Overtime contingency will be provided for both software engineers and end-users.

d. The availability of hardware maintenance people to correct any hardware problems during scheduled working hours.

3. Testing new products

In-house testing is required before a product is considered for use by the software engineers and/or end-users. The IT software support coordinator may pre-test new products, but testing new products for software support engineers will involve both the help desk software support unit and the IT software support coordinator. New products considered are of two kinds: new software support used by the help desk software support engineers and Beta software that may be used by the help desk software support engineers and/or end-users.

a. New help desk products

New help desk products may come in the form of new hardware and/or new software. The term "new" is not to imply that it has just entered the market, but to say it is new to the company. While pre-testing of new products by the IT software support coordinator may be conducted on or off the company's site, testing new products will be done on site if at all possible. The testing should utilize the following benefits:

• The help desk software support engineers know the end-user's needs more than vendors would.

• They know the type of help most likely required by the end-users.

• They know the limitations of the end-users. The turn-around time requirements of end-users is a known key factor.

• The help desk software support engineers know what is expected of their help desk manager.

• The software support engineers have the day-to-day technical skills required to evaluate a new product.

- The software support engineers are aware that they will have to live with the product that is approved.

- If the product is selected and tested, there will be an experience level to be gained if the product is later implemented.

b. Beta testing

The help desk software support unit is a good place to try Beta programs. As the support unit gains experience with the Beta program selected, end-users may be asked to participate in the program. The IT software support coordinator will be require to be involved with Beta programs before they are utilized. He/she should know the status of the running Beta program.

There are some procedures that apply to Beta programs before they can be utilized. The following apply to the use of Beta programs:

- Before a Beta commitment is made, the IT computer operations manager will be required to give approval.

- No end-user will be involved in a Beta program without the consent of his/her manager and the help desk software support manager.

- No online end-user files will be available for use by the Beta programs.

- The relationship with the vendor providing the software will be conducted by the person selected by the IT computer operations manager. This person will also be the source of information for IT personnel and involved end-users.

- Beta programs employed by end-users will be monitored frequently by the help desk software support unit.

B. Support desk models

Support desk models are used to help define the support structure needed for managing end-user problems to resolution. The first selection will not always be assured of success; therefore, an alternate model should be available. It is better to cut losses at this point than to go on with trying to patch up a poor candidate. Finding the successful selection should include the research of other models. The models will be ranked in order of preference. This data will be filed and provide a basis for the next selection.

The model selected should be one that minimizes the help desk software support engineer's work effort and provides the end-users with what is required for their needs. There is no assurance that all parties will get what they all want. The end-user manager may have to determine what is absolutely essential to his/her software support users. When internal billing for software support is done, the end-user manager may have a wider latitude for selecting the service level desired. When the service is provided at the expense of IT computer operations, the IT computer operations manager makes the final decision. This can be appealed by the end-user manager to the head of IT. A compromise may be reached when next year's budget is planned.

1. End-user service levels

   The support desk service levels can vary with different end-users. These levels are determined by end-users' requirements and budget funds available. These needs can, in part, be resolved with end-user training. Training can target the items in question. The model selected would reduce the operating cost if it could deliver different levels of service.

2. End-user paid service level

   User budget paid support is a better gauge for a more actual service level required. End-user management tends to be less satisfied with an IT computer operations budget paying for the service than an internal charge being made to their own budget.

3. Service level cost information

   The service level cost information will be provided to the end-user's management. This information will be provided, if desired, for both IT paid services or end-user paid services.

4. User training model

   end-users will be provided training for the level of service they are to receive. They need to know how to provide information and work with the help desk software support engineer. This will reduce the interaction time and benefit both parties. Training will be provided by IT. The first form of training will be a class, after which individual training will be available to new end-users. Model update training may be in one form or the other. The person responsible for the training should know the end-users and their needs, as well as the software support engineer. He/she should also be knowledgeable about the support desk model selected.

5. Model selection

Software support model selection is predicated on several variables. Choosing the right model for both the end-user and the help desk provider may first start with management. Management knows the requirements and should therefore provide the decisions necessary to properly select the correct model. Management should be able to rely on the following information to help them make the selection:

- The financial status of the company.
- The end-user's skill profile.
- IT management's expertise and risk-taking ability.
- The current help desk software support operations' level of technical and people skills.
- The software support staffing levels.
- Future short- and long-range planning of the IT organization.

From the above information, IT management should provide answers to the following questions:

- What are the spending limits?
- What is the configuration of the help desk/user software support system(s)? Will more than one center be employed by the IT department? If more than one is to be utilized, how will they be deployed? Who will have the overall responsibility and authority for all software support?
- What judgment criteria will be used to evaluate software support performance? Not all services deal with the same complexity of problems. Not all end-users have the same technical skill level, communication level, tolerance level, or job demands. This issue is covered in S3.6.3 D.
- What will be the relationship of the help desk software support organization with IT computer operations and the IT software support coordinator?
- Who will provide the software support service? Will it all be in-house, all vendor provided, or a combination of the two?
- How will the help desk software support units be organized? This is covered in S3.6.4 A.
- What help desk software support will be part of the IT computer

operations' budget? What services will be charged back to the end-user's budget? This is covered in S3.6.4 D.

- What provisions are to be made for required funds that have not been budgeted? Changes to the service levels cannot always be planned.

C. Software support desk implementation

There is a two-step procedure for the software support desk implementation. The first step is the pre-implementation procedure. The second step is the post-implementation procedure.

1. Pre-implementation procedure

When the selection of an operating system has been made, there will be different skill levels of the end-user software support engineers. The skill should be of the level to fully test the model. Not all support engineers employed by the help desk unit will be at the same skill level when the selection is made. Training of these lesser-skilled support engineers will be required. The availability of self-paced tutorial programs, with any other available training tools, will be employed to bring all skill levels to the required level.

End-user training will be done as close to the implementation date as possible. Employing overtime pay may be employed as needed. It should be budgeted as part of the implementation expense. The group training could be provided for one half of the end-user unit at a time. This will allow for a more efficient operation of the end-user unit. End-user tutorials and self-learning models used for introducing new employees to the end-user software support will be made available to all end-users. Current end-users should feel free to use this available training as needed. Each end-user will be provided an operations manual. The end-user should study the manual. There will be a person in the software support unit who can be contacted for any assistance needed. Depending on the need, an after-work-hours telephone contact will be available.

The pre-implementation procedures cannot be considered completed until the following have been completed:

- All end-user software support unit procedures are verified as completed, correct, and in place.
- All end-user unit procedures are completed, are verified as correct, and are in place.
- All end-user software support engineers' operations manuals are in place and confirmed as being read.

- All end-user unit operations manuals are in place and confirmed as being read.
- All the system's hardware has been inspected and tested as operational.
- All the system's software has been tested as operational.
- The total system has been tested, with software support engineers acting as end-users. It is recommended that the testing be observed by end-user personnel.
- The total system has been tested with a system failure. The backup and recovery procedures will be tested.
- Vendor assistance response will be tested and documented.
- A day, that is not a normal work day, will be used by end-users and the support engineers to test the installed software support operations. This should be completed without any correctable incidents.

2. Post-implementation procedure

After the software support operations have been placed into service, the system will be monitored very closely. The IT computer operations manager will assign assistance to the end-user software support unit from his/her staff to help with this procedure. Any irregularities will be duly noted and investigated. Depending on the complexity of the operation, the voice communications may be recorded and studied. Identifying the persons involved is optional. Response and solution times will be averaged, and the shortest and longest times reported. A daily e-mail report will be sent to the IT computer operations manager. After the first week, the software support manager will send the IT computer operations manager an activity report noting whether the expectations were on target and whether there were any additional problems yet to be resolved.

The end-users will record, on provided daily questionnaires, any problems they have encountered. Candid interviews will be conducted with end-users by the person monitoring the process. The daily questionnaires and interview information will be summarized and shared with the software support manager.

The software support manager will do his /her own observation of the operations. He/she will conduct after-work meetings, as needed, to get feedback from the software support engineers. Any problems are encouraged to be brainstormed by the group.

The software support manager will meet with the end-user manager on an as-needed basis after the end of the first week of the new operation. The first week, the software support manager should observe, at random times, get feedback from the end-user manager and random end-users with any problems.

Any problems that tend to persist after the first week may require close monitoring to be carried on until it is no longer needed. The software support vendor will be contacted for any solutions that they may be able to provide. If problems persist, the IT computer operations manager will call a meeting of all parties concerned. The meeting will cover what is needed to resolve the problem. If need be, the operation can be stopped until it is resolved or replaced with another solution. If it is a disaster, it may be necessary to scrap the system.

After the system has been operational and very much debugged, a final report will be completed by the software support manager. It will be sent to the IT computer operations manager, the IT software support coordinator, and the end-user manager. The report will summarize whether the new end-user software support system has met its expectations. If it did not, the report will give the reason why it did not accomplish its objective. Anything learned that would be of assistance with any other similar undertakings will be recorded.

Comment:
To celebrate the project completion, a post-implementation party should be planned for all persons concerned with the project. The party will be held off the company premisses but should be paid for by budgeted monies. It is good for the morale of all those concerned with the project and provides an opportunity for users and software engineers to meet in an informal environment.

D. Measuring software support performance

There can be two kinds of software support services: the internal help desk software support and vendor-provided software support. Both software support services will have an ongoing program of performance measurement. The measurement conducted for both services will not be the same because of the limitations of the vendor software support.

1. Measuring in-house software support performance

The performance measurement for the in-house help desk software support operations allows for a large arsenal of tool selection. One or more measurement devices can be employed simultaneously. A determination must be made as to what is wanted from a performance measurement. Management may want to measure different items at the same time or at different times. There can be more than one kind of management concern with measurement, depending on who the manager is. The following can have justifiable concerns for their own interests:

- The head of the IT organization.
- The IT computer operations manager.
- The IT software support coordinator.
- The help desk software support management.
- The IT and/or company training management.
- The end-user management.
- The company controller and/or the IT internal auditor.
- Vendors that have provided software and/or hardware.

2. Measuring vendor software support performance

The measuring of vendor software support performance has a more limiting span of management concerns. Section S3.6.3 D-3, Software support performance measuring instruments, has listed a selection of report programs identifying various aspects of software support operations. Any required vendor software support performance data will be specified in detail in the purchase order and/or contract. The specified details will require the approval of the firm's legal counsel, before the agreement is completed. This information will be in the request for bid sent to software support vendors. Therefore, they should be aware of the necessity for the reports. The following can have justifiable concerns for their own interests:

- The head of the IT organization.
- The IT computer operations manager.
- The IT software support coordinator.
- The IT and/or company training management.
- The end-user management.
- The company purchasing agent assigned to the IT purchases and/or leases.

3. Software support performance measuring instruments

The main differences of measuring instruments lie in their measurement-gathering techniques. Instruments can be in-house developed or purchased off the shelf. Some different instruments are used for the type of information needed. An online in-house call tracking system used for a help desk software support system will provide a whole host of different information reports. Reports should target the information wanted by different managers. Vendor support systems will require that contract arrangements be made with the vendor. An available reports menu will be provided to management, listing:

a. Contact volume

The volume of contacts by end-users can be provided by hour, day, week, or month. For software support engineers, scheduling hourly and daily volumes would be of more interest, while monthly contact volume would be of more interest to the head of IT computer operations and end-user management. Besides the incoming calls, the percentage of those calls that are closed during the contact provides a rough idea of the efficiency of the software support engineers. The difference between incoming and completed calls will indicate the backlog being carried. A small backlog is preferred over having no backlog. A consistent no-backlog situation could indicate that the support unit may be overstaffed.

If there is a consistent backlog, the kind of backlog inventory is important to know. If it represents only complex problems, is the backlog developed because of solving the simple or urgent calls first? If callers are not provided services according to the need of the firm in the most optimum manner, then there must be some other arrangement made to find a better solution.

Comment:

Enough people think that their problem comes first, which can be a dilemma. If this be the case, end-user management will have to identify which calls are rated as "code blue." This gets the software support engineer off the hook, because end-user management knows best what is needed first by his/her department.

b. Volume of calls by end-users

Calls per end-user report (by month) are important. This report should be sent to end-user management and IT and/or company training management. The report should contain the following information:

- A listing of the number of calls by each end-user for the month, the average per day, and the days worked.
- The average number of calls made by all end-users for the month.
- The range of daily calls for the month (the lowest number and the highest number made) within the end-user's unit.

c. Problem resolution time

Problem resolution time is how long it takes to resolve each call. This is the time between the point that a software support engineer answers the call and the point that the end-user has his/her problem resolved. This time may cover more than one call: the time (days) that a return call by the software support engineer requires to resolve the problem. If successive calls are required for solving the problem, the total number of calls should be recorded. The total time, of one or more calls, to resolve a given issue should be available. This report should be produced monthly and made available to:

- The end-user software support head.
- The end-user management.
- The IT computer operations manager.

A confidential monthly report by a help desk software support engineer will be provided to the software support head. A confidential monthly report by an end-user of the help desk will be provided to the end-user's management.

d. Software support response time

This is a measure of a call-back system: how long it takes the software support engineer to get back to the end-user. In a direct contact system, the number of times the support engineer greets the end-user caller is a barometer of the support unit's work load. If the service is new, the software support will have to contend with the user's learning curve. Later it could be a work load problem.

The need for staffing increases will have to be studied by working hours: which days and shift hours require the increased staffing, the rearrangement of support engineers' work hours, and other solutions considered before any new people are obtained. If there is a peak load time problem, investigate the possibility of encouraging end-users to contact the support service during this time only if the need requires immediate attention and is of high priority. If IT is providing more than one software support unit, consider the possibility of software support engineers being loaned between units.

Response time should be measured as a percentage of contacts meeting a predetermined threshold time limit. The greater the percentage of calls meeting the objective, the greater will be the cost. Adding one more software support engineer to a current group of two people would increase the service level and the non-productive time. Management will have to consider this when the non-productive time is more than the added work time—is this something they are willing to pay for. Adding one more software support engineer to a group of 50 may meet the service level wanted and not be a problem with non-productive time.

Access percentage of time limits not meeting the planned time standards should be of concern to IT management. The problem should be isolated. It could be a group of software support engineers needing more experience and/or training, that is responsible. A monthly software support response time report, by support engineer, will be run to identify which software support engineers require individual training. The training will be designed to meet the needs of the support engineer. After the training has been completed the software support response time report will be studied. Hopefully, there will be an improvement. IT management may also want to consider that the response time requirement level may be too high. To confirm this, compare other similar services. The vendor and/or other firms would be a source for finding other services for comparison.

e. Backlog aging

This is identifying the number of contacts that have not been resolved. A weekly backlog report will be run. The report will list calls that were resolved that week by the days they required; unresolved contacts by the day they were made will not be listed. Unresolved contacts at the weekend cutoff will be grouped, listed by the number of unresolved days. Any contacts that have gone unresolved after 10 work days will be identified on the report by the end-user making the contact. If the software support is provided by a vendor, copies of the report will be sent to the IT software support coordinator and end-user management.

If the service is provided by the IT end-user software support service, the software support engineer with an unresolved contact of 10 or more days will be listed along with the end-user identification. This weekly report will be provided to the IT end-user software support unit's head. Copies, without the software support engineer identified, will be sent to the IT software support coordinator and end-user management. The IT end-user software support head will contact the software support engineer about his/her listed unresolved contacts of 10 or more days and provide any assistance possible. He/she will note the contact made and date on the listing sheet. The number of selected work days, an arbitrary 10 days, may be changed at the discretion of the IT software support coordinator or the IT computer operations manager.

f. Other monitoring methods

If the software support is vendor provided, it would be prudent to know what performance monitoring reports they have to offer. If the reports identified with the bid package are what the IT management wants, so much the better. Inquire what other reports are available, and the service cost.

The report types listed in this procedure are not the only kinds that are available. There are other productivity measurement methods available and ones that can be devised for special management needs. These reports can be for a one-time need, used as required, or used on a continuous basis. The basic management needs are:

- The end-user is satisfied with the service, if not why not. How does the provided service compare with other end-users for the same cost. Will end-user management be willing to pay for what they want? If the software support service cost is paid from the IT budget, IT will have to prove that the end-user is getting its share of the IT software support service that top management allocated. This can be a problem when the service is free to end-user management.
- The efficiency of the in-house software support service.
- The productivity of each software support engineer.
- The best communication methods to inform the software support engineers employed by the end-users.
- Support response times. The response time performed compared with what was planned.
- The backlog ratio of incoming calls.
- The kind of call aging reports are wanted by IT and end-user management.
- The timetable of the reports wanted, the less often the better.

Surveys can be used by management to gather information from end-users and in-house software support engineers. They can be used as needed. The survey should be designed to collect information without identifying the person completing it. A remarks section could be provided at the end of the form. The survey could be followed with another survey to collect more informative data.

g. Telephone monitoring

All telephone calls will be monitored the first few weeks of the software service. These calls will be randomly selected to be analyzed by the software support head. The caller will be notified that calls can be monitored "for the benefit of better customer service." Whether phone calls are monitored as needed by the end-user software support engineer or on an ongoing basis is determined by the IT software support coordinator or the head of IT computer operations.

h. Other monitoring methods

Other contact audit trails that do not rely only on telephone communications should be considered. The audit trail will have to be designed for the media, such as:

- Memos received or copies of ones sent will be filed for one year or the lifetime of a project plus one year. The filing can be in a digital format on a removable secondary storage file.

- Faxes received or the copies sent will be filed for one year or the lifetime of a project plus one year. The filing can be in a digital format on a removable secondary storage file.

- E-mail received or sent will be down-loaded to a removable secondary storage file and held for one year.

S3.6.4 In-House Software Support Service Operations

The structuring of in-house end-user software support operations can take many forms. There is the centralized system and the decentralized system service concepts. There is also the concern of the location of the service units. Political influences can play a role with the location and structuring of these service centers. The end-user software support system can be a mixture of in-house and/or vendor-provided services.

Microcomputer end-users usually are provided with an unstructured software support program when their operations are just getting started. The service will most often be a mixture of software vendor support and in-house service. The vendor support is most often provided as part of the software purchase price. Some software vendors will upgrade the level of support for a fee. The in-house software support will be a mixed bag of assistance from one or more sources, which can be: a lead or key operator, microcomputer manager, the IT training unit, other more experienced operators, and other departments that are using the same software or an end-user software support unit. If the software was developed in house, the IT programming unit can be a source of software support.

A. In-house help desk organization

When the volume of needed software support approaches two people, IT management should evaluate the need of an in-house help desk software support unit. The operation may be justified when two people are needed, but after a final evaluation, two or more people may be required. There could be a problem if only one person is required. A one-person help desk operation cannot sustain full-time support during normal work hours. The unit will be part of the IT computer operations organization. This would be the starting point with most in-house help desk software support organizations.

The software support engineers should be carefully selected. IT and end-user staff may be the areas to recruit from. The selection would be based on the skills required for the new position. Programmers should not be considered for this position. They make very poor candidates for end-user software support engineers. The IT computer operations manager will discuss the software support needs with the end-user manager. After the initial contact, IT will draft a survey to seek input from end-users. These users can be employing one or more forms of software. The software can be in-house developed and/or purchased. The current support services should be studied for their good and bad features. From the collected information, the requirements for the in-house software support unit are determined.

1. Help desk operation structure

    Aside from having centralized or decentralized end-user software support services, there are other considerations that can be explored. The first is whether to have one or more software support operations. The design would be based on benefits received by the IT and end-users. There are many variables to consider before reaching a design.

    • The size of the total company organization.

    • The location of the end-users and whether they are all in a central location or in two or more locations.

    • The time zones in which the end-users are found.

    • Time span support hours required.

    • End-user software support services needed by foreign subsidiaries.

    • The vendor-provided services currently being used that will be converted to an in-house service.

    • Beta testing software support needs to be addressed.

    • How the help desk operation structure is involved in a pre-planned secession of growth steps.

2. Help desk reporting structure

    The help desk software support responsibility ultimately lies with IT, whether the service provided is by vendors, in-house IT, or non-IT support units. The total success of all the software support units is only possible through a completely integrated system command structure. To reach the final planned structure may require succeeding organization and reorganization efforts.

The size, diversity, complexity, and dispersion of the company are dependent variables in the design formula. For a small limited complexity, one-site company organizations may require only one end-user software support unit. The support may be augmented by one or more vendor-contracted software support services. The vendor software support services will be contracted and controlled by the IT organization. The IT computer operations manager will be responsible for the total software support organization. Depending on the needs and planned growth of the software support services, the responsibility will be delegated to the IT software support coordinator. Operation of an in-house end-user software support unit requires two or more people. There will be a person appointed as the head of this unit. The title of the head of the support unit will be in keeping with the size and function of the unit.

3. The number of in-house software support units

The help desk geographic dispersal will depend on some or all of the following factors:

- The total number of software support engineers—there is a minimum size a software support unit must be to be efficient.

- It is better to have two or more small software support units under the same roof. They can be supportive of each other and assist the software support training effort.

- The concern for disaster planning can justify the dispersal of the support units.

- Wider hours of support coverage may be less of a staffing problem if placed into different time zones.

- A larger software support unit is more efficient.

- Having operations in areas that use a different language would justify having a support unit in each language's area. Dialects of the same language could also create a problem.

4. End-user technical support needs

End-users that have a complex support need may require that the software support unit be acquainted with the technical area of the user. This would place the support engineer more allied with the user than the IT department. To resolve the end-user's problems, the software engineer must speak the technical language of the end-user. Examples of this would be engineering, production control, etc.

This type of environment requires special organizational attention. The software support unit head would still report to IT computer operations manager. The operations manager and the IT software support coordinator will provide the software support technology needed for the software support engineers. End-user management will provide the training required for their help desk software support engineers. If necessary, they may also provide candidates that are skilled in their area of technology for the position of software support engineer. The special software support unit head will be required to indirectly report to end-user management. End-user management should provide an annual performance evaluation of the unit to the IT software support coordinator. The IT software support coordinator will be in contact with end-user management about any new IT technology that may assist the end-users and will be informed about any staffing need changes or problems by end-user management.

Another in-house help desk organization for this special need would be to employ specialized teams within a larger centralized help desk software support structure. This structure would be of greater value if the same type of need were required by other end-users. See S3.6.4 B for more information.

B. Software support internal structure

The internal structure of software support organizations is uniformly similar throughout the industry. There are differences which are based on the end-users. These end-user differences are:

- The number of end-users.
- The specialized needs of end-users.
- The geographic distribution of end-users.

An IT organization may justify more than one software support structure depending on justifiable needs. The following organizations are available:

1. Small software support unit

The software support unit head will report to the IT computer operations manager. The IT computer operations manager can delegate this reporting responsibility to the IT software support coordinator, who will also continue to be the coordinator for the software support vendors.

A small software support unit may have from two to 18 software support engineers. The organization would provide general software support for multiple end-users or one specialized end-user. With two to six support engineers, one will be a lead support engineer. Having over six software support engineers would justify a supervisor, which would also perform the duty of an administrator. This staffing would be for a normal day-shift work load. Ten to 12 software support engineers would justify a full-time administrator.

2. Large software support department

The large software support department head will be the director of software support. He/she will report to the CIO. The IT software support coordinator, who will coordinate the software support vendors, will report to the director of software support.

A large software support department can cover more than one shift. The director of software support will have two or more software support managers reporting to him/her. Each shift will have a shift manager. There will be specialized end-user software support supervisors by type of service provided. If there are two or more special software support supervisors, they will report to the special software support manager; otherwise the supervisor(s) will report to the director of software support. The special software support manager or the day-shift special software support manager will be the department head when the director of software support is not present.

A software support administrative manager will work the primary shift but be responsible for all shifts. The other shifts will have administrative supervisors in charge.

Other software support specialists will be grouped by specialty. If there are enough people in each unit, they will have a supervisor; if not, the person responsible will be the lead specialist. The specialist supervisor(s) and lead specialists will report to the support specialist manager. These people can perform the following functions:

- Beta software support engineers.
- Planning software support engineers.
- Dispatchers.
- Software product support engineers.
- Technical support advisors.
- Hardware support engineers.
- Help desk support trainers.

3. Multiple support centers

When there are multiple support centers, two or more centers can be similarly structured as the large software support department. The center that is located at the same site as the CIO will have a director of corporate software support services. The other support center heads and the IT software support coordinator of software support vendors will report to the director of corporate software support services. There can also be small end-user software support units that would provide general software support for multiple end-users or a specialized end-user head(s) who will report to the director of corporate software support services.

C. Software correction procedure

Software product defects, bugs, should be found by the software support engineers before the end-users. This should be done before the software is released to the end-users. Not all bugs will be discovered this way. It is normal to have end-users discover bugs. Bugs will be found with in-house–written programs, Beta programs, and purchased software. Purchased software should have less bugs than the other software, especially if the release version is other than number one. When bugs are made known to the software support group, they should be corrected as soon as possible. Until the problem is corrected, the end-users affected should be informed about the problem. Newsletters can contain the details of the problem and the alternate process to be pursued until a final solution is available. If the notice cannot be delayed until the next newsletter is issued, e-mail notices will be sent to all end-users concerned. The e-mail notice will go out under the name of the head of the end-user software support unit.

The software source will determine the procedure that will be used to resolve the problem.

1. Beta software

Beta software, which is not involved with day-to-day operations, will be shut down if it brings the system down or has severe bugs. It will not be used until the problem is resolved by the provider. Very minor bugs may be worked around with the help of the in-house Beta software support engineers. The same Beta software support engineers will contact the developers, be it in-house or vendor Beta software, to resolve the problem. Beta software developed in house or by a vendor can experience operation bugs. If this were not the case, the software would not be called Beta software.

2. Purchased software

This is software that is purchased or leased from a vendor, often called third-party software. Try to avoid version one; it will more than likely contain more bugs than later versions. The end-user software support engineer will contact the software product support engineer unit about the software problem. The software product support engineer will contact the vendor support unit to resolve the problem. After the problem is resolved and corrected, the software product support engineer will contact the software support engineer about the current status of the software. End-users will be e-mailed the needed information. E-mails will be sent to the IT software support coordinator and the software product support unit's management informing them of what happened and of the current status. Replacement software will be down-loaded to end-users' microcomputer systems that are licensed for their use. Bugs not fixed by the vendor will require a "work-around" procedure.

> ***Comment:***
> **Vendor software most often comes in sealed containers. Read the small print! The small print can even go as far as to not guarantee that there is an enclosed disk. There are very good vendors, but we seldom hear about what they did for their customers unless it is passed on by a happy consumer.**

Purchased software that includes the source code can be fixed in house. The software support engineer will patch the program after discussing it with the vendor's development people. The patched version will be tested at length and approved by the vendor development programmer(s) as being safe before placed into service.

3. Proprietary-developed software

Proprietary-developed software is software developed by the firm's IT development staff. The programs may be entirely in-house written or shell developed and supported by leased or purchased program modules. This software provided by an in-house programming project will require all the same documentation as expected from vendors. The help desk software support engineers will be provided operation support manuals and training. After it has been debugged and is ready to be turned over to the end-users, there will be an end-user IT training program presented. Also provided will be a self-learning program for new end-users and software support engineers.

This software is subject to maintenance and bug patching after it has become operational. The end-user software support engineers will document all problems experienced by end-users. A weekly report will be sent to the head of end-user software support and the authors of the software. As long as the software is still operational, the corrections will be made without having to turn off the software. A network problem identification and chat room will be maintained to provide quick end-user feedback. The remedy suggestions by the software support engineers will be posted onto the chat rooms.

D. Software support tools

When IT management is considering having an in-house help desk software support unit for the first time or software support management is proposing a replacement or addition, a software support project is initialized. The number of people assigned to the project will depend on its complexity. The people assigned will be used as needed for the life of the project. A project leader will be appointed; this may be a full- or part-time job.

To satisfy end-user support needs, maintenance support tools have become available. These tools are competitively priced. Therefore, it is seldom that one can justify developing and constructing support tools. The third-party providers have tools for software support, which allow for modification to the buyer's special needs.

The head of end-user software support should be proactive for the end-users' future needs. To do this, the CIO will require privileged information about future planning that must remain confidential. The planner or project leader responsible will be asked to consider several different scenarios, which will be most confidential. The CIO will most likely be the only one to actually know which scenario will become the plan.

Tool selection requires a sequence of procedures to arrive at a final solution. The first major element the project leader will be concerned with is the allocated budget. The budget provided should be guided by the best configuration required, with room for management-planned growth in a span of time of expected hardware obsolescence. The guide for the final selection is based on the best return for the financial investment. This is the measurable tangible return on the investment. Intangible benefits should not be overlooked; they should be noted and reported.

Comment:

Hundreds of millions of dollars are spent each year by school boards in the United States for computers without any identifiable tangible benefits. School boards try to out-spend each other without any identifiable tangible benefits. The object is how many dollars they spend that counts, and not what are the measurable tangible benefits. Dollars are what these people can identify and count along with most of their supporters.

A Toledo suburb went through such an experience. To save money, they planned to keep their microcomputers for up to 10 years before replacing them for the first 10 years. The plan was to replace 10% of the computers each year. After 10 years, each group being replaced would be only 10 years old. This must have made up for not having any tangible education goals.

The project team will follow a series of procedure steps required for tool selection. These procedure steps will proceed in the following sequence:

1. Identify requirements

   The project team will collect a comprehensive list of requirements. The information input will be from the members of the in-house software support staff and end-user management. The collected input will be sorted by similar requirements. Performance statistics from software support administrative services will be available by day and hour for:

   • Volume of service contacts.

- Response time.
- Degree of problems.

Other logged information will be collected from administrative services. This collected information will be evaluated to identify the current requirements' status. Any trends will be extrapolated to project future conditions.

The requirements will be documented by the project leader. They will be reviewed by all parties concerned. After all parties have completed reading the document, they will sign off with their approval. It would be wise to have people that are strong supporters sign off first.

2. Selection process

   Any selection of resource tools will require that the project team complete the following, in the order they are addressed, before the solution is considered realistic. A consensus of weighted priorities has been developed. These are the element items required, ranked by importance.

   - Required funding must be available.
   - Define what is required for the tools to comply with existing systems.
   - An RFP (request for proposal) will have to be developed for possible vendors. The RFP will request purchase and lease bids. The RFP will contain the description of the current system, if there is one, that is to be expanded or replaced. A detailed description of what is expected will be provided. The performance expectations will be defined—what will be expected for user operation manuals, training needs, on-call operation support, and maintenance.

   After all items have been addressed and approved, the project leader will send a copy of the RFP to each vendor. A copy will also be sent to the head of end-user software support, purchasing, and other involved parties. A cover letter will be included, naming the contact person for the project (the project leader). The vendors will be asked to provide customer names that can give testimonials. The letter will provide the cutoff date for accepting bids and sales presentations.

3. Acquisition process

   The acquisition process can start after funding has been provided.

The vendor bid proposals will be evaluated and compared by the software support project team. Selected vendors will be invited to make a presentation before the software support project team, the head of end-user software support, a selection of senior software support engineers, and software support management. The presentation provides an opportunity for both vendor and customer to clarify any issues and reach agreement on what is to be expected.

After the vendors' presentations, the software support project team will evaluate the proposals. This will be followed by site visits to confirm that the vendor's product is performing as reported. Please see 15.5.2 Evaluating Vendor's Proposals and 15.5.3 Vendor Selection in the *Information Systems Policies and Procedures Manual.* These two sections will provide the procedures required to complete the acquisition process.

The software support project team will continue to be responsible for the installation of the support system until it is operational and approved by its users. Other tasks required to make the installation operational are:

- Providing software support engineer training and a new support engineering self-learning program.
- Providing end-user training and a new end-user self-learning program.
- Providing operator manuals for the software support engineers and end-users.
- Testing the system.
- Having a backup and recovery procedure in place.
- Testing the backup and recovery procedure.
- Having software support management approve the system as operational and approve vendor invoice for payment.

S3.6.5 Managing Software Support Staff

Software support engineers have one of the highest job burnout rates in the country. These workers are also known to have high turnover rates. The object is to get the best people that can be found and do the most to keep them. The effort to keep software support engineers takes more than money alone.

A. Proactive staff planning

The corporate culture will influence the planning style. How proactive

Comment:

I did a study of about 1700 people who as a group worked in a very stressful job environment. This group were known for their high absenteeism and job turnover. Within the work group were semi-professional and professional segments. The semi-professional segment was found to be paid more than any of its counterparts in the area. This group were notorious for their absenteeism. They would seldom leave for employment elsewhere, because it would require a substantial pay cut. The professional segment was not paid the top dollar. It had less absenteeism, but a high turnover rate. Its employment record will have shown a employer change, but a good attendance record.

Management was myopic about the problem. The problem was eventually resolved. All the employees and management were let go when the organization went out of business.

IT management can be will depend on this factor. In turn, IT management will have a profound influence of what kind of management style will guide the software support unit. The ability to attract and retain the kind of people needed to best serve the end-user will hinge on this factor.

Comment:

A good illustration of this is the Strang/Montross syndrome. Rating IT proactive management on a scale of 10 to 0, the top proactive manager is a 10 and the opposite is zero. Strang was a GE engineering manager that first forsaw the use of computers to design electric motors by artificial intelligence. The first internally programmed computer procedures were written by one of his people in his engineering unit. He was more than a proactive manager; he encouraged others working for him to also behave in the same way. He rates a 10 on the Strang/Montross scale.

> **Montross was an IT manager who represents the zero. He was the inverse of a proactive manager. He was a micro-manager. A rating of 10 provides the breeding ground for an IT success story; a five is a 50-50 chance of success, while a zero is doomed for an IT disaster even before it starts. The higher the Strang/Montross rating, the better the chance for success of IT management.**

1. Software support management

Managing software support engineers requires a special proactive management style. The skills required to be a top-of-the-line end-user software support engineer are seldom found in one person. The person must be very current and proficient with their technology, be able to hold their composure under stress, and have an end-user hand-holding personality when needed. Technology and people skills are seldom found in the same person, so an effort is required to get and hold on to these people. The management process will comprise the following:

- Planning proactively.
- Defining support staff needed—as the IT culture fits into the corporate culture, the support staff needs to fit in with IT.
- Acquisitioning software support staff.
- Managing software support staff.
- Educating and training software support engineers and end-users.
- Monitoring software support management and engineers.
- Retaining software support morale.

The first person to be the end-user software support manager will most likely be hired from the outside. The person should have two or more years of proactive software support management experience. The experience should be from a firm that has the same type of corporate culture. The experience brought with this person should assist the installation with much less lost effort. Other factors that are important to software support management (this would also apply to any person selected from within the company for the position) hiring success are:

- Managers that have worked in similar IT and software support environments.
- People with good mentoring skills—this is needed to develop the next level of support people.
- Managers that have utilized the same support system successfully.
- A person that demonstrates a proactive management style.
- A person that has good human relation skills.
- A person that can perform under stress.
- The ability to plan and implement a budget.

A good job description and benefit package should be prepared before the search is started. The recruiting sources for such a person are limited. IT management with networking opportunities would be a good place to start. A national recruiter that works with this type of placement should be contacted for possible candidates. The human resources department will be contacted to assist in the search and provide psychological testing. Internet recruiting is now available.

2. Software support staff

After the first manager has been successful selected, internal software support personnel should be candidates for future promotions. Promotions from within the software support unit(s) are good for both the person and the company.

The human resources department will provide psychological testing for all software support job candidates. The testing will be requirements profiled for the type of position. All promotion candidates within IT and the software support unit will be tested for the position under consideration. Testing is essential to determine whether the candidate has good people skills and can survive stress. These weaknesses have been known to have been concealed by knowledgeable technical people. To discover the weakness during a crisis is not the best time to find the defect.

B. Software support evaluation and compensation

To attract and keep good people, wages must be competitive. Providing other financial rewards will also be helpful. Overtime should be

Comment:

A few years ago, a Northeast IT person totally lost his cool and threw his microcomputer system out the window. He became entangled in the wiring and was pulled out the window by the system. Unfortunately, the window was not on the bottom floor.

Some years ago, a nationally known company, located in Chicago, was still using tabulating card input. The corporate controller was so upset with data processing errors that he ran into the data processing room and threw cards, still in their card trays, out the windows. The wind—Chicago being known as the windy city—scattered the cards and trays as they descended down to the sidewalk and street.

discouraged, but paid for. There are annual wage surveys published for the IT field by "Computer World" a weekly, and "Datamation" a monthly, etc. These can be helpful guides to ensure that the compensation is realistic. The human resources department will be contacted to work in concert with IT to ensure that the compensation is satisfactory. The compensation may need to be within the top 20 percent of the prevailing wage for the industry and area of the country to attract experienced personnel.

1. New software support personnel

    New hires or transfers to the department will be assigned a mentor for the first six months. The time may be extended upon mutual consent. The first month, the new employee should meet informally with his/her mentor no less than once a week. Before the first week comes to an end, the person's supervisor will meet informally with him/her. This should be followed by an informal weekly meeting. These meetings are to be held any place but the supervisor's office. The meetings can be held over coffee, at lunch, or even after work hours. Formal review meetings will be held no less than every other month for the first year.

2. Annual increases

    Annual increases will be based on performance. Part of the end-user software support operations will have an ongoing service monitoring system. Information about the unit, shift, and individual software engineer's performance will be recorded and maintained. When annual salary increases are given, they should be based on the person's performance. This is the time to review the performance as compared to the department average. The year's performance will be reviewed by the manager. The manager will review not only the department performance records, but will also rely on end-user surveys and peer performance reviews. Peer reviews will be in the form of ranking peers, without any two or more being equal. All software support members will receive peer reviews and subordinate reviews. A weighted scale will be used for all collected input. Any areas that need attention should be discussed. What options are available to the employee should be pointed out. The employee's career path plans should also be the subject of consideration. Any advice or assistance will be provided by the manager.

3. Work shift differential

The human resources department will be contacted to find out if any work-shift pay incentives are offered. If there is no company policy, the human resources manager will be contacted to explore the issue with other firms in the area. Human resources people exchange this kind of information at their own professional level. If need be, IT will have to work out with human resources the pay differential to be used. IT can recommend pay scales but cannot establish company policy for this issue.

4. Standby support

Software support engineers that are on call will be compensated. This can be problem area if the personnel are non-exempt. There are federal laws that can govern this work assignment. The human resources department will be contacted to find out if there is a company policy regarding this situation. If there is none, the human resources manager will have to explore the issue if the software engineers are not salaried. If the software engineers are salaried, they should be paid a standby or on-call premium. IT can recommend a premium pay plan but cannot establish company policy for this issue. A suggestion would be to have an on-call beeper rate for telephone services to be provided. The pay may require adjustment depending on the number of calls.

A standby rate will be provided for the number of hours a software support person would be on standby. This is to have backup on call as needed. This should be a person that is scheduled to work the next shift. This would be a much lesser rate than providing an on-call software support. The renumeration rate will have to be resolved with the human resources manager.

5. Software support bonuses

In addition to a person's base pay, there should be bonuses. For bonuses to be effective, there should be more than one kind provided, and not all at the same time. Bonuses can be any of the following:

- Monthly bonuses by individual.
- Quarterly bonuses by shift and/or work group.
- Annual bonus based on department performance.
- Annual bonus based on IT or company performance.

Several types of bonuses may be considered: short-range (low cost) and long-range monitory benefits, a paid bonus vacation day(s) that must be taken in the month awarded, and performance grab-bag awards of special surprise items. The surprise items could be something unique: air line tickets, watches, a paid month's lease for an upscale sports car, a wall plaque, a leather briefcase, a gift certificate, etc. These items will be part of the department's budget, along with the bonuses.

If there is a problem with retaining support engineers, a special year-end bonus plan can be implemented. This would pay a sizeable bonus once a year, but the bonus payment would be over a three- to four-year time span. Any earned bonuses would be forfeited at the time of employee termination.

6. IT/software support fringe benefits

The fringe benefit package should be a wide array of cafeteria-style fringe benefits. Not all employees have the same needs in this area. This can be a plus factor to maintain a healthy and loyal support staff. Part of the fringe benefit offers will be paid education. All job-related IT training will be paid for by the company and provided on company time. Self-improvement IT training will be paid for by the company, and half of the training time will be on company time and half on the employee's time. Education at accredited institutions will be paid for if it applies to the employee's career path as a subject or a degree. A course grade of C will have 50 percent reimbursement, a grade of B will receive 100 percent reimbursement, while a grade of A will receive 100 percent reimbursement for the class, books, lab fees, and mileage.

Comment:

If top management will not approve this type of approach, there is the outsourcing route. In this case, it could be your own employees that are outsourced to gain a better benefit package.

C. Acquiring software support staff

Software support staff vacancies should be filled from within the company if possible. The IT area will have the first priority selection. End-users that are knowledgeable about the software and lead operators may be a talent source. People without any prior end-user software support experience will require some training and on-the-job training to be brought up to a desired performance level.

To be considered for a position as a software support engineer, reference checks are required, even for non-IT internal transfers. Psychological testing and interviews will be conducted to determine whether the candidate conforms to the profile requirements. Tests should also be utilized to assure that the candidate can also master the knowledge skills required. After positive results are obtained, the candidate will be interviewed by software support management and their possible peers. After the interviews, the people conducting the interviews will meet to compare notes. One of the things that will be noted is the point of view of the candidate concerning the different pre-planned views of the interviewers. This can be called the "honesty" test.

Depending on the needs status for the end-user software support engineers, skilled and/or non-skilled recruiting will be done. The following are sources that may be considered:

• Internal referrals: your own employees may refer people they know. The fact that a poor referral will be something that the employee will have to live with encourages them to refer better people. After the person has been hired, a reward will be given to the finder; it could be something other than money. After the person has been on the job for one year with a good review, a second part of the finder bonus can be given.

• Professional recruiters: these recruiters are a likely source for experienced software support engineers and other support personnel.

The placement fee will have to be paid out of the IT budget, which can be around 20 percent or more of the first year's salary. Select a national firm that will do the pre-screening. The recruiting firm will be sent a batch of IT application forms. The completed forms will be attached to the résumés and returned. The IT application form will present information in a comparable order. Make sure the IT application form is approved by the human resources management to assure there is no EEOC violation.

- University recruiting: recruitment of pending university graduates provides a good source of candidates. This recruiting should be done by the end of the first month of the fall term. The students will have a formal IT education, but IT students that have worked at the student computer help desk will also have a level of experience that can be utilized. A good time to recruit them is in their third year. The week before they go on spring break might be a good time to interview. For proactive managers that can get funding for student interns, this is the time to find them for summer internships. They can discover the real world, and IT can find some potential talent.

- Advertising: a good place to advertise would be in "Computer World." Read several weeks of ads to get an idea of how best to place your ads. When résumés are received, screen them for ones that will be sent an IT application form. Others will be sent a standard form letter. File the good résumés by name and attach them to the returned IT application form. The IT application form will present information in a comparable order.

- Internet recruiting is now available.

D. Managing support staff

Support staff management requires proactive management skills, as well as people and technical skills. The manager will be a strong supporter of department teamwork. The goals of all department members will be department goals first and personnel career goals second. Personnel career goals rely on the completion of department goals.

There must be a clear definition of what the objective and goals are. The goals will be a fine balance of productivity and end-user satisfaction. Beware that some end-users' demands can be unrealistic and costly to satisfy. A record of time spent by end-users will identify these problem end-users. End-user management will be informed of the problem. Service calls that are paid out of the end-user's budget will get the attention of end-user management.

The manager's performance objectives should be easy to understand and realistic. There are three basic objectives a manager will be concerned with.

1. End-user satisfaction

    The primary objective is end-user service satisfaction. Feedback will come in the form of a monthly survey. The survey will be one page, rating item satisfaction on a scale of one to seven. The lower part of the form will be used for comments. Seven will be excellent, four fair, and one very poor service. See Exhibit S3.6.4-1 for an example of the form. The survey items are:

    • The average response time.

    • The average resolution time.

    • The technical quality of the service.

    • The attitude of the support service.

    • The overall level of service.

2. Software support performance and morale

    Software support morale can be measured by the employee turnover rate and subordinate evaluation. The turnover rate for the software support unit will be compared with the IT turnover rate. If it is equal to the IT department rate, it is outstanding. If it is twice the IT department rate, it indicates a problem. The subordinate evaluation ratings should be averaged by item to compute the department average. See Exhibit S3.6.4-2 for an example of the form. The calculation will be done by the manager and will be for his/her own information.

    Each software support engineer will be evaluated for quantitative and qualitative performances. The average item values will reflect the unit's performance profile. The profile averages will be compared with each software support engineer's average performance. This information will identify any areas that might need attention. The same information will also be used for the employee's annual evaluation, for guidance, and for salary consideration. The information collected will be seen in Exhibit S3.6.4-3. The information items of concern are:

    • End-user's average rating of the software support engineer (user survey information).

    • End-user's quality ranking of the software support engineer with that of other software support engineers (user survey information).

SOFTWARE SUPPORT EVALUATION SURVEY
For the month of _____

As an end user of software support, please rank the following on a scale of one to seven. One being very poor and seven excellent.

The average response time .... _____

The average problem resolution time .... _____

The technical quality of the service .... _____

The attitude of the support service .... _____

The overall level of service .... _____

Please list the names of the software support engineers that you have been in contact with this month, the number of contacts, and your rating of one to seven for each.

Comments:

Exhibit S3.6.4-1

- The number of end-user service contacts that were completed, compared to the unit's average.
- Call monitoring evaluation—done by the manager. This will be the average of no less than three calls that were monitored by the manager. If there is a quality problem, the sample size will be expanded. The quality average will be rated as: excellent, good, fair, needs improvement, and having a problem.

SOFTWARE SUPPORT DEPT. SURVEY
For the month of _____

This survey is to collect information that may assist the department's operation. Please rank the following on a scale of one to seven. One being very poor and seven excellent.

The software support tools provided are ...._____

The training we receive is .... _____

The end users know how to ask for assistance ...._____

The end users understand our instructions .... _____

Our work environment is .... _____

Management understands our needs ...._____

Comments may be typed, and use back page if need be.

Exhibit S3.6.4-2

3. Budget control

   This is the third factor; it cannot be good at the expense of the other two. If the service is charged back to the user, there can still be a concern when the user's budget has been exceeded. There are real problems when end-user evaluations are poor and their budgets have been exceeded. End-user management should be contacted for a resolution to the problem. Any budget variations by line item of more than 10 percent (or a dollar quantity) will require written justification by the manager.

E. Working environment

   The working environment will be ergonomically ideal. The work sta-

---

EMPLOYEE'S PERFORMANCE EVALUATION

EMPLOYEE _____ DATE _____

JOB TITLE _____ MONTHS OF SERVICE _____

END USER'S RATING (1-7) _____ END USER'S RANKING _____

END USER'S SERVICE CONTACTS _____ FOR MONTH(S) OF _____

END USER'S SERVICE CONTACTS COMPLETED ON FIRST CALL _____

NUMBER OF USER COMPLAINTS _____ COMPLAINT VALIDITY _____

NUMBER OF MONITORED CONTACTS ____ QUALITY _____

TRAINING NEEDS _____

COMMENTS:

Exhibit S3.6.4-3

tions, chairs, lighting, and colors selected will be pleasing and comfortable. Each person's work area should provide a level of tolerance for his/her own tastes, as long as it does not conflict with co-workers. Dress codes will be relaxed, but some kind of footwear and clothing tops are required.

Work breaks should allow a person to leave the work area for a distraction. There will be several breaks a day. The extra breaks will be made up with a shorter lunch time. A handy break room will be provided, with adjoining rest rooms. The break room will contain:

- Different kinds of comfortable chairs.
- Tables with comfortable chairs.
- A refrigerator that also makes ice cubes and has room for lunch bags.

- A microwave.

- Hot coffee and hot water for tea, hot chocolate, Ovaltine, etc. Possibly, a small sink to help keep the room neater.

- Candy, treats, and soft drink machines—these dispensed items are free or at a very nominal cost. The profits received will pay for the hot drink and expendable items.

- A rack for personnel cups.

- A bulletin board for work and personnel information.

- A telephone for personal calls.

- A room that is nicely decorated, with soft lighting (at daylight color temperatures) and background music—the room will be carpeted and have drapes to absorb sound.

S3.6.6 Outsourcing Software Support Services

There can be a host of reasons to outsource software support. Outsourcing may start with software vendors providing extended software support services. This can be extended to more than one source for vendor software support services. Installing an in-house end-user software support service for the first time can be a complex and challenging undertaking, as well as a sizable investment. Starting a limited software support system for the first time will garner valuable experience that can be built on. In a large software support undertaking, a consultant may be justified.

Large well-known companies are outsourcing this service. They prefer to concentrate on their core IT services. Some firms have even outsourced both their IT operations and end-user software support services. The microcomputer operations are now with the end-users that require end-user software support. There is a need for someone at the firm to coordinate the outsourcing services. Firms employing total outside services should have someone coordinating the effort and overseeing that the services rendered are what has been paid for. This person will be the IT software support coordinator. His/her duties are to:

- Forsee what kind of software support is needed by end-users.

- Determine how the services will be charged—by end-user or one budget company account.

- Request vendor proposals.

- Evaluate vendor proposals.

- Make final vendor selection.

- Sign vendor contract.
- Monitor vendor performance.

A. Vendor proposal request

The vendor request for proposal will be sent to all potential software support vendors. The request for proposal will contain:

- The format of the proposal to be followed.
- The company contact person for the project.
- The due date of the proposal and presentation.
- The expected date of the service to come on line.
- A description of what will be required of the software support service.
- The number of end-users.
- The required time window for software support services to be provided.
- The proposed cost of the service.
- A provided list of current customers utilizing the vendor's services.

B. Vendor evaluation

The original manual covers this area in 15.5.2 Evaluating Vendors' Proposals. In addition, to be considered will be:

- Other service offerings that are available.
- Whether there are other days and hours of coverage.
- A chance to visit the call center and listen in on live calls.
- Plans for disaster recovery.
- What nationality and/or region of the United States the software support engineers are from.
- The type of call tracking system to be used.
- Total call volume.
- The average wait time.
- The percentage of call problems resolved on the first call.
- The method of measuring end-user satisfaction.
- The service reports available.
- The corporate culture, management style, and business philosophy of the service company—in as much as the interaction of the two firms will be close, this is an important issue.

C. Vendor selection and contract construction

After the first selection is made, arrange for a contract meeting with the selected vendor. Notify the other vendors that you have received their information and are finalizing which vendor is to receive a contract. Before the final contract is presented by the vendor, inform them that service-level definitions are required in the contract. Also, tie financial consequences to what is not delivered. The legal representative of the firm will review the document and approve it before it is signed. After the contract is signed, notify the other vendors that the selection was made and they were not selected.

D. Vendor performance monitoring

The IT software support coordinator will monitor all software support that the company has paid for. This will be done with reports provided by the software support vendor(s) and information collected by the IT software support coordinator. The information collected will be in the form of random contacts with end-users and end-user management. These contacts will be made for all software support received from all vendors. Monthly end-user software support surveys will be conducted for each provider. See Exhibit S3.6.4-1 for an example of the form.

The software support vendor will provide contracted reports. The software developers that provide support for their product are not known to dispense any reports for this service. Firms that are software support organizations will provide monthly and annual reports that the contract has identified to be furnished.

The IT software support coordinator will analyze the inputs for each vendor and complete a report that identifies each vendor's level of provided service as compared to what was expected and sent to IT or the IT computer operations head. Any vendors that are not doing what was contracted for will receive information as to what course of action the IT software support coordinator will take. This will be followed up with a memo as to the completed resolution to the problem.

Comment:

The subject of software support entails much more material than can be covered in detail within this procedure

section. This section of the procedure manual covers the procedure aspect of software support for both vendor-provided service and in-house software support services. The art and science of software support requires a separate book, and there is a book on the market. Francoise Tourni-aire and Richard Farrell have authored just such a book, *The Art of Software Support,* published in 1998 by Prentice Hall PTR. The ISBN number is 0-13-784497-2. It is recom-mended reading for IT management with concerns about software support.

SUPPLEMENTAL ADDITIONS TO CHAPTER 3

6. SOFTWARE SUPPORT

S3.6 End-User Software Support

S3.6.1 IT Software Support Operation

S3.6.2 Designing a Software Support Package

S3.6.3 Defining Support Structure

S3.6.4 In-House Software Support Service Operations

S3.6.5 Managing Software Support Staff

S3.6.6 Outsourcing Software Support Services

Chapter 4
END-USER SYSTEMS AND PROCEDURES

1. POLICY

S4.1 END-USER/WORK GROUP SYSTEMS AND PROCEDURES

The development of work group computer systems has established the next logical step of work group systems and procedures. This has been done with varying degrees in companies for years. Not all internal units found within companies have the same knowledge or talents available. With more company dollars being spent at the end-user level, there is more concern that the dollars are being spent wisely. Therefore, company policies are needed to establish a uniformity of this kind of development throughout the company.

S4.1.1 Scope

The scope will start with departments that have existing work group computer systems in place. Company sites that do not have a systems and procedures unit can partake if they have available industrial engineering and/or others with ISO 9000 documentation skills. This talent pool can provide for the leadership of a project manager, which will qualify this effort to be within the policy scope. Microcomputer technology can be part of the site's resources. The first successful departments that will foster others to follow and eventually may even broaden the scope. Successful units may later be tapped for their knowledge and provide in-house consulting.

The work group computer system and its work group computer coordinator have established an organization within the department with which to generate an end-user systems and procedures function. The first department to start will be a pilot project. The department that is selected first should be the one most likely to succeed. After that, other departments may start the process one at a time. The success of each department may broaden the scope. The selection process will be done by a committee appointed by top management at the main facility. It will be called the end-user systems committee. Plant or operations site managers will make this decision at other company sites.

Departments may already be doing this within the organization. The policy is to not curtail this activity if it has met with success. The policy does require that standard procedures be used. If the department has a procedure that has proven successful, it should be considered to be incorporated in the company's procedures. The policy fosters the continuous improvement of this process.

S4.1.2 Policy Objectives

An objective is to have only successful work group computer system operations attempt the transition to systems and procedures and end-user reengineering. End-user systems and procedures or reengineering is not a solution to a failing work group computer operation—it will only make things worse. The objective is to encourage the activity of end-user reengineering as the next step after a successful development of end-user systems and procedures by the work group.

The policy objective is to provide the constraints that such undertakings are not following different procedures. There are needs for standard policies and procedures throughout the company. The policies will be defined into procedures that all departments will use. Successful departments can then communicate with other company departments with a uniform understanding of end-user/work group procedure methods. Companies can be as successful with this as they have been with ISO 9000.

The responsibility to maintain and disseminate the end-user/work group systems and procedures publication will report to the IT systems unit head. This person, the end-user coordinator, will provide the procedures that will be tools for the end-user to develop their own systems and procedures. All end-user/work group systems and procedures changes will require the final approval of the end-user systems committee. The committee can grant a one-time waiver for special circumstances that a department may have. The committee must be flexible and proactive to be successful.

2. THE ORGANIZATION PROCESS

S4.2 THE PROJECT ORGANIZATION PROCESS

For end-user systems and procedures to take place, a project organization is needed to take on this activity in one form or another. This organization can later be involved with the end-user reengineering process. The knowledge gained with the end-user systems and procedures experience will be most helpful to any user reengineering task.

S4.2.1 The Innovative Project Management Organization

There is a major difference between the end-user/work group systems and procedures project organization and the traditional project management organization. The traditional project management organization, such as often found with the IT systems or programming units of information systems, has a one-cycle project life cycle. At the end of a project, the project members are disbanded from the project responsibility. The next project may have a different project manager and more likely more members from different company departments. One major concern of the project manager is the loyalty the project members have to their own department. Different members within a project group do not necessarily have the same objective.

As new projects start up there is a loss of labor hours because of the learning curve. Such aspects as the internal and external politics, what new skills require time to hone, the users, etc. must be learned. The time loss is expediential as to the size of all people involved with the project grows in numbers. The communication formula for this is

$$\frac{n(n-1)}{2} = X$$

Where

n = the number of people communicating

X = communication complexity

If n would equal 2 (people), X would equal 1, but if n would now equal 5 (people), X would equal 10. We see that complexity of communication increases by ten when adding three more people to a project.

The reason that "The Innovative Project Management Organization" is given its name is that the one employed by end-user systems and procedures projects is so different than the traditional one. There are several noticeable differences between the two. The end-user one has particular advantages noted here.

A. Project size

The number of end-users involved will be noticeably smaller. This will reduce communication complexity significantly.

B. Project members

Project members will most likely know each other. This reduces the learning curve problem.

C. Departments representative

Most—if not all—project members will work in the same department. This reduces the loyalty problem.

D. The project head

The end-user project coordinator is a permanent entity. Because all projects have the same project coordinator, there is no problem learning the style of each coordinator.

E. Department knowledge

Most—if not all—project members will usually work in the same department. They will know the department and will save time asking each other about the department.

F. Procedure knowledge

Members of given projects will be acquainted with the policies and procedures. Some will even know what documented procedures are not being followed and why.

G. Objective

Most—if not all—project members will have the same goals. These goals most often are the ones that the department head will have.

H. Terminology

The project members will be speaking the same language. The terms that will be used are already used in the department.

I. Hardware familiarity

Most—if not all—project team members will know the hardware already in use. The idiosyncrasies of some of the equipment will be known by most project members.

J. Software familiarity

Most—if not all—project team members will know the software already in use. The idiosyncrasies of some of the programs will be known of most project members.

K. Known skill level of project members

The end-user project coordinator will be acquainted with many of the project members (e.g., which ones can be depended on and which cannot, and which ones will underestimate the time to accomplish a task and which ones will overestimate or be right on the button). The ones that underestimate task time can provide a project with disaster. The end-user project coordinator can plan for a contingency for these people with their first task.

L. Authority

The project coordinator title as well as the traditional project manager is misleading. The traditional project manager is really a coordinator, because he/she has little authority over all the people on their project team. The end-user project coordinator has much more authority because they are working for the head of the whole department.

Comment:

Having worked on many projects of both kinds, I favor the end-user project. Looking back at 23 years of experience in this field, I feel very fortunate to have worked for the companies that I did.

S4.2.2 Project Assignments

When there is a work group microcomputer organization in place, the work group computer coordinator is the most likely candidate to become the end-user project coordinator. To have the personnel skills to be the work group computer coordinator and the knowledge of the department operation is all in his/her favor to be the end-user project coordinator. There may be reasons why the person may not hold both positions. One of which is that both positions would become a full-time responsibility.

The project may take place where there is no work group computer coordinator or the coordinator is too preoccupied with other responsibilities. In this case, a candidate that best meets the requirements for the responsibility will be selected by the department head. The time required in the early stages may avoid full-time commitments through delegating tasks to the end-user project members. A successful end-user project coordinator can expect the end-user project will continue with other projects, but not always with the same project members. At times, the end-user project coordinator will have more than one project simultaneously going on. The time involved should not diminish the importance of his/her regular full-time job. There may be times that the task of being the end-user project coordinator will place greater demands on his/her time than the regular job.

Members of the project will be assigned tasks, and a schedule of when these task duties are expected to take place. This will be in addition to their regular job responsibilities. They will know beforehand what hours they may be required to devote to the project. This will be in accordance with the status of the project schedule. In cases of hourly personnel, monies may be required to be budgeted for overtime work. Some firms even budget monies for salaried personnel. This is usually done at the pro-rated hourly rate these employees earn.

A weekly status report will be sent to all project members. This will not only inform the status of the project, but also inform project members their forthcoming work schedule. A copy of the weekly status report will be sent to the department head. This will provide the department head with an idea of what demands will be placed on his/her employees in the future.

S4.2.3 IT Assistance

When there is no one available within the end-user department, the department head may ask for IS assistance. This individual would be from the IT systems and procedures unit or the IT systems analysis unit. The person would be assigned to the department head that is proceeding with an end-user systems and procedures project. The person assigned is called a consultant end-user project coordinator. While working on the project, the IT person would have the duties of a project coordinator and internal consultant. Their goals are to:

- Train department project and operation workers.
- Develop department project workers with the hopes that one employee can be groomed to become an end-user project coordinator by the time the project is complete.
- Introduce technology that is needed for this and future projects.

- Complete the project on time and within budget, with limited future assistance needed.
- Be loyal to the department with his/her project needs.

There are advantages for having an internal consultant over an external (i.e., vendor) consultant. Internal consultants are often preferred because they:

- Know the company.
- Know the policies and procedures to be used.
- Are available and accessible.
- Will still be with the company after the task is completed.
- Are loyal to the company.
- Are less costly than an outside consultant.

There can, however, be some disadvantages with having an internal consultant. Any of the following may present a problem:

- Problems with company politics.
- Any past project problems or failures the IS unit has had, the memories, will live long after the project is finished.
- The candidate selected for the position of end-user project coordinator may want to keep status quo.

S4.2.4 External Consultant

The external consultant (vendor) can also provide advantages. The tasks that would be expected of an internal consultant could be much the same as for the external consultant. External consultants can provide advantages because they:

- Arrive with a credibility halo.
- Have a perceived objectivity.
- Have no political involvement.
- Can have the freedom to experiment with new technology.
- Arrive with outside contacts that they can rely on.

They may arrive with some disadvantages. The following items will not cover all eventualities:

- They have to acquire an internal advocate.
- They arrive with very little true information.
- The consultant will need time to build trust within the company.

- The cost can be higher than an internal consultant.
- They run the risk of reading the internal climate incorrectly.
- The external consultant can be too much of an outsider.
- When they leave they may never be seen again.

3. END-USER PROJECT MANAGEMENT

S4.3 COMPONENTS OF END-USER PROJECT MANAGEMENT

End-user project management is a marriage of different skills of people brought together for a given undertaking. Coordinating a project requires both technical and managerial skills. The project coordinator's task is to use the resources for a given project.

S4.3.1 Project Objectives

The major reason for the end-user project group's existence is to complete a given task. The task projects are to undertake systems and procedures analysis and reengineering projects. There should be specific results expected from the end-user group before any effort is expended by the group. Items such as the following should be addressed:

- How will the results be defined?
- How will progress be measured?
- What time frame is the project to be completed?
- What are the priorities with end-user project items and other related items?
- When team resources become less than the required need, which results may be minimized or ignored?
- What criteria will define a successful completion?

S4.3.2 Required Project Human Resources

The end-user project group will comprise a collection of unique skills required for successfully completing the project. The people assigned to the project will be mostly part time. If any special skills are not available within the department they can be requested from other parts of the company. If the skilled people are not available from within the firm they may be contracted from vendors providing such services. If the skills are needed for more than what is available in the project budget, extra dollars will be required to be found. If the vendor's service is for more than $1,000, quotes will be asked from no less than three vendors. Cooperate policy can change the dollar amount figure for needed competitive bids.

End-user employees will represent resource man-hours. Their hours are to be consumed within the allocated calendar time of the project. Their special skills or training will be needed at given time slots of the project schedule. If their scheduled time slots change due to other department commitments or unforeseen circumstances, they may not be available at the time needed. If their tasks cannot be done at a later date, the end-user project coordinator will have to seek help from another source or adjust the projects schedule.

> *Comment:*
> **People and hours are not interchangeable. If it takes one person 20 hours to knit a sweater, 20 people cannot do it in one hour.**

When the time arrives, there is no assurance that the person will be available as planned. Others in the department will be preselected as alternates for key tasks found on the PERT chart. If there is still a problem, the department head will be asked for over time. If this is not available the department head will be informed that the project will be delayed. The end-user project coordinator will inform the department head as to the extent of the delay by memo. A copy of the memo will be placed in the project documentation folder. The more distant a project member is scheduled, the less the chance that they will be available at the timed planned. A weekly status report will be sent to the department head and all members of the project. A copy of the end-user project coordinator's current Gantt chart will be attached to the report.

S4.3.3 End-User Project Coordinator's Duties

The end-user project coordinator's duties are not supposed to be a full-time permanent job. Under extenuating circumstances it could become a full-time activity for an undetermined length of time. The responsibility of the coordinator could be jointly shared with the duties of the department work group computer coordinator. There would be some advantages with both responsibilities being given to one person. The department will not be prevented from performing end-user or work group systems and procedure activities when not having a work group computer coordinator.

The exact duties may vary from department to department, a lot will depend on the department's objectives, function, resources, and management style. The title of coordinator befits the responsibility of using people that already have a job within the department to join a common goal of completing an end-user developed project. The end-user project coordinator will have duties involving many different activities. There will be new skills to develop as he/she is carrying out the duties.

The duties of the end-user project coordinator start with planning. Planning required before the project starts are:

- Approving general plan.
- Performing current procedures study.
- Analyzing current procedures.
- Defining needs for feasibility study.
- Doing feasibility study.
- Analyzing feasibility study.
- Approving the project.

The coordinator will develop a work plan for each project. The work plan is the procedure with which to complete the project. People will be assigned tasks in a given sequence as part of the project's process of completion. The selection of members for the project should also consider their present job obligation. The coordinator should have an option to work with flexible alternatives such as flex-time, compressed work week, etc.

A major concern of the coordinator is to organize the activities needed to complete the project. The Gantt chart will be helpful in performing this task. The Gantt chart will inform he/she what has been completed, what is currently being done, and what there is yet to be done. It will also indicate whether or not the project is on schedule. Refer to the main volume for Gantt charts and task schedules. PERT charts will also be used to optimize task assignments. When the PERT chart is completed it will be a source of information for completing the Gantt charts. This can be done manually or by any one of the marketed software packages. See the main volume for information about PERT and Gantt charts.

The end-user project coordinator will also have tasks that can be seen on the Gantt chart other than administrative duties. The following are possible tasks that may be done:

- Perform work sampling.
- Perform analysis.
- Document procedures.
- Write simple computer programs.
- Write proposed procedures.
- Write operators manuals.
- Design forms.
- Perform training.
- Develop Gantt charts.
- Develop PERT charts.

End-user project coordinators must also be communicators. There will be formal and informal communication methods employed. Verbal communications can be both formal and informal; written communications are most often formal. Project members and other invited people will attend project meetings. The final form will be influenced by the department culture and management style.

A. Meetings

Meetings can be conducted for different purposes and with different numbers of people. The kind of meetings that involve end-user projects are:

1. Two-people meetings

These two-people meetings are done for both formal and informal reasons. A formal meeting of two people is conducted in the office of the senior member. Notes may be taken by both people. The end-user project coordinator will hold their formal meeting with vendors in his/her office. If they do not have an office, a conference room will suffice.

Informal meetings can take place anywhere. When the end-user project coordinator would like to meet with a member of the project team, it can take place over a cup of coffee or at the project member's work area. A formal meeting takes place in the end-user project coordinator's office or a conference room.

2. Information presentation meeting

When meetings are held to present information, such as status meetings, the number of people attending can almost be unlimited. Information flow is one way and a close agenda can be followed. Handouts can be given as people come to the meeting. This reduces the need to take notes. Graphics can also be used in the handouts to help define items presented at the meeting. There can be more than one speaker presenting information. The length of the meeting should not run over one hour. The use of visuals can enhance the presentation.

If the information is about the project status, is it on schedule? Some questions to ask if it is not on schedule include:

- What is the reason it is not on schedule?
- What impact will this have on the project?
- What can be done to correct the delay?
- What alternative action is needed?
- When will the project be back on schedule?

Comment:

When using overhead transparencies, lay them on the floor. If they cannot be read from a standing position, your audience will also not be able to read them.

3. Brainstorming meetings

The size of a work or brainstorming meeting should be a limited number, three to nine people. It should be held in a conference room without interruption, including beepers or cellular phones. There should not be a boss and his/her subordinate present. The end-user project coordinator will chair the meeting.

The meeting can have an air of informality by providing refreshments. All the attending people will have a chance to speak. The chairperson will keep the meeting moving. All brainstorming should be encouraged. The chairperson may have to prod the silent types. The best ideas can come from these people. A voice-activated tape recorder can be used, if there is no major objection, to recall just how something was said. If need be, the tape can be erased before the meeting is over. Notes will be taken of the good solutions that were arrived at by the group.

4. Project presentation

This meeting is held for presenting a proposal to the department management. It could be a feasibility report presentation with a recommended course of action or a reengineering proposal. About a week before the project presentation, hand deliver the feasibility reports with a cover memo.

The meeting presentation should be well prepared. It will require a well-executed presentation. There should be a presentation aid. One of the best aids is a flip chart. If the audience is a small group there will be no problem seeing the flip charts. The charts will be drawn before the meeting. Colored markers will enhance the charts. The presentation notes can be written in pencil on the edge of the flip chart pages. Rehearse the presentation in the room it is to be given a day before the presentation. Walk through the presentation with the flip charts. Leave blank sheets covering the next item, when the last drawn chart is no longer needed.

The day of the presentation, get there about a half hour early to get set up. Bring a couple of different colored markers to use on the flip chart as needed. The blank pages can serve as a place to write on if need be. If there are more hand outs, have them ready to pass out when the time arrives to do so. Open the meeting with a general statement. Then proceed with the presentation. End it open to questions.

B. Written material

Written material can come in many forms. The distribution can be to one or more people. It can provide a formal audit trail over time for the project.

Comment:

A company in Michigan maintains a central file for projects. A copy of all correspondence related to the project is sent to the file. Correspondence can be addressed to the file only. This provides an audit trail for the life of the project. E-mail can work the same way by CC:ing the project folder.

1. Letters

   Letters will follow standard universal procedures when written, unless there is company policy provided. This is a formal document and most often used when corresponding with non-company people.

2. Memos

   Company-provided memo forms or formats will be used if provided. The head of the memo contains the sender's name, date, receiver's name, and subject reference. With e-mail use today it provides a fast and convenient way of sending memos.

3. Documentation material

   When documentation is in a written form it should look as if the same person wrote it, because more than one person will write documentation material. When writing this material, consider the reader that has to understand what has been written. Check with the IT systems unit to find out if they have anything on administrative manual procedures. This material is provided in several forms:

   - Documentation of procedures.
   - Proposed procedures.
   - Operator instructions.
   - Policy and procedure manuals.
   - Feasibility report.
   - Reengineering proposal.
   - Machine operation instructions.
   - Training manuals.
   - Troubleshooting instructions.

Comment:

Years ago the Association for Systems Management published *Documentation Standards Manual for Computer Systems*. I still have a copy and find it a good reference. Some years ago the American Management Association published *Improving Administrative Manuals*, written by Robert E. Harmon. I keep a copy of it in my reference library. If it is out of print, they may have replaced it with something else. It is a good book on the subject.

S4.3.4 Why Projects Fail

Knowing why projects fail can provide insight as to what to look for during project development. There are several areas that can be of major concern.

A. Analysis

Poor analysis or even no analysis has been the reason for many project failures. When cutting costs for competitive bids, this is one of the first areas that vendors reduce costs.

B. Training

Too little concern is given to training. It is a cost-cutting area for vendors. Do not underplay the value of training. Good training can be 5% or more of the cost of the new system. However, the cost becomes much higher after it is too late.

> **Comment:**
> **While down in Florida I learned that a local chain store gave their baggers two days of training. I then asked a check-out cashier of a national chain how much training she received. She said she received none, but she noted that she observed someone else for an hour or so. That may have explained why one store was so busy and the other was not. I have no plans to buy any stock in the well-known company.**

C. Crash programming and testing

When programming schedules are met no matter what, it will not provide bug-free programs. Program testing can take more time than writing the program. Rushed test data will more likely not look for all possible problems.

D. Poor systems testing

Yes the programs work, but will they work with the other systems programs?

E. Poor selection of hard/software

Hybrid systems are more popular than they were many years ago. It saves money; however, problems can come from mixing brands.

F. No or poor follow-up evaluation

When there is no or little post implementation follow-up, it may be due to an effort to save time. As more time passes there will be more noticeable problems occurring.

There are early danger signs to be concerned with. If the end-user project coordinator spots any of these there could be problems ahead. Some major signs to notice are:

1. Isolation

   When a member(s) of a project shows signs of isolation, he/she may be avoiding being questioned about how things are coming along.

2. No schedule changes

   When there are no schedule changes allowed, it is an early sign that corners will be cut to save time and get there no matter what.

3. Late or no reporting

   Late or no reporting of progress is a sign that there is nothing to report.

4. Premature programming

   Any programming effort before all the details are hammered out will be time wasted. This allows for less programming time available when it is needed at the end.

5. Staff reassignments

   Departments that allow staff reassignments are wasting time. If there is a replacement, it is not easy to pick up where someone else left off—in addition to the learning curve problem. It also takes time from other project members to help the new person.

Comment:

I cannot confirm this with any research, but there are some people who think the number one reason that projects fail is because of a lack of planning.

6. Vendors not returning phone calls

When the vendor has a contract in process and does not return phone calls, it is a signal to the end-user project contact person that there might be a problem.

S4.3.5 Project Management Tools

There are tools available that can assist the project management effort. Some of these items may be available or loaned from the IT systems unit. The end-user project team may consider:

- Form rulers and form layout sheets to assist the design of paper forms to be printed by a forms vendor. These devices are provided free by most paper forms vendors or can be purchased.

- Computer forms design software is available for in-house–generated forms. Most word processing and desk-top publishing software can also be used to generate camera-ready copy for in-house printing.

- For graphic flowcharting, templates and computer software are available.

- There are many computer software packages produced for project management. The prices start at shareware levels and go into the thousands. Today, there are some effective packages for PC's and Apple systems.

Comment:

There have been some very good reports about Timeline and Microsoft Project. There are some excellent self-paced instructional packages to help a user learn the system. According to various studies, no significant correlation has been shown between price and the package rating.

Shapeware Corporation of Denver has a software package called VISIO. It produces graphic symbols for: standard flowcharting; network diagrams; office space planning; electrical, chemical, biotechnology, and mechanical engineering; home planning; landscaping; etc.

When selecting a project management software package, first look for software that will run on the hardware that is already installed. Secondly, one should choose the less-complex package that will do the job. Other features that must be considered are:

- User support.
- User friendliness.
- Reliability.
- Work breakdown structure (WBS).
- Single-source data entry.
- Calendar support.
- PERT and CPM charting.
- Online tutorials.

It should be able to:

- Perform "what if" scenarios.
- Identify critical path and compute slack time.
- Produce graphics.
- Support capture of resources for allocation to tasks.
- Compare planned to actual Gantt charts.
- Plot milestones.

Other features that may be worth considering:

- Can it be networked.
- Can handle multiple projects.
- Have resource leveling.
- Training is available.
- Have individual resource calendars for vacation and training.
- Can show work-completed versus budgeted milestones.

S4.3.6 Project Management Technology

There is a wide range of project planning technology available. Some of the techniques require a computer with its supporting software, while others can be applied using manual methods. No one technology provides all project management needs.

A. PERT charts

PERT charts can display the total project with all scheduled tasks shown in sequence. These can be produced manually or using computer project management software. The displayed tasks show which ones are in parallel that can be performed at the same time.

PERT and CPM charts look alike. The only difference is how the task times are determined. The CPM method uses one value (most likely time) for the determined time each task will take. PERT requires a calculation as follows:

$$\text{TASK TIME} = \frac{\text{To} + \text{Tp} + 4\text{Tn}}{6}$$

To = optimistic time
Tp = pessimistic time
Tn = most likely time

The critical path of the PERT/CPM chart computes the project duration. This can be done manually or using a project management software program. The critical path can be worked backwards from a needed finish date (to determine a start date) or forward from a start date to determine a finish date. The critical path is the minimum time in which the project can be completed if all the required resources are available.

The PERT/CPM chart will show the slack times. Slack time occurs when a task takes less time to do than a parallel critical path task. This information can be valuable. For example, suppose the critical path needs to be reduced in total time by two days. Assume a critical path task of 12 days is found that has a parallel slack time of 10 or fewer days. Simply have the critical path task work overtime two Saturdays, and the total project time is reduced by two days. This is a very simple illustration. More complex solutions for reducing the total project time can be found by using a project management software program. See the *Information Systems Policies and Procedures Manual* for more information about PERT/CPM and Gantt charts.

The PERT/CPM chart can provide input data for the Gantt chart. Each leg of the PERT/CPM chart can become a Gantt chart. The Gantt chart will display the scheduled calendar days for the task. The chart can be available on a monitor from a project software package and/or on hard copy placed on the office wall.

B. Gantt charts

Gantt charts are used to show calendar time task assignments in days, weeks, or months. As the task progresses and reaches a milestone, the milestones can be shown on the chart. The number of days required to complete a task that reaches a milestone can be compared with the planned number. The actual work days, from actual start to actual finish, are plotted below the scheduled days on the Gantt chart. This information can be a warning that the person is not meeting the estimated time schedule. Depending on priorities, project resource adjustments can be made.

Gantt charts can also be used to show dollars allocated versus dollars spent information. This can be compared to the status of task work completed. Tasks can also be broken down into subtasks, and both can be used to identify the persons assigned. Gantt charts can be produced to show a person's task-type assignment by projects. The overall project status displayed by the Gantt chart allows the project manager to assign or reassign personnel as needed. It also shows when there is a need for shifting project schedules and can provide warning flags of problems yet to arrive.

Gantt charts can be produced on graph paper, overhead transparencies, or magnetic boards. If computers are used, the charts can be available on networked computer monitors and hard copy.

4. SYSTEMS AND PROCEDURES ANALYSIS

S4.4 CURRENT PROCESS ANALYSIS

The current process observed by user management is the starting point for thinking about the need for a preliminary feasibility study. General observation of operations is like that of icebergs in that what you cannot see is often greater than what you can see. The study of a current process analysis gets down below the water line of the operation. What really happens there is unknown to management. Each unit wants to be successful, so it does what it can with its own below-the-water-line effort to keep things moving.

Comment:
When workers are not allowed to strike, they just follow the procedures sent down from management to slow things down. The central developed procedures do not work and the workers know it. It is something like government.

The current process needs a preliminary procedures feasibility study to determine that it is worth the effort to do a complete user-feasibility study. A preliminary procedures feasibility study may come about in the form of a management request as to why something is happening. The request leads to finding an answer. Is it feasible for the department to do something or not? The answer can be yes or no. No means it is simple enough that it will not require any further effort. Yes means let's do it because it has merit. From here, the next task is the systems and procedures analysis.

S4.4.1 Examination of Current Documented Procedures

The status of the current official documentation compared to the actual procedures being performed will determine the time needed by the analyst. An analyst or the end-user project coordinator acting as an analyst will perform the study. To start, the analyst needs to know what are the current official documented procedures. These are found in the latest published documentation that the unit supervisors have. The next steps are to:

A. Define the area of study

The process, activity, or operation starts at one or more places and ends in one or more places. The task is to find the starting place. The area of study will cover all the areas of the process, activity, or operation. The area to be studied may not be the same as the actual area when the study is completed.

B. Follow the process

The process study starts with input from another area of the company or an outside source. Start with the unit that is believed to be the one. If it is not the starting place of the study area, ask which unit they receive their input from. Work backwards until the starting point is reached.

At the starting unit, find out the source(s) of their input. After the process it is completed follow it to the next step. Record this information and follow any process that remains in the area of study.

Go to the unit that receives the item next (in the area of study). Confirm which unit it was received from, and find out what becomes of the item after their process is completed. Document the input and output information. The documentation procedure is repeated with each unit within the area of study until it is sent out of the study area or is discarded.

There may be items that leave the area of study and then are returned to the department. The item may be returned to the same unit it came from or another unit for further processing.

C. Examine the operating procedures

Start with the first unit of the process. Talk to the unit head and explain that a study of the current documented procedures is being done. Ask to borrow them for a day or two so they can be examined. A comparison will be made with any other procedures management may have. Make a copy of the borrowed procedures before returning them. This procedure process will continue until the last unit of the study has it documentation returned.

D. No printed procedures

There is no assurance that any formal manuals will be available. Do not embarrass the unit head if they do not have a manual. The analyst will make an offer to buy them a cup of coffee if they provide some needed information. Collect from the unit head the procedure information and any printed material that is relevant. Use a shorthand pad to take notes. Ask if it is permissible to take notes so that you will not recall incorrect details. Do not use your office or conference room for this informal communication. Use the lunch room, or if the unit head has to be at his/her work area go there. Anything the unit head says off the record, stays off the record. Do not write a word about the information.

E. How to dress

The area required for the contact with the unit head may need to be considered when dressing for the day's visit to the unit. Some areas require that you wear safety glasses, and that you do not wear high-heeled shoes, dresses, or skirts.

Comment:
A worn-out shorthand pad is nice to collect information, folded documents, or notes. It looks a lot less intimidating than an expensive briefcase. Do not try to overprotect it, because it gives the wrong signals.

F. Communicating

Mix the conversation with other unrelated things. Let the person know something about you. But, most of all listen to what, how, and why it is said. Listening is a learned skill. Listening will be enhanced if you:

- Listen with your mouth closed.
- Do not jump to conclusions, and have all the information.
- Listen for what the user's words mean.
- Ask questions—you are not required to know what the person means from the start.
- Do not become a defensive listener. It may stop other information from being received.
- Avoid preconceptions. That is the reason for identifying people by the job they do or the occupation they have. It is not how they are saying something, but what they are saying that counts.

> ***Comment:***
> **At a large hospital a person called for a clinic appointment. She was told to bring a plastic plate with her when she came. When the patient arrived to be registered she was asked for her plastic plate. The women said she did not know what size plate to bring so she brought two of them.**

S4.4.2 *Study of Current Operating System*

The information collected is management's record of what is being done. It will be examined. The documentation will be arranged in sequence. If the procedure documentation is developed by the same source, it increases the continuity. An example would be ISO 9000 documentation. Documentation that depends on the unit heads will have less continuity. The more complex the operation is the less likely will be the continuity. The following procedures will be used to study management's concept of the current system.

A. Develop system flow

   The information collected will be studied to determine its flow pattern. This is management's documentation of the flow. The documentation collected and studied will be pictured as a system flow.

B. Systems flowchart

   A system flowchart will be drawn from the information collected. The chart will be drawn with a number two pencil. The chart will be copied. The original chart will be filed. The copy will be used for later activities.

> **Comment:**
> **There is software on the market that will simplify the drawing and redrawing tasks. It is available at a competitive price. It may be worth looking at if drawing flowcharts becomes a common activity.**

There are several options for selecting flowcharts (See the main volume, Chapter 2, section Seven—Flowcharting Standards.) The system flowchart drawn will be the level zero dataflow diagram.

C. System flowchart validity

The dataflow diagram will be shown to the unit heads to confirm that it is correct. Corrections will be noted on the chart.

D. Identify key workers

Ask each unit head to identify the key input and output personnel. These are workers who receive incoming items in their unit or release items from the unit. The names and job titles will be posted to a work copy of the systems chart.

Items can be received and released more than once from a unit. The item can be released to another unit within the department or to another department for a process and then returned. After it is returned to the unit it may require other actions to be completed. After the activity is completed it will be released. Any other corrections to the flowchart will be completed before leaving the unit. The unit head will be thanked for his/her time and contribution.

E. Revise the system flowchart

After all the data has been corrected on the work copy of the flowchart, the original will be updated. A new copy of the level zero dataflow diagram will be made or amended.

S4.4.3 Study of Current Operating Procedures

The current system will be documented in detail at the procedure level. The process will start with the examination of the completed systems flowchart, after which each unit head will be contacted for a consultation visit. The order of the visits will follow the procedure sequence. The analyst will read the procedures furnished by the unit heads just before each visit. If no procedure documentation was furnished, the analyst will refer to his/her notes.

Studying the current procedure for a given end-user operation will require several factors to be considered. The following will provide a guide and structure to the process.

A. The end-user analyst

With an end-user/work group project, there may be a chance the analyst is from a unit to be studied. In this case the end-user project coordinator will study the unit. If this can not be done, an analyst should be obtained from another department or the IT systems unit. To work as an analyst in the unit the analyst is from is a total waste of everyone's time. An analyst cannot be objective in such an environment.

B. Unit head relationship

During the visit, the unit head will be informed why the analyst is there. He/she will be asked to introduce the analyst to the operational employees. If the employee(s) already knows the analyst, the introduction will not be required. The analyst will ask the employees when would the best time to talk to them.

After the date and time has been established, the analyst will return to proceed interviewing the employees at their work stations. The unit head will be informed each time the analyst arrives in the unit area. It is a simple protocol courtesy. It can be a simple waving of a hand. If the unit head is not there, just proceed. If they do return while the analyst is there, acknowledge their presence.

C. Tools needed

Bring a shorthand pad and some pencils. An $8^{1}/_{2}''$ by $11''$ pad attached to a plastic binder may be considered. There are binders that have pockets that provide room collecting sample documents. If the interview is to be structured, the analyst will find a question checklist useful.

D. Skills needed

The study of the unit's operating procedures is collecting information from each employee. The most important means of gathering the correct information is the procedure interview. A skillfully done interview is not an easy accomplishment. To some analysts it comes naturally. The person needs a level of objectivity that produces results. Interviewing workers takes a passive, friendly attitude that begets a level of confidence to gather the required information. An analyst that is a work group member can be very helpful to both the analyst and the person being interviewed. When interviewing, personal conversation is encouraged to a degree. It places the interview on a more friendly level. But keep the business talk on the subject at hand.

Comment:

There is help available if the analyst has a problem with communicating. Toastmasters International has a chapter in most towns of any size. They are friendly people with a need for helping each other. Call their national office at (248) 398-1892 to locate a chapter near you. The cost is not much more than a reasonably priced meal.

E. Checklist

Regardless of how well-qualified an analyst is of knowing his/her particular department, computers, or areas of operations, a checklist is a useful tool. Without such a list, the analyst may overlook some of the more important aspects of the study. A checklist need not be an endlessly complex compilation of every conceivable item. Checklists are not one size fits all. Checklists will require revising as the assignment requires.

Each of the primary areas influencing the procedures should have its own short list. The replies to these questions should be checked against what will be asked in other areas not yet interviewed. There should not be a problem to go back to a person interviewed earlier to ask an additional question.

Another use of checklists is to trigger ideas. This is an end-user project that all users can contribute. Make sure the person and unit get the credit for their ideas. Keep the idea on the back burner until it is design time. The design phase should not precede the analysis phase.

There is the standard "universal why" that should not be overlooked. It should be part of the checklist in most cases.

• What is done and why is it done?

• Where is it done and why is it done there?

- When is it done and why is it done at this time?
- Who does it and why does this person do it?
- How is it done and why is it done this way?
- Should it be done at all and why should (or should not) it be done?

F. Sample documents

Sample documents will be collected as the procedure information is being recorded. Any computer monitor screen displays will also be duplicated to be part of the information collected. Any controlled documents, such as a payroll check, will be copied and voided by the unit head.

Sample reports generated will contain the following information:

- The title of the report.
- The form number, if it is a preprinted form.
- How many copies of the report are made.
- When the reports are generated.
- Who receives the reports.
- What computer files are used for the report.
- What computer files are changed when the report is made.
- What files are from the file server.
- What transaction data are input for the report.
- How the files are backed up.
- Whether there is a disaster recovery procedure. Make a copy of it.
- How the transaction data are stored.

G. Operations manuals

Which operation manuals that are available to the operator are used more often than others? Make a list of the operation manuals and their source. Note which manuals they do not use and why.

H. Computer

If a computer is used, the questions will be on the checklist.

I. Provide time for the worker to get data

If the person cannot provide the correct information at the time it is asked for, come back when he/she will have the information. If the person is pushed, he/she will furnish what he/she thinks is correct. This is not what is wanted for the procedure study.

When all the information is collected from the people that perform the procedures, it will be sorted into a system sequence. Review the procedures for continuity. Place the recorded information into a binder along with the samples that will be the supporting exhibits.

S4.4.4 Documented Current Procedures Confirmation

The information collected is difficult to work with in its current form. The information will be transferred to a media that will be easy to follow and be the focal point of a discussion. If a level zero dataflow diagram is drawn, it can be followed up with the next, which is a level one dataflow diagram. The department head would have no problem with a level zero dataflow diagram. The unit head should be equally able to follow the level one dataflow diagram.

The level one dataflow diagrams will be taken to the unit heads for confirmation that the documentation is correct. Attached to these are copies of the exhibits. If needed, the workers will review their part of the chart to ensure that it is correct.

The procedure flowchart will be used when the procedures of the current system must be compared with that of the proposed system. Procedures of both systems are drawn on the same document. The current procedures will be drawn on the upper portion of the document. The end-user analyst will find it easy to draw. There are drawing templates available, which will make the task easier. More information is provided in the original IS manual.

The procedure flowchart is also an excellent method for documenting a manual operation. It illustrates all the procedures that comprise a system on one document.

It is placed on a horizontal roll of paper. The paper comes in different widths and lengths. Because it is stored as a rolled-up document, lengths present no problem. The only limitation to length is where it will be displayed for viewing. Procedure flowcharting is easy to follow, even for people that have never seen one. There are only six symbols used, which are easy to understand and follow. It is an industrial engineering tool that has found its way into business-systems analysis applications.

The analyst can confirm that the procedures recorded are correct by having the end-user operational personnel view the section of the chart that pertains to their actual procedures. It also gives the analyst an easy-to-follow source of information when writing or dictating (into a continuous speech recognition programmed computer) documentation procedures.

Preparing a procedure flowchart requires the following procedures:

- The direction of the flow is left to right.

- Charts are drawn with a number two pencil.

- One must identify the system in the lower left-hand corner with the following: project title, project number, date, and the end-user analyst's name.

- All input documents will have a receiving process, a procedure, and a ending action. The ending action may be: filing, destroying, or sending it from the unit.

- The standard symbols will be used.

- A work copy can be provided. This will allow for comments or changes posted to the document.

The analyst will take the work copy to each unit from which procedure information was collected. The process followed by the actual people that were interviewed. These people will examine their part of the procedure flowchart and confirm whether it is correct. Corrections will be made to the copy and any other data will be provided as needed. After verification that the documentation is correct, it will be taken back to the end-user analyst's work area and have the corrections applied to the original procedure flowchart.

5. END-USER FEASIBILITY PROPOSAL

S4.5 END-USER FEASIBILITY PROPOSAL COMPONENTS

The end-user feasibility proposal is different than the IT feasibility study. The end-user preliminary feasibility study is a scaled-down version of the IT feasibility study. End-user management is much more in tune to the needs of the department's end-user/work group operation. This knowledge provides the end-user department head the opportunity to approve the feasibility proposal. The feasibility proposal is just that—a user/work group effort to provide a proposal that merits feasibility. These terms were developed to differentiate the end-user/work group projects from that of the IT units.

The feasibility proposal can be done for two reasons. The first is the revision of an end-user/work group system, and the second is the development of a system that does not currently exist. Both of these undertakings are end-user/work group project efforts.

The revision of an end-user/work group system requires the process done in section 4.4—CURRENT PROCESS ANALYSIS. The collection of the actual procedures being done will be analyzed. The information elements collected will be synthesized to produce a new system. The revised system will have to try to achieve the end-user's goals. The I/O components will be the what is wanted. Are changes to be made to these components? If so, what will they be? Will new software be a component change? Will the hardware component be affected? How will the process component be affected? These and other components can be addressed in light of the requirements for a new replacement system.

The development of a system that does not currently exist is the second item for an end-user feasibility proposal project. The project will be led by the end-user project coordinator or a possible alternate selection of a project leader. The requirements will be addressed in light of what funds and calendar restraints are placed on the project. Will all components of the system have equal priority? If not, what are management's priorities?

S4.5.1 End-User Replacement System

Replacing a system requires that the current system be studied in detail. This is why section 4.4—CURRENT PROCESS ANALYSIS was written. The information elements collected of the current system and the requirements mandated for the new system will all be synthesized. The replacement system can consist of one or more of the following requirements:

- New software.
- New hardware.
- Modified or upgraded software.
- The upgrade of the system network.
- The installation of a network.
- Upgrading of the system.
- Gateway installation on the LAN system.
- Simplification of the system's procedures.
- Duplication of the system at another location.
- Expansion of the work group/user size.
- Replacement of the current system with a totally new system.
- Changes to the server's database access.
- Additions to the server's database information.

The replacement process involves several items that must be considered before the replacement is made. The following will be considered before the replacement takes place.

A. The conversion process

   The other consideration to be made is how will the change take place? This depends a lot on how extensive the change will be. Some changes can be made during the system's operation while others will require a weekend conversion. There may even be a need for two systems running in parallel for a given amount of time.

B. Training requirements

   A person will be selected for coordinating end-user training. The person should be assigned as an ongoing trainer for the end-user projects. Training needs will be appraised. Who will be trained will be considered. Also, training techniques will be evaluated.

C. Acquisition of new hardware

   Hardware acquisition may require a department budget before the equipment can be purchased. Or the purchase may be made from existing department budgets. Refer to Chapter 1, section 3—COMPUTER HARDWARE BUDGETS for more information that would apply to the project.

D. Computer software acquisition

   There is a wide range of software acquisitions that can be made for end-user/work group projects. If money is needed for the acquisition of end-user/work group software, it may require a request of budgeted monies for the needed year. One or more software acquisition selections can be made by a department. A selection of one or more of the following may be considered:

   - End-user–developed software.
   - IT programming–developed software.
   - Acquiring a contract programmer.
   - Purchasing a turn-key system.
   - Leasing a turn-key system.
   - Have a system contractor develop the end-user system.
   - Purchase or lease packaged software.

   For more information, contact the IT software asset manager or the IT programming unit head. Chapter 2 can provide more information.

For the maintenance of current software, the selection scope is reduced to:

- End-user software maintenance.
- IT programming software maintenance.
- Contract programmer maintenance.
- System contractor maintenance.

The IT programming unit may be called on for advice. For any programs the end-user has had IT programmers write, the unit head will be contacted. For purchased software packages, the best that could happen would be a software upgrade.

E. Documentation requirements

Documentation requirements start before the actual project is formed. It continues after the project is completed. The time devoted to documentation after the project is completed will be for project maintenance. Documentation comes in many forms, of which not all are prose. Information not found in the supplement should be looked for in the main volume. The following are forms of documentation that contain a minimum of prose.

- System flowcharts.
- Procedure flowcharts.
- Programming flowcharts.
- Program documentation.
- Work sampling form.
- Questionnaires.
- Time/documentation log.
- Interview guides.

F. Procedure manuals

Procedure manuals, programmed learning manuals, instruction manuals, and troubleshooting manuals require a minimum level of reading skills. The writing level should be geared to the minimum level of the expected reader. Some word processing software, such as WordPerfect, will analyze the reading level of the prose that it is processing. For writing prose, general college grads should not be above the tenth grade level, while office workers today should not be above the eighth grade level, and hourly workers the sixth grade.

Writing documentation is not popular with end-user project team members. Prose or even IT documentation for end-users does not require a writer's identity style. The concern should be the reading level of the person needing the written information.

Comment:

The systems analysis four-year degree program that I developed for The University of Findlay required technical writing. This information came from a Delphi study done some years ago on practicing systems analysts across the United States. Some of my foreign students who were returning to their home countries were encouraged to do the technical writing in their native language. I received a good-grade bottle of wine from a former student who got a job at Microsoft. He headed up the Spanish technical writing unit of Microsoft before he left the United States.

Procedure manuals are one of the tools used by management to provide structure to the organization. It provides a formal means of recording administrative policies and providing communications to the employees for instruction in the methods of conducting the firm's business. The format of a particular manual depends upon how it is to be used. The manual could be an:

- Overall company policy manual.
- Step-by-step procedure manual telling workers how to perform a task in a uniform manner.
- Training manual.
- Single-page instruction attached to a machine.

Small companies may use only one manual to satisfy all their procedural requirements. A large company may have many types of manuals. It is important to remember to keep the number of manuals to a minimum. The work of controlling and updating a procedure increases when a change in one manual requires a change in a second manual.

The nature of the company's business affects the type of manuals it will maintain. A company organized according to function requires the pattern-type procedures to explain the methods of operating between divisions. A firm organized by product lines needs policy procedures issued at management level.

There are several basic rules that must be followed if a procedure manual is to be effective:

- It must be up to date.

- The procedure statements must be well written. The technical skills of the reader should not be taken for granted.

- The manual must be well organized. The procedures within must be easily found.

- The procedures must be adequately coordinated and accepted by the employees.

- The manual distribution must be kept current so that the people who should have manuals actually receive them.

- The procedures must work.

- The procedures must be approved and revised by a person with appropriate authority. This person is not required to write the procedures, but only to sign their approval.

To expend all the effort and cost to develop a policies and procedures manual does provide a return for the investment. Because of ISO, the value of documented procedures in the United States has risen significantly. There have been many books printed on the subject, and many companies use them, which shows there must be some merit to the subject. The following are advantages of policy and procedure manuals:

- When a manual is initiated for the first time or even being updated, management is forced to make decisions on polices and procedures.

- By maintaining consistency and continuity, the printed manual becomes the "bible" within its field to settle arguments, save time, and provide a level of confidence. People come and go, but manuals stay for the new people to follow.

- Manuals are used for training new employees. The manual shows how a specific job is performed and how it is part of the overall process.

- Policy manuals provide an avenue for the executive to issue guidelines. They also provide answers to problems by stating "it is the policy" that we have to do that.

- It allows for management by exception and it relieves executives from repeat decisions on the same problem.

- By documenting standardized work routines, it facilitates financial performance audits.

- Manuals identify responsibility areas to eliminate overlapping, voids, obsolete activities, and the burden of routing and filing unnecessary forms.

Comment:

Some time ago, the British Army was doing studies to minimize unneeded procedures. A team was sent out to study artillery procedures. They noticed that one man was posted 50 yards back behind the cannon. When asked why this was done, the answer was a familiar one: "It has always been done this way." The experts—not wanting to do the wrong thing—performed a thorough study on the procedure. They discovered that the man standing 50 yards back had the job, at one time, of holding onto the horses when the cannon was being fired.

S4.5.2 End-User New System Development

Developing procedures for an end-user's new system has benefits that are not available when replacing a current system with a new system. The benefits are that the employees does not have to learn a new system while trying to forget the old one. The old system may have some procedures that the employee may prefer over the new one. The major benefit is the installation process. Installing a new system is not hampered by the problem of going from one system to another. Each type of conversion presents problems in going from the old to the new. Learning the new system process while still retaining the old is required with a parallel conversion.

The first consideration in designing a system that is not replacing a current system is to adopt a broad approach. The broad approach can be started with a brainstorming meeting of the end-user project group being chaired by the end-user project coordinator. Many of the problems can be resolved by an analysis of the objective of the new system. The objective is what the project team has to consider. The objective may be a requirement for an end product that should be well defined. The solution to the objective that starts with a broad approach becomes more narrow until the solution for a system design is reached. The development of the procedures required for system design comes from the procedure elements needed to process the system.

The system may start with a simple content dataflow diagram on a flip chart. It will continue to a level one. At this point, process considerations are made. Will it be a manual or a computer process? If it is a computer process, what kind of software is needed? Will the new system use existing hardware or will new hardware be used? The option of new hardware can expand the software selection.

The software selection can have more than one kind of software source (e.g., already available software or software that requires programming). There may be money and time considerations that will force an arbitration regarding the software selection.

S4.5.3 Develop Feasibility Proposal

The end-user feasibility proposal will contain all the information to install the new system. It will not contain operation and procedure manuals. A copy of the feasibility proposal will be furnished to department management.

A formal presentation will be made by the end-user project coordinator and the project team. The presentation will be made to department management and any guests that they may have invited. The presentation is not to sell a replacement system, but to furnish information for a system wanted by management. The question is: will the presented system satisfy their needs with the resources they have granted the project to work with?

S4.5.4 New System Startup

With management approval, there will be a start date for the systems operation. There will be time needed to:

- Obtain the required software.
- Obtain any new hardware.

- Write the procedure manuals.
- Write the operation manuals.
- Select and train operational personnel.
- Develop test data.
- Run operation tests.

The system will start on a given day. The process will be followed by the end-user project coordinator or a member of the project team. After the system has been running without any problem for a while, the end-user project coordinator will write a memo. The memo will be addressed to the department management and all project team members. The memo will state the status of the completed project as now being an operational system.

6. END-USER REENGINEERING

S4.6 END-USER REENGINEERING COMPONENTS

Most success stories about reegineering involve department operations. With end-user computing in place, end-user reengineering is the next logical step. The components needed are already in place to empower the department to do their own reegineering. The components are microcomputers, department project teams, and systems and procedures tools. Proactive management is also a major component. What may be lacking can be acquired and developed within the department. End-user–developed microcomputer operations can be the foundation stone for constructing end-user reegineering programs.

Comment:
An article, "The Real Trick to Reengineering" in the July 1993 issue of *PC World,* reported a study by Lester C. Thurow, dean of MIT's Sloan School of Management, which showed that white-collar productivity declined during the 1980s despite the use of microcomputers in the workplace.

> *Comment:*
>
> **An Indiana manufacturing VP once admitted that it took five days to process a customer's order to get it to the plant. His plant took only three days to build the product for the order.**

Tools are available at the end-user level to proceed with reengineering projects. Before the advent of computers, some firms had system and procedure units that performed what may resemble reengineering. Many of the tools the systems and procedures analysts used are still available and used today. Some of the tools are used with end-user systems and procedures. The main thing the systems and procedures analysts did not have is the microcomputer. This tool properly used can be a real assist for end-user reengineering.

End-user reengineering project components include:

- A project team.
- Required tools.
- A pilot project.
- Process redesign.
- Project implementation.

Not as a component as much as a department policy, employees should feel safe from downsizing. With the low unemployment rates, company transfers can provide worker opportunities and employee attrition should take care of the rest. Workers that do not have to worry about their jobs can feel free to play an active role in reengineering.

S4.6.1 Reengineering Candidates

Candidates for reengineering can come in many different sizes and complexities. The first project selected should be one that has the best possibility to succeed. As the project team gains experience they may take on more complex or larger projects. Reengineering candidates can come from several sources.

A. Department head

The department head may have his/her own thoughts of what needs attention. They may have their own priority list. These can be problem areas that higher management has been disturbed about or budget overruns, etc. They are not the only source for projects, but a source that should be of concern.

B. Customer complaints

Whether it be a service problem or a product problem with the customer, it should be of major concern. Some businesses have top managers that monitor customer service. Other firms have web sites that collect customer information. Customer complaints can be an excellent source for end-user reengineering projects.

C. Cost analysis

Some professional or industrial organizations have cost information that would flag areas for user reengineering attention. The cost for a given product or service is available from some of these organizations. If the professional organization does not publish the information, it may be obtained from a member of the organization informally at a meeting. If no one has an answer, they may be able to provide a name that can.

D. Personnel discontent

Areas that have a high turnover and/or absenteeism are a problem that may warrant the attention of the end-user reengineering project team. If it is a supervision problem, it is something that reengineering cannot resolve.

E. Overtime

Continuous overtime may in some cases warrant reengineering studies. The study alone may solve the problem. There are certain times of the year when workers need the overtime pay, while at other times it is not popular.

Comment:

In one case, a hospital medical records unit needed more overtime than what was budgeted. A simple work sampling study showed that the workers were non-productive 35% of the time.

F. Bottlenecks

When there is a bottleneck in a system, it warrants attention. The rest of the system can process only at the pace of the bottleneck. An end-user reengineering study and solution can often resolve the problem.

G. Low-volume high-cost processing

Some operations' costs cannot be reduced because the volume will not warrant cost-cutting investments. An end-user reengineering project team study may find an alternate solution.

S4.6.2 *Corporate End-User Reengineering*

A corporate end-user reengineering program manager should report to the CFO, executive VP, or CEO. This would give the program credibility. Corporate direction, goals, standardization, and assistance would be provided to end-user reengineering projects teams. There would also be the benefit of having a corporate budget.

The corporate effort could enlist a consulting firm to assist with the organization of the end-user reengineering program. They could also recruit the corporate end-user reengineering program manager. The program manager would be a full-time position with a supporting staff as needed.

The person filling the manager's position should have most all of the following qualifications:

- Knowledge of the kind of business the company is in.
- A bachelor's degree in industrial engineering and an MBA.
- Microcomputer experience.
- Have held a supervisor's or coordinator's position from three to five years.

The duties of the corporate end-user reengineering program manager would consist of:

- Developing a company-wide end-user reengineering plan.
- Computing a budget for the end-user reengineering program.
- Providing an end-user support program.
- Coordinating needs of end-user reengineering programs with: end-users, information systems, and consultants.

Support for end-user projects could be in the following forms:

- Maintaining an end-user reengineering help desk.
- Overseeing reengineering education and training.

- Providing consulting service for management and end-user team members.
- Working with labor relations as needed.
- Being the main source for vendor contacts.
- Assisting end-users with vendor contracting.
- Providing cost savings confirmation.
- Assisting with end-user reengineering startup teams.

A corporate steering committee will be formed to guide corporate reengineering efforts. The committee will be the final judge of last resort for any allocation of resources and disputes. Any union contract changes will require approval of the committee and the head of labor relations.

S4.6.3 End-User Reengineering Team

The end-user reengineering team is responsible for operations and/or processing systems in their department. The department can be a company unit at a location site removed from the main operations. If the reengineering effort is not a company-wide program, it should be sanctioned by a higher level of management. When the executive who has an area of responsibility decides to initiate an end-user reengineering program, he/she should discuss it with his/her next level of management.

The end-user reengineering effort will be done by a project team. The team is responsible to the person that has given its authorization to be formed. The project team will have a team leader. There will be a project team assigned to each reengineering project. The project will be given a project name and number. The name will identify the area of the project. The project number will be a sequence number.

A. Project leader

The project leader will be selected by the person that has given the team the authorization to be formed to do end-user reengineering. This person will not need to devote full time to this effort, unless told to by the person who appointed them. There can be a different team leader for each project team. There are advantages of having more than one end-user reengineering project leader. One advantage would be having a backup leader available. The other advantage would be having the ability to have more projects going on at the same time.

Having one permanent leader also provides advantages. A permanent team leader could coordinate resources between projects. Project reports should go to management from just one source, so there will be less chance of conflicts over resources with more than one team leader.

It is suggested only one team be launched with the first end-user reengineering project. A team leader should:

- Be a salaried worker.
- Have an air of maturity.
- Have administrative skill.
- Be respected by other workers.
- Have some familiarity with the operation.
- Be a delegator.
- Have good presentation skills.
- Have good writing skills.
- Be an innovator.
- Be a good leader.
- Have a good work ethic.
- Have a reputation that can be trusted.
- Be familiar with the workings of the firm.
- Know both the formal and informal organization structure.

Unless an experienced team leader was hired specifically for this responsibility, they will require some training. There can be some merit to bringing in a trained person, but it is limited. Knowing the people and the operations is far more important. Bringing in an experienced person to assist the project leader and train team members does have merit.

B. Project team members

Project team members will be assigned as needed from the department workforce. The project leader will request that people be assigned as needed to the reengineering project team.

If this is a company-wide effort, the project leader should be able to ask for assistance from the corporate level party that has that responsibility. With a company-wide program, assistance could be obtained from other department reengineering project leaders, industrial engineering, and the information systems unit. People may be available to advise or even become a part-time member of the project team. With any company-wide end-user reengineering, there should be budgeted funds available to hire contract workers or consulting assistance. They could also be part of the project team.

S4.6.4 Reengineering Team Training

The project leader should receive his/her general training and whatever other training deemed necessary before the project team is formed. Most, if not all, team members will require training. Training will be a two-phase program. The first phase will be general training that all members receive at the company site. This may be presented by a consultant or the project team leader. The contents of the training will cover the merits of end-user reengineering. It will also cover how reengineering will help the department with its problems and how they may be corrected.

The second phase of the training will cover the tools used in reengineering. Not all project team members will receive this training at the same time. The training will be available in several forms and be paid for by the company. Arrangements for the payment of any hourly people for off-site training should be cleared with the personnel unit management before any of the training starts. These forms of training may consist of the following:

- Classroom lecture.
- On-the-job training.
- Short courses away from the company site.
- Correspondence courses.
- College classes.
- Reading.
- Consultant instruction at the company site.

Comment:

A good place to start looking for assistance would be the Institute of Industrial Engineers' journal, *Solutions.* For information, contact the Institute of Industrial Engineers, Technology Park/Atlanta, Norcross, GA 30092. Their phone number is (770) 449-0461, Fax number (700) 263-8532, and e-mail WWW.iienet.org.

H. B. Maynard and Company is still advertising in the journal. They have provided training in this area. Their address is: 8 Parkway Center, Pittsburgh, PA 15220. The phone number is (888) 629-6273, e-mail inbox@hbmaynard.com, and their web site www.h.b.maynard.com

S4.6.5 Using Reengineering Tools

There are several tools available to the reengineering team. These tools are for investigating current operations. Many of the tools have been developed by the industrial engineer, but their use is not limited to them.

A. Flowchart

Flowcharts are a good source to display the current operation and to propose the reengineered version. Information is available in the original IS manual in Chapter 2, section 7—Flowcharting Standards.

1. Level zero dataflow diagram

This is showing the system all on one page. It can be used to display the current system or the proposed reengineered system. This can be used for both manual and computer systems. There are software packages that will perform the dataflow diagrams. It simplifies the task of drawing and correcting the diagrams.

2. Level one dataflow diagram

This is for showing the procedures within a system. Each page provides procedure detail of a given part of the level zero dataflow. It is useful for manual and computer operations. If needed, parts of it can be expanded further.

3. Procedure flowchart

This has been long used by the procedure analyst. The procedure flowchart will be used when there is a need to compare the procedures of the current system with that of the proposed reengineered system. Procedures of both systems are drawn on the same document. The current procedures will be drawn on the upper portion of the document. The end-user analyst will find it easy to draw. There are drawing templates available that will make the task easier. A working copy will be made to post any corrections.

The analyst will take the work copy to each unit from which procedure information was collected. The process will be followed by the actual people that were interviewed. These people will examine their part of the procedure flowchart and confirm whether or not it is correct. Corrections will be made to the copy and any other data will be provided as needed. After the verification of the documentation is correct, it will be taken back to end-user analyst's work area and the corrections will be applied to the original procedure flowchart.

B. Work sampling

Work sampling is a tool used by analysts for years to find out how workers are spending their time at work. There will be a required listing of the tasks workers perform. They are observed at given random intervals of time. At that split second, their activity is marked on a sampling tally sheet. They are allowed 10% of their time to be personal time. If they are not in the area, they are counted as not being there. When they are using the telephone it is recorded. The only question then is was the telephone time personal or business? The nature of their work should present some idea as to how much of their time should be on the telephone.

This study can be conducted in a open fashion or undercover. It is best, in most cases, to have a open study. Some studies are done by identifying what each person is doing—this is harder to do. The percentage of activities spent on particular tasks is what is being measured. One other activity that can present a problem is employee thinking time. Is it related to the job or not? Always give the person the benefit of the doubt. If it is a union shop, there will be a concern about the study. For more information, refer to the main volume, section 3.3.5—Work Sampling Studies.

C. Questionnaires

This tool is used to collect information from a large number of people at the same time. It can be also used to collect information from outside the department. It is less time-consuming than interviews. The questionnaire should be short. It is better to send out several small questionnaires as opposed to one large. There can be a space provided for other input. If a second questionnaire is sent out, it can be revised based on data collected from the first one. Information provided from repeated answers from the other input space may be included in the next questionnaire.

To tally the response, provide for a yes or no answer, a check-marked box, or an odd number scale. Avoid written responses as much as possible. The responses to the questionnaires must be tallied and provide the information wanted with the minimum of time.

D. Activity log

A worker keeps track of the number of times a given activity occurs. This may be followed by a work sampling study or interview later. It should be done over a number of representative days. The log could be furnished for the study and collected daily.

E. Interview

For a person doing this for the first time, an interview guide is recommended. The interview will be performed as follows:

1. The end-user analyst

   The person performing the interview should not be from the area being studied. An analyst from the department cannot be objective in such an environment.

2. Unit head relationship

   During the visit, the unit head will be informed of why the analyst is there. He/she will be asked to introduce the analyst to the operational employees. If the employees already know the analyst, the introduction will not be required. The analyst will ask the employees when would be the best time to talk to them.

   After the date and time have been established, the analyst will return to proceed interviewing the employees at their work stations. The unit head will be informed each time the analyst arrives in the unit area. This is a simple protocol courtesy. It can be a simple waving of a hand. If the unit head is not there, just proceed. If they do return while the analyst is there, acknowledge their presence.

3. Tools needed

   Bring a shorthand pad and some pencils. An $8^1/2''$ by $11''$ pad attached to a plastic binder may be considered. There are binders with pockets that provide room for collecting sample documents. If the interview is to be structured, the analyst should bring a question checklist.

4. Skills needed

   The study of the unit's operating procedures is collecting information from each employee. The most important means of gathering the correct information is the procedure interview. A skillfully performed interview is not an easy accomplishment. To some analysts it comes naturally. The person needs a level of objectivity that produces results. Interviewing workers takes a passive, friendly attitude that begets a level of confidence to gather the required information. An analyst that is also a work group member can be very helpful to both the analyst and the person being interviewed. When interviewing, personal conversation is encouraged—to a degree. It places the interview on a more friendly level. However, it is best to keep the business talk on the subject at hand.

5. Checklist

Regardless of how well a person knows the department, a checklist is a useful tool. Without such a list, the analyst may overlook some of the more important aspects of the study. The same checklist should not be used for all studies. Checklists will involve revising as assignments required.

Each of the primary areas influencing the procedures should have its own short list. The replies to these questions should be checked against what will be asked in other areas not yet interviewed. There should not be a problem to return to a person interviewed earlier to ask a question.

An additional use of checklists is to trigger ideas. This is an end-user reengineering project to which all users can contribute. Make sure the person and unit gets the credit for their ideas. Keep the idea on the back burner until it is design time.

There is the standard universal "why" that should not be overlooked. It should be part of the checklist in most cases.

- What is done and why is it done?
- Where is it done and why is it done there?
- When is it done and why is it done at this time?
- Who does it and why does this person do it?
- How is it done and why is it done this way?
- Should it be done at all and why should (or should not) it be done?

6. Sample documents

Sample documents will be collected as the procedure information is being recorded. Computer monitor screen displays will also be duplicated as to be part of the information collected. Any documents that are controlled documents, such as a payroll check, will be copied and voided by the unit head.

7. Sample product

Collect any processed items that require altering in the area of study. Samples will start with what comes into the area and how it is identified. A sample of each procedure performed in the area and a copy identifying information that moves with the product will be collected. A sample of the item that leaves the area, and the move tag or ID markings will be collected. If the samples are too large to handle or too expensive to collect, photographs of what would have been collected will be taken.

Samples of reports that are generated will contain the following information:

- The title of the report.
- The form number, if it is a preprinted form.
- How many copies of the report are made?
- When are the reports generated?
- Who receives the reports?
- What computer files are used for the report?
- What computer files are changed when the report is made?
- What files are from the file server?
- What transaction data is input for the report?
- How are the files backed up?
- Is there a disaster recovery procedure? If so, make a copy of procedure.
- How is the transaction data stored?

F. Layout flowchart

The system process takes on a physical flow of material or information. The movement can be graphically illustrated on a layout flowchart. The unneeded movement of material or information costs money and time. Drawing a layout flowchart of a current operation provides the opportunity to study the flow as a continuous one. Manufacturing companies have known this for a long time. The cost of moving material can become a good part of a product's cost. The evolution of the production line reduced the cost of making a product substantially. Job shops have set up short production lines within their operation to also reduce the job shop cost of manufacturing.

The extra movements cost time, money, and process delays. The movements that cost the most in time and money should be given first priority. The 80/20 rule states that 20% of the items represent 80% of the activity. These are the items that have the first priority when rearranging the process flow.

A current physical system flow diagram will be drawn on graph paper. A proposed physical system flow diagram will also be drawn. The two flow diagrams will be compared to show the difference. Software is available for this same process. It can come up with better solutions than a human could in much less time. The software has been used by manufacturing engineers for some time. The manufacturing engineering or industrial engineering department should be contacted for assistance—they may have the software in operation already.

G. Process chart

Process charts are preprinted forms that are used by industrial engineers and systems and procedure analysts when studying procedures. The form may change a little from one company to another. It basically collects the same information. It can be used by the end-user reengineering team. The forms are placed on a clipboard and provide lines for each operation of the procedure.

The form goes by several different names: analysis charts, procedure study sheet, process analysis chart, etc. Some require the drawing of procedure symbols, while others have them printed on the form. Distance between procedure steps are recorded on some sheets but not others. This information can be transferred to a flowchart. It can also provide distance information for the layout flow chart. A sample of this form is found on page 4-50.

H. Time studies

Time studies are still used today. Time studies merely measure the time required to do a particular operation, with the use of a stopwatch. It should be used mostly for time-paced machine operations. This is the time a machine may take to do a job (e.g., tape backup or the copy speed of a scanner, etc.). The task being time studied should be broken into elements of the total task. These elements should be at least a half a minute in duration. Sometimes videos can be made of the operation and studied later. If the video has a running time in the frame, that information is useful. It is advisable that the company's industrial engineering unit be contacted for some training in this procedure.

This can be a fearful instrument among workers. Any use of this tool with workers should be considered first before using the stopwatch. Unions have some very serious concerns about its use.

I. Work measurement

Work measurement was started by Frederick Taylor. It has been around for some time. Later, Maynard and Stegmarten developed MTM (Methods-Time Measurement). Today, the H. B. Maynard and Company has earned a well-deserved reputation with their efforts of

| | Present |
| | Proposed |

PROCESS ANALYSIS CHART

Name of Procedure _____

Department or Section _____

_____ Date _____

Step #	Description of Each Step Show WHAT Is Done — WHO Does It	Opera-tion	Inspec-tion	Storage	Transp.	◯ Travel in Feet	△ Time in Minutes
		◯	☐	△	◯		
		◯	☐	△	◯		
		◯	☐	△	◯		
		◯	☐	△	◯		
		◯	☐	△	◯		
		◯	☐	△	◯		
		◯	☐	△	◯		
		◯	☐	△	◯		
		◯	☐	△	◯		
		◯	☐	△	◯		
		◯	☐	△	◯		
		◯	☐	△	◯		
		◯	☐	△	◯		
		◯	☐	△	◯		
	TOTALS:						

work measurement. The use of work measurement is particularly good for repetitive and routine tasks. These tasks can be found in the office or factory.

These work measurement standards are published and easily used. The use of the work standard manuals does not require any special training. The standards do not account for employee personal time or working conditions. The work standards manual can provide information for staffing new operations. It can be used to compare with current operations. The end-user reengineering team can use it as a guide.

Any task not listed in the standards can be computed. Work standards are developed by analyzing the task in detail and employing methods-time data tables for body motions. The table's unit of measurement is .00001 hour. One TMU (time measurement unit) is equal to .036 of a second. A task is studied using TMUs to develop a standard for a given task or proposed task. Published work standards are MTM computed standards.

The MTM is too complex to be covered as part of one chapter. The computation process can now be done with microcomputer software for tasks not listed. This makes the task analysis easier to perform. If there is no one with these skills available in the company and reengineering is a company-wide effort, one person should be trained and the MTM software purchased.

The following are some of the benefits that work measurement can provide:

1. Forecast work time needed

   Work measurement will compute the time needed to do a proposed operation. It will also do it fairly.

2. Human factors

   It will consider the skill level and attitude of workers. It will optimize human factor limits.

3. Uncover poor operations

   It will identify poorly designed manual operations.

4. Optimize manual operation designs

   It will optimize the design of a given operation.

5. It is fair

   If it is used as it is intended to be used, it is a very fair way to study a current operation and provide options for improvement.

S4.6.6 Reengineering Design

The end-user reengineering process has several steps before it is complete.

A. Data analysis

All the data collected from the current operation requires analysis to start the end-user reengineering process. Data from a worker's suggestion box system can be very helpful. This information will be studied by each member of the end-user reengineering team. After the team has analyzed the data, they will meet to verify that all team members have the same view of the current operating system. If anything has been overlooked, the information will be obtained.

B. End-user reengineering the operation/system

When end-user reengineering starts, it will be a broad approach. The broad approach can be started with a brainstorming meeting of the project team and chaired by a project leader. Many of the problems can be resolved by an analysis of the objective of the new system. The objective is what the project team has to consider. The broad approach examines the reengineering task in relation to entire organization and to compare it against known industrial standards.

Many reengineering tasks can be solved by an analysis of more than the unit under study. Reviewing the process being done to an item before it is sent to the unit under study may reveal what can be done to reduce time and costs for one or both units. Also, looking at what becomes of the item after it is sent from the unit under study may also reduce time and costs for one or both units. There may even be more to be gained by examining the whole process or organization. A series of questions by the brainstorming meeting of the project team should be considered.

- Are any procedures being duplicated?
- Are there functions being done by a unit that are not needed and must be redone after it is received by the next unit?
- Is the span of control overextended?
- Can functions be reassigned?
- Are there any overlapping procedures?
- What makes each bottleneck?
- Should a subunit be established to speed up operations?

- Can operation supplies be moved closer to the task using them?
- Is there too much unnecessary control?
- Is control missing?
- Is the absence of a delegation of authority limiting flow?
- Is the delegation of authority at the correct place when needed?
- Is there more than one source giving orders?
- Is there lack of operator training?
- Are there training problems?
- What is the English reading level of the people that have to read the instructions?
- What level are instructions and procedures written?
- For areas that depend on color coding, are the operators given color blind tests? About 12% of males are color blind.
- Can the system process flow be reduced?
- Do the operations people have the required tools handy when they need them?
- How often is a function not being done because supplies are not available?
- How adequate is machine preventive maintenance?
- How long does an employee have to wait for needed information?
- Is the process needed or can it be combined with another process?
- Why is the function or process done?

A second guiding principle in end-user reengineering is to look for eliminations. Eliminations are more profitable than simplifications. It also reduces the reengineering effort required. The less tasks to be performed within a system, the lower the cost and the faster the process. Look for the largest yields for the end-user reengineering time by examining:

1. Operations that take the most time

   Find out if all the tasks within the operation are justified. What is needed to reduce this?

2. People assignments

   Are there not enough people to do the work or are there too many? When there are too many people, they make work to look busy.

3. Inspection practices

If the process to move items being inspected costs more than the cost of the inspectors doing the moving, have the inspectors go to the item.

Comment:

A Milwaukee company found this not only saved money but reduced the process time. It was also a strong union shop that required six forklift truckers to move the product to the inspection area and then on to the next operation. The union contract specified that all moves from one area to another not be done by the same trucker. A unit trucker would move a finished, processed item to the pickup point. The inter-plant trucker would move it 16 feet to the inspection receiving area. The inspection unit trucker would move it to be inspected. After inspection, a trucker would move the items to the units pickup. The inter-plant trucker would move the items to the next unit's receiving point. Then that unit's trucker would move it to the next machine to be processed.

There was nothing in the contract that would prevent the inspectors from inspecting the items before they were picked up by the inter-plant trucker to be taken to the next unit.

4. Are people matched to skill requirements?

Are overqualified workers doing tasks that could be done by less skilled workers? Are underskilled people trying to perform tasks that they are not qualified for? Are replacement workers trained for the tasks to be performed?

The tools available for the reengineering process design may start with a simple content dataflow diagram on a flip chart. It will continue to a level one. If the current process is shown on a procedure flowchart, the reengineered process will be drawn below the current one. The two can then be compared.

If a physical rearrangement is needed for the new process, it will follow the redesign process. The operation will be the best that the space can provide. The operation will continue in the same area or a new area will have to be considered.

C. The reengineering proposal

The end-user reengineering team will write a proposal. The reengineering proposal will contain all the information to install a pilot operation or a new system. The proposal will proved detailed information about the benefits of the reengineered design. It will provide information about the current operation and the proposed operation. It will not contain operation and procedure manuals. Copies of the proposal will be furnished to the department management.

D. The Reengineering presentation

A formal presentation will be made by the end-user team leader and the project team. The presentation will be made to the department management, key workers and any guests. The presentation is to sell the reengineered operation or a pilot operation version.

S4.6.7 Operation Testing

After the parts of the system have been tested or simulated with correct expected results, the total system will be tested. The new total system will be an operation test under normal work loads. Dummy data will be used with predetermined end results. This should represent a normal work cycle. It will be conducted when the department using the system is not at work. If the department works around the clock, a pilot operation will be required to test the system. A pilot operation test will also be required if a new operation will start that is not replacing some other operation.

A backup and recovery test should be conducted after a successful operation test has been completed and evaluated. There should be more than one backup and recovery test. After a test has been fully evaluated, then the next test can be conducted. The backup and recovery testing can be considered complete after two successful tests have been completed. One of these tests should be conducted by the operational personnel that will be using the system. The project members will observe the process but not be involved or even lend any kind of assistance. After all testing, with operational personnel involved, has been run and evaluated, it will require acceptance. Management that will be responsible for the new system's operation will require approval for the reengineered startup.

S4.6.8 The Reengineered Startup

With management approval, there will be a startup date for the reengineered pilot operation or new system. Time will be needed to:

- Obtain any new equipment.
- Write the procedure manuals.
- Write the operation manuals.
- Select and train operational personnel.
- Rearrange the process work area.
- Test the operation.

The system will start on a given day. The best time to do the startup at the plant site is if the plant has an annual shutdown. The next choice would be over a long weekend. All the team members will be working during the changeover process. The project leader will monitor the conversion procedure.

S4.6.9 Follow-up

If the operation is a pilot study, the end-user reengineering project team will monitor and study the results of the operation. If changes to the procedures, flow, or equipment are required, a report will be prepared for the department head by the project leader. The results of the pilot study will be reported and any recommendations needed to overcome the problem will be provided in the memo.

With permission from the department head, the changes will be made to the pilot operation. After the pilot operation has proved that it is operational, the project leader will write a memo to the department head of the success. The memo will also contain information that will be required to start a the new reengineered operation if any changes will have to be made to the original reengineered design.

If the new operation is the result of a pilot study, the operation will also start at the best time. If the plant site has an annual shutdown, that will be the date selected. The next choice would be over a long weekend. All the team members will be working during the changeover process. The project leader will monitor the conversion.

The reengineered operation will be monitored for a month by the project leader, after which a study will be conducted regarding the success of the project. A report will be written and sent to the department management. A copy of the report will be placed with the rest of the end-user reengineering project documentation and filed.

Comment:

There is now a journal for end-users called the *Journal of End-User Computing*. It is published quarterly by Idea Group Publishing, 1331 East Chocolate Avenue, Hershey, PA 17033-1117. Their telephone number is (717) 533-8845, Fax number (717) 533-8661, and e-mail: jtravers@idea-group.com.

SUPPLEMENTAL ADDITIONS TO CHAPTER 4

> *S4.3.5 Project Management Tools*
> *S4.3.6 Project Management Technology*
> *S4.6.7 Operation Testing*

Chapter 5
WORD PROCESSING/DESK-TOP PUBLISHING

1. POLICY

S5.1 MICROCOMPUTER OPERATION

The microcomputer operation policy covers all computers, computer-related hardware, and other devices that support information technology throughout the company organization. The organization consists of units that use information technology hardware that requires an authority to set standards and provide optimum use. Corporate policies for microcomputer operations covers computers from desk-top to the notebook. These policies apply whether the computer systems are on or off company property. The polices cover ancillary information processing devices throughout the organization. This policy mandates the endorsement and support by the CEO/head of the organization.

S5.1.1 Scope

The scope covers all freestanding and networked word processing and desk-top publishing operations. This is from the input of raw data to the disposition of output documents and computer-stored data. All raw data source material is company property: correspondence addressed to the company, dictation tapes, and employee-generated hard copy. All raw data, stored data, and output documents are company property.

Output documents that are intended to be released to any party not in the service of the company is the firm's property until it is released to the recipient. The release can be in the following forms: United States Postal Service or a foreign postal service, fax transmission or Internet transmission, or an authorized passing of the document(s) to the receiver or the receiver's representative.

S5.1.2 Operation Policy

Information systems is responsible for maintaining and enforcing a company-wide operation program for computer software, hardware, and ancillary information processing devices. The head of information systems will assign the responsibility to an IT unit to coordinate end-user microcomputer and ancillary devices. An end-user computer committee will be formed. The committee will contain no more than seven or less than three end-users and a purchasing department representative. A representative of the IT unit will be the chairperson of the committee. The committee will follow management's policy and define it for company-wide policies and procedures.

All user unit heads will comply fully with the policies. There will be procedures to enforce these policies. Each unit head will be provided with a policy and procedure manual, which will also contain a recommended equipment list. The approved equipment list will be referred to for acquisitions. In cases of word processing and desk-top publishing special hardware needs, a request memo will be sent to the committee chairperson. A waiver may be granted by the committee. Special waivers will be also be granted for any software needs that is not on the approved list.

Personally owned computers and other equipment of any kind are not allowed on the company's property. Special permission can be granted by information technology management to vendors. Personally owned computer software, disks, electronic devices, mobile phones, pagers, and magnetic devices are not allowed on company-owned property. The unit head can grant permission for personal word processing and desk-top publishing after work hours. The only thing permitted to be removed from the company grounds are hard copy documents of such activities. The documents will not contain any company information.

2. STAND-ALONE WORD PROCESSING

S5.2 STAND-ALONE WORD PROCESSING SYSTEMS

Stand-alone word processing systems will be required to comply with the approved list for the purchase of new microcomputer equipment. Each unit head will have the option to retain word processing software purchased with their budgeted funds. The help desk may or may not support the software after a given date.

International firms may provide the same brand of word processing software for other languages. The help desk will support users in the spoken language of the word processor software.

The unit head will have the end responsibility that the word processing meets with all policies and procedures of the company. The unit head will contact the information systems asset manager whenever any hardware is relocated. The unit head will comply with software licensing changes. The unit's computers cannot operate any pirated or unlicensed software.

S5.2.1 Daily Operating Procedures

There are standard operating procedures that apply to all microcomputer operations. The procedures are as follows:

A. Turning on the system

To turn on the system the operator will perform the following operations:

- Use the operator's password after the machine is turned on.
- Follow the manufacturer's prescribed procedures.
- Check to see that the monitor display and all peripheral equipment are operating properly. If not, the operating manual is consulted. If there is still a problem, contact the help desk.

Portable computers that have access to AC power supply will be checked for the status of their batteries. If the batteries require recharging (or to prolong battery life), the available AC power supply will be used. If the power supplied is outside of the USA, be sure that it is compatible with your hardware requirements.

B. Turning off the system

When the operator turns off the system, he/she will:

- Exit from the operating system.
- Turn off peripheral equipment.
- Turn off and lock the computer.
- Remove disks and store in a locked container.
- Turn off the surge protection switch.
- Check battery-powered microcomputers for recharging needs, and when necessary, recharge as soon as possible.
- Secure or destroy confidential hard copy.

> *Comment:*
> **A night janitor for the top management office area had a habit of reading the wastebasket documents before taking them away. He was aware of things that only a few people in the company knew.**

C. Supply items

The operator will maintain a stock of items needed for the computer and word processing operations. Supply requests will be submitted for needed items. The items can be picked up or delivered.

S5.2.2 Operation Rules and Procedures

The following rules and procedures apply to the operation of all free-standing microcomputers:

- No food or beverages are to be placed on or near the hardware or software.
- No smoking is permitted near the hardware or software.
- A clean, cool, and dry environment is recommended for the computer.
- The computer disks and reading heads must be at least two feet from telephones. Other magnetic devices should be kept away from the computer, disks, and tapes.
- All computers and peripheral equipment must be plugged into a surge protection unit.
- Non-computer electric devices should not be plugged into the surge protection outlet or into the same wall plug with the surge protection device.
- Only grounded electrical outlets are to be used.
- No illegal copying of software is permitted.
- No personal word processing is permitted during work hours.
- No personal hardware, software, or disks are allowed on the premises.
- Floppy disk labeling will be done before the labels are applied to the disks.

- Floppy disks will be kept in their disk containers.

- Confidential disks are stored in a locked container.

- The operator will make the computer inaccessible when he/she is gone from the area.

S5.2.3 Stand-Alone Word Processing Operations

Word processing is one of the most often used applications by stand-alone computers. Larger organizations will license a given number of copies of the software in use. Their are several brands of word processing software on the market. Each software package will require a given hardware configuration and operating system. Freestanding word processing consists of several components.

A. Forms of input data

Manually inputting data for word processing consists of the following:

- Text data source documents—keyed input.

- Text data source documents—text-scanned input.

- Graphics source documents—scanned input.

If the raw input data are to be returned to the sender, the original documents will be scanned into graphics formatted computer data files. If it is not returned to its source, it will be held for the time limits dictated by the law or IT systems unit's recommended time limit. The graphic files will be off-loaded to secondary storage and kept as long as the law requires or IT systems unit's recommended time limit.

File data is information already on disks. The files may be on hard drives or disks. The input data may take the following forms:

- Uncompleted document forms.

- Boiler-plating, standard phrases, or paragraphs down-loaded to the document being constructed.

- Form letters or documents. Attorneys make use of this feature for making out wills, contracts, etc.

- Correspondence name and address files.

B. Text document creation

Word processing software assists a person in creating a text document by automating certain procedures. The person operating the word processor can control page layout and other features. Time-consuming tasks such as creating tables, line centering, underlining, or bold lettering are simplified with word processing. Word processing software feature samples are:

1. Page formatting
   - Center lines.
   - Column formatting.
   - Set edge of page margins.
   - Automatic paragraph indention.
   - Set vertical line spacing.
   - Set type font.
   - Set page numbering.
   - Set and clear tabs.

2. Screen layout
   - Full vertical page.
   - Full horizontal page.
   - View document in text mode.
   - View document in graphics mode.
   - Windows for calling up files, edits, layouts, graphics or help, etc.

3. Cursor movement
   - Move the cursor up or down by line, paragraph, page, or to the beginning or end of a document.
   - Move cursor to specified page.
   - Return cursor to location prior to save.
   - Move cursor to select windows and items within the windows. Keystrokes can be used in place of the mouse to perform cursor movement. Moving the cursor with keystrokes is preferred by some people because it can be faster and have a lower error rate.

4. Automatic features
   - Wordwrap.
   - Margin justification.
   - Pagination.
   - File backup.
   - Footnotes.
   - Reformatting after edits.

C. Text/document editing

Editing documents is simplified if the software provides procedures for insertions, deletions, and moving blocks of copy within document and between documents. The equivalent of a cut-and-paste approach to editing text can be accomplished in a few seconds. The ability to boiler-plate text from files saves time and provides consistency.

Other editing features on high-end word processing software overlap low-end desk-top publishing. Editing features include the ability to search for words, phrases, or blocks of text are now more common features to be found. Other writing tools include spell check, thesaurus, and a grammar check. Some of the features of text/document editing are:

1. Insertions and deletions
   - Insert paragraphs, lines, or words.
   - Insert date, time.
   - Delete blocks of text.
   - Can use insert or type mode.
2. Reformatting
   - Sort lists of words.
   - Reform paragraphs, or sections of documents.
3. Block operations
   - Move a block of text from one location in one document to another.
   - Reproduce blocked text and place it in the same document or another document.
   - Delete a block of text.
   - Block text and have it become bold underlined or italicized.
4. Search operations
   - Find and replace text.
   - Search and delete.
   - Repeat last command.

D. Printer control

Word processing software contains printer controls. The software may contain a selection of printer fonts, varying size of type, bold face, underline, italics, or shadow. Word processor software must be installed for a particular printer for it to work.

1. Control of printing
   - Bold face.
   - Shadow printing.
   - Proportional spacing.
   - Line, form feed.
   - Color or black and white.
   - Print alternate pages.
   - Pagination.
2. Printer manipulation
   - Begin and/or end printing at specified page.
   - Multiple copies of each document.
   - Print banner copies.

E. File management

Documents produced by word processing are usually stored on hard drives, backup copies on secondary storage devices. The word processing software controls these files. All files should be backed up in more than one file form. The automatic word processing backup is done on the same hard drive. A disk crash cannot call up the back up. Long-term backup should be saved in another form.

The word processing software provides commands for operations. Some of the commands are:
- Rename files.
- Delete files.
- Copy files.
- Sort files.
- Alphabetize.

F. Other applications

There are many different applications in dissimilar word processing software packages. The more complex a word processing software becomes, the more time it takes to master its applications. The best one for a person may be the one that provides what is needed with the least amount of training required. The following features may not be found all on one word processing system:
- Voice input translation.
- Automatic spell check with audible warnings.

- Word count.
- Analysis of the reading level of text material.
- Security controls.
- Fax transmission.
- Provide output in another word processing form.
- Math capability.
- The writing of micro programs within the word processing software.
- Placing a border around text.
- Inserting clip art.
- Drawing.
- Inserting drawings.
- Positioning a picture in a document.
- Editing a document picture.
- Words not in the dictionary may be added.

S5.2.4 Voice-Input Word Processing

Voice-input word processing can be done with a desk-top or lap-top computer. It requires voice-input software, a sound card, and microphone/speaker hardware. This technology inserts the human voice in place of the use of fingers. Some software even learns each user's voice. The output improves with use, because the software adjusts to each speaker's voice. It may take a while to master a user with a heavy accent.

The software specifications include the operating system requirements. The operating manuals are simple to use and even weigh less than a notebook computer. The voice-input word processor software is a lower-end word processor. Its use opens up a whole new system of concepts and applications.

When dictating for shorthand recording or into a dictating device, the person tends to slow down their dictation so that it is not misinterpreted. With voice-input word processing the results are better if one would speak at a normal rate. A little faster than a BBC (British Broadcasting Corporation) news broadcaster or an American national network news broadcaster would be a good rate to speak.

The text appears on the monitor screen as one is speaking. This is accomplished by the operator wearing a head set that contains a microphone and earphone. This allows the hands to be free for other activities. The input procedure should not have to contend with any loud distracting background noise.

Depending on the software selected and the way it is set up, the dictation can be recorded and then transferred to a word processing system. This allows for files to be stored with other word processing files.

Comment:

The software provided by Dragon systems allows for the Dragon Naturally Speaking Preferred software to be input directly in Microsoft Word used by Windows 98. The user manual is small and easy to follow. It can have more than one person using the system and will adjust to each persons voice. It comes with a headphone set. Dragon also allows the use of a handheld line scanner. The IRISPen scanner reads text material and it can be mixed with the voice-generated text. They are on World Wide Web and can be found at http://www.naturalspeech.com or http://www.dragonsys.com, and e-mail is support@dragonsys.com.

Comment:

IRISPen consists of two components: an OCR (optical character reader) scanner and a PCR (pen character recognition) text-recognition technology. The IRISPen line scanner is not much larger than a marker and is stored in an easy-to-access holder. The IRISPen runs under Windows 98. It is easy to use and can read up to 100 characters per second. It can read paper text material one line at a time and stop with a flick of a button. It can paste to Windows or read to Microsoft's Word with Dragon Naturally Speaking software. They have a small, easy-to-read manual. They can be found at http://www.irisusa.com or reached at support@irislink.com.

While speaking into a voice-input word processing system, any changes or corrections can come from the keyboard if it cannot be voice corrected. The text-line scanner along with voice, mouse, and keyboard input provides for a very versatile stand-alone word processing system. Besides having a word processing input, e-mail input can be furnished by this system. The following are some of the available procedure operations for voice-input word processing:

- Dictate continuously, speaking naturally without pausing between words.

- Dictate and say voice commands concurrently, simply by pausing before and after saying a command.

- Correct recognition errors and revise and format text by voice or keyboard.

- Correct while in process or revise text later.

- Spell naturally while correcting, using the names of the letters.

- Increase recognition accuracy by customizing vocabulary with specialized subjects.

- Use only each person's speech file.

- When you have a cold or voice problem, do not allow the system to adjust to this because it will have to be recorrected after the voice returns to normal.

- A utility can read aloud (in a computer-generated voice) the text that is in the document window.

- Play back what was said in the person's own voice.

This information is for voice-input word processing as a freestanding computer operation. For more information about freestanding word processing procedures, see section 5.2.3—Freestanding Word Processing Operations.

Comment:

Voice input beyond word processing and telephone communications is in the pipe line. There are many applications that are potential candidates for voice input. It would be wise to start considering in what areas this application would be effective.

S5.2.5 Training

Training for stand-alone word processing will be provided by the information system's IT training unit. If the site does not have an IT training unit, training material will be made available by the local training unit. If this is not available, the company information systems organization will provide the training material.

Stand-alone word processing training will be available as individualized training. The material will be loaned to the operator and then returned to the unit that provided the material. The training provided will be one of the following forms:

A. Tutorial

The operator will learn via a tutorial. The tutorial will be purchased if one is suitable. The operator—at his/her own pace and as time is available—will learn about the system. The operator will be provided with a copy of the tutorial software, a copy of the software manual, a copy of the operator's manual, and a learning guide. After the operator has completed all the items on the learning guide, he/she will return the tutorial software and the learning guide.

B. On-the-job training

The OJT (on-the-job training) will be done by an experienced word processing operator. The OJT instructor will have a learning guide provided by the information systems organization. The IS organization will provide the operator with a copy of the operator's manual and software manual via the instructor.

The OJT instructor will follow the learning guide when working with the student. They will proceed as time and student's learning skills permit. A skill test will be provided with the learning guide. When students pass the final exam, they will receive a certificate from the IS unit. Anyone receiving company development and training will receive notice of the certification in the newsletter.

C. Vendor instruction

Vendor instruction may be purchased by the company. The instruction can be provided at the company facilities or at another location. If hourly employees are required to attend the classes on their own time, the human resources department should be contacted as to the requirements for any overtime pay. If the employee attends a local college word processing class for a credit of their own choice, the reimbursement for this will follow company education policy.

S5.2.6 System Upgrading

When it becomes time to upgrade the word processing systems, it can occur in more than one way. The technicians making the changes will record the machines converted each day, so the information technology asset manager can update their data files about the machines that were converted.

A. Current system software upgrade

Upgrading current systems software may require some computers to also have hardware upgrades. The selection can be made for many different reasons that would benefit the company. These upgrades usually follow the first version of the software being used. If any difference is noticed by the operators, it will be for the better.

The people using the revised software will be informed about the changeover before it is placed into their freestanding computers. The process cannot occur all at the same time. Each computer will have a tentative schedule as to when to expect the change. The word processing user will be furnished a new manual and any machine operating amendments. This will be sent to each word processing user by information systems no less than two weeks before the conversion. The operator should plan to not use the computer at that time. The removal of the old software and the installation of the new should take less than an hour of the IT technician's time.

B. New word processing software

When new software is to be used by stand-alone word processing users, a training program will be required. The options for training are:

1. Tutorial after installation

The operator will learn via a tutorial. The furnished tutorial will be purchased if possible. The operator will learn at his/her own pace and as time is available after it is installed. The operator will be provided with a copy of the tutorial software, a copy of the software manual, and a learning guide. After the operator has completed all the items on the learning guide, he/she will return the tutorial software and the learning guide.

2. Tutorial before installation

There is a second option for the tutorial training, which is the preferred method. A workstation will be set up at the IT training unit or the computer store. The operators will learn via a tutorial. The tutorial will be purchased if one is available. If one is not available, the IT organization will devise one. The operators at their own pace will learn about the system before it is installed. The training machine will require appointment slots to schedule users. This will be done by the unit furnishing the learning machine. The operators will use the setup provided with the tutorial software and the new word processing software. A copy of the software manual and a learning guide will be furnished. After the operators have completed all the items on the learning guide, they will have completed their training.

The people using the new software will be informed about the changeover before it is placed into their freestanding computers. The process cannot occur all at the same time. Each computer will have a tentative schedule as to when to expect the change. The word processing user will be furnished a new manual and any machine operating amendments. This will be sent to each word processing user by information systems no less than one month before the conversion. The operator should plan not to be using the computer at that time. The removal of the old software and the installation of the new system should require about an hour.

C. New computer hardware system

The people who will be using the same software, but will be receiving a new computer system, will be informed about the change a month before it takes place. The process cannot occur all at the same time. Each computer will have a tentative schedule as to when it will be replaced. The machine user will be furnished a new machine operating manual. This will be sent to each freestanding microcomputer user by information systems no less than three weeks before the conversion.

A new computer workstation will be set up at the IT training unit or the computer store. The operators will learn via a tutorial. The tutorial will be purchased if one is available. When not available, the IS organization will devise one. The operators, at their own pace, will learn about the new hardware system before it is installed. The training machine will require appointment slots to schedule users. This will be done by the unit furnishing the new machine. The operators will use the set up provided with the tutorial software and the current word processing software.

The operator should plan to not use the computer when it is scheduled to be replaced. The changeover should be done in less than an hour.

D. New operating system

The stand-alone computers will be using most of the same software, but will be receiving a new operating system (for example, going from Windows 98 to Windows 2000). They will be informed about the change no less than a month before the replacement will take place. The process cannot occur all at the same time. Each computer will have a tentative schedule as to when it will be replaced. The machine user will be furnished a new machine operating manual. This will be sent to each stand-alone PC user by information systems no less than one month before the conversion.

A new computer workstation will be set up at the IT training unit or the computer store. The operators will learn via a tutorial. The tutorial will be purchased if one is available, If not available, the IS organization will devise one. The operators at their own pace will learn about the new hardware system before it is installed. The training machine will require appointment slots to schedule users. This will be done by the unit furnishing the new machine. The operators will use the setup provided with the tutorial software and the current word processing software.

The operator should plan to not use the computer when it is scheduled to be replaced. The changeover should be completed and tested in an hour or two.

E. Totally new hardware, operating system, and software

When new word processing software is installed into new hardware with a new operating system, it presents a training challenge. The training must be well orchestrated to be successful. The training will involve one or more vendors, in-house instructors and the coordination of a training unit. If information systems have no IT training unit, the company training unit will be called on to do the coordination. If the company does not have a training unit, an IT training vendor will be required to coordinate the training project.

The training project will require planning on the part of the training coordinator. Stand-alone PC users that will also require training and are not word processing users can take part in the training project. They will not receive any word processing training. The training for stand-alone word processing users will cover the following:

- New hardware training.
- New operating systems training.

- New word processing training.
- Other help desk–supported software.

The training project will be divided into the following groups. Each group will have its own training program.

1. New hardware and operating system training

   New hardware and operating system training program will be conducted in a lecture class setting. Each class member will be given a machine operation and operating system manual three to four weeks before the class meeting. The manuals will be user friendly. If need be they can be purchased or written in house or by vendors. There will be two or more classes given so that departments will not have their operation's understaffed. There will be a class size limit. The class size will depend on the room size available and the number of microcomputers available.

   The people attending will have read the manuals before coming to the class. The class presentation will be designed with supporting audio visual aids. Vendors or in-house trainers will make the presentation. The presentation will be no more than four hours with a break at the midpoint. After the presentation the people attending may ask questions.

   The classroom will serve as an open lab. The open lab will be for both hardware and software skill development. A variety of software will be available for the computers. There will be a staffed help desk in the computer lab will be available at all times the lab is open for use. The computer lab will have tutorial software available for use on all the new help desk supported software. Quick reference guides will be available for any employee to use or take.

2. Word processing

   The word processing instruction will be conducted in a lecture class setting. The class members will be given a word processing manual and a quick reference guide three to four weeks before the class meeting. The manuals will be user friendly, and they can be purchased or written in house or by vendors. There will be two or more classes given so that departments will not have their operations understaffed. The class size will be limited, depending on the room size available and the number of microcomputers available.

   The people attending will have read the manuals before coming to the class. The class presentation will be designed with supporting audio-visual aids. Vendors or in-house trainers will make the presentation. The presentation will be no more than four hours with a break at the midpoint. After the presentation the people attending may ask questions. If needed, a second class meeting will be held the following week or two.

The people attending the class will be encouraged to make use of the computer lab. They can contact the lab help desk at any time it is staffed. If need be, the user departments will have overtime funds available to cover needed training for hourly employees.

3. Other class training

Classes will be conducted for other popular new software. The training will be designed for the complexity and demand for this form of instruction. The computer lab will be open and staffed for any of these employee's needs. Help desk–supported software information will be available in the computer lab.

4. Other instruction

Software that will not have enough users cannot justify having a class, will have other kinds of instruction available. Hourly employees attending company-required instruction will have to be cleared for overtime compensation. The instruction will be in the following forms:

- Tutorials.
- Vendor-provided training.
- Computer training school short courses.
- Self-paced video instruction.

S5.2.7 Word Processing Budget

The word processing monies for stand-alone word processing can come from the corporate lump-sum budget, the department lump-sum budget, or the department itemized budget. This all depends on the company budget policy. The following items may not all be budgeted in the same way.

A. Hardware

PC hardware can be acquired by all three methods of budgeting. When word processing is acquired for an area, it often requires the computer hardware.

B. Software

Software can be acquired by all three methods of budgeting. When word processing upgrades are made, itemized department budgets may not have the money provided. Itemized budget planning may not foresee software upgrades. These upgrades may also require added hardware.

C. Supplies

Supplies are budgeted as corporate lump-sum budgets or as department lump-sum budgets.

D. Help desk

Help desk expenses most often are a corporate expense item. But department usage could be charged.

E. IT technical assistance

This IT service most often comes under corporate expense. Depending on corporate policy, this service could be charged back to the department.

3. NETWORK WORD PROCESSING

S5.3 WORK GROUP SYSTEM

The network word processing work group has replaced the typing unit. Stand-alone word processing computer systems have reduced the number of typing units. These procedures are for the current work group word processing operations.

The work group will have a unit head. If the size justifies it, the unit head will have a key operator. If there is no key operator, the unit head will perform the duties of a key operator or assign some one to perform the duties on a permint or rotating bases.

S5.3.1 Key Operator

The systems administrator is responsible for maintaining the word processing hardware. These duties are:

A. Turning on the system

To turn the system on, the operator will perform the following operations:

- Use the password after the computer server machine is turned on.
- Follow the manufacturer's prescribed procedures.

- Check to see that the monitor display and all peripheral equipment are operating properly. If not, the operating manual is consulted. If there is still a problem, contact the help desk.

B. Supply items

The printers will be checked at the start of each day and throughout the day to ensure an adequate paper supply. A stock of items needed for the computer and word processing operations will be maintained. Supply requests will be submitted for needed items, and can be picked up or delivered.

C. Turning off the system

When the key operator turns off the system they will:

- Perform a file backup.
- Exit from the computer server operating system.
- Turn off peripheral equipment.
- Turn off and lock the computer.
- Remove disks and store in a locked container.
- Turn off the surge protect switch.
- Secure or destroy confidential hard copy.

The key operator will also be responsible for the unit when the unit head is not present. The operator will also assist with OJT.

S5.3.2 Work Group Computer System

The work group microcomputer word processing system will consist of a computer server and microcomputer work stations. Work stations will have text-line scanners and/or headphones as needed. There will be online peripheral devices serving the system. The devices will consist of the following:

- Text-line scanner. Also used as a backup device.
- Page scanner(s).
- Work group style printer(s).

S5.3.3 Work Group Operation Rules and Procedures

The following rules and procedures apply to the operation of the computer server and all work stations:

- No food or beverages are to be placed on or near the hardware or software.
- No smoking is permitted near the hardware or software.
- A clean, cool, and dry working environment is recommended for the work group area.
- The computer disks and reading heads must be at least two feet from telephones. Other magnetic devices should be kept away from the computer, disks, and tapes.
- All computers and peripheral equipment must be plugged into a surge protection unit.
- Non-computer electric devices should not be plugged into the surge protection outlet or into the same wall plug with the surge protection device.
- Only grounded electrical outlets are to be used.
- No illegal copying of software is permitted.
- No personal word processing is permitted.
- No personal hardware, software, or disks are allowed on the premises.
- Confidential disks and tapes are stored in a locked container.
- The operator will make the workstation inaccessible when he/she is absent from the area.

S5.3.4 Work Group Word Processing Operations

There will be a licensing for a given number of copies of the software used by workstations. There are several brands of word processing software on the market. Each software package will require a given hardware configuration and operating system. Work group word processing consists of several components.

A. Forms of input data

Input data for word processing consist of the following:
- Text data source documents—keyed input.
- Text data source documents—text-scanned input.
- Graphics source documents—scanned input.
- Voice dictation—keyed input.

If the raw input data is to be returned to the sender, the original documents will be scanned into graphics-formatted computer data files. If it is not returned to its source, it will be held for the time limits dictated by law or IT systems unit's recommended time limit. The graphic files will be off-loaded to secondary storage and kept as long as the law requires or IT systems unit's recommended time limit.

The file server data is information already on disks. The files may be on hard drives or disks. The input data may take the following forms:

- Uncompleted document forms.
- Boiler-plating, standard phrases, or paragraphs downloaded to the document being constructed.
- Form letters or documents. Attorneys make use of this feature for making out wills, contracts, etc.
- Correspondence name and address files.

B. Text document creation

Word processing software assists a person in creating a text document by automating certain procedures. The person operating the word processor can control page layout and other features of word processing. Time-consuming tasks such as creating tables, line centering, underlining, or bold lettering are simplified with word processing. Word processing software feature samples are:

1. Page formatting
   - Center lines.
   - Column formatting justification.
   - Set edge of page margins.
   - Automatic paragraph indention.
   - Set vertical line spacing.
   - Set type and style of font.
   - Set page numbering.
   - Set and clear tabs.
   - Line spacing.

2. Screen layout
   - Full vertical page.
   - Full horizontal page.
   - View document in text mode.
   - View document in graphics mode.
   - Windows for calling up files, edits, layouts, graphics, or help, etc.

3. Cursor movement
   - Move the cursor up or down by line, paragraph, page, or to the beginning or end of a document.
   - Move cursor to specified page.
   - Return cursor to location prior to save.
   - Move cursor to select windows and items within the windows. Keystrokes can be used in place of the mouse to perform cursor movement. Moving the cursor with keystrokes is preferred by some people because it can be faster and have a lower error rate.

4. Automatic features
   - Wordwrap.
   - Margin justification.
   - Pagination.
   - File backup.
   - Footnotes.
   - Reformatting after edits.

C. Text/document editing

Editing documents is simplified if the software provides procedures for insertions, deletions, and moving blocks of copy within a document and between documents. The equivalent of a cut-and-paste approach to editing text can be accomplished in a few seconds. The ability to boiler-plate text from files saves time and provides consistency.

Other editing features on the high-end word processing software overlap low-end desk-top publishing. Editing features include the ability to search for words, phrases, or blocks of text are now more common features to be found. Other writing tools include spell check, thesaurus, and grammar check. Some of the features of text/document editing are:

1. Insertions and deletions
   - Insert paragraphs, lines, or words.
   - Insert date, time.
   - Delete blocks of text.
   - Use insert or type mode.

2. Reformatting
   - Sort lists of words.
   - Reform at paragraphs or sections of documents.

3. Block operations

- Move a block of text from one location in one document to another.
- Reproduce blocked text and place it in the same document or another document.
- Delete a block of text.
- Block text and have it become bold, underlined, or italicized.

4. Search operations

- Find and replace text.
- Search and delete.
- Repeat last command.

D. Printer control

Word processing software contains printer controls. The software may contain a selection of printer fonts, varying size of type, bold face, underline, italics, or shadow. Word processor software must be installed for a particular printer in order for it to work.

1. Control of printing.

- Bold face.
- Shadow printing.
- Proportional spacing.
- Line, form feed.
- Color or black and white.
- Print alternate pages.

2. Printer manipulation

- Begin and/or end printing at specified page.
- Multiple copies of each document.

S5.3.5 Work Group Word Processing Training

Training can be provided for different needs.

A. New word processing operator

New word processing operators will receive tutorial and OJT instruction. The OJT can be provided by the unit head or key operator.

B. Current system software upgrade

When current system software is an upgrade. This may require some computers to also have hardware upgrades. The unit head will be furnished new manuals and any machine operating amendments. The unit head will conduct a class on the software changes. Handouts will be provided for the operators.

The unit head will be informed about the changeover before it is placed into their work group server. The unit head will receive a tentative schedule as to when to expect the change. The removal of the old software and the installation of the new should take less than one hour of the IT technician's time. It will be done when the unit is not in operation.

C. New word processing software

When new software is to be used, a training program will be required. Classes will be conducted for the operators by the unit head before and after the new software is installed. The unit head and key operator will receive tutorial training for the work group computer file server.

The unit head will be furnished new manuals and any work group machine operating amendments. This will come from information systems no less than one month before the conversion. The removal of the old software and the installation of the new system should require about an hour for each machine. This will be done when the unit is not working.

D. New computer hardware system

The work group will be using the same software, but will be receiving a new computer system. The unit head will be informed of the change one month before it will take place. This information will come from information systems no less than one month before the conversion.

The unit head will conduct classes for the new hardware. A new computer workstation will be set up at the IT training unit or the computer store. The unit head will assign operators to the these training machines for practice.

The unit head will work with the technical people to schedule the changeover, which will be done during the time the unit is not in operation.

E. New operating system

The word processing work group system will receive a new operating system. The unit head will be informed about the change no less than one month before it will take place. The unit head will be furnished new machine operating manuals, which will be sent from information systems no less than one month before the conversion.

The unit head will conduct new operating system classes for the operators. Each operator will receive a new operating manual. A new computer workstation will be set up at the IT training unit or the computer store. The unit head will assign operators practice time for the new operating system.

The changeover will be planned by the work group unit head and the technician. The changeover will be completed and tested when the unit is not in operation.

F. Totally new hardware, operating systems, and software

When a new word processing software is installed into new hardware with a new operating system it presents a training challenge. The training will be well orchestrated by the unit head. The training can involve one or more vendors, in-house instructors, and the assistance of a training unit.

The training project will require planning on the part of the unit head. The training for the work group will cover the following:

- New hardware training.
- New operating systems training.
- New word processing training.

The training project will be divided into the previous groups. Each group will have its own training program.

1. New hardware and operating systems training

New hardware and operating systems training program will be conducted for the work group by a vendor. Each class member will be given a machine operation and operating systems manual three to four weeks before the class meeting. The user-friendly manuals can be purchased or written in house or from the vendors.

The people attending will have read the manuals before coming to the class. The class presentation will be designed with supporting audio-visual aids. Vendors will make the presentation. The presentation will be no more than four hours with a break at the midpoint. After the presentation, the people attending may ask questions. Each student should have their own computer station.

The classroom will serve as an open lab, which will be for both hardware and software skill development. There will be a staffed help desk in the computer lab at all times the room is open for use. The computer lab will have tutorial software available. Quick reference guides will be available for employee to use or take.

2. New word processing system

The word processing instruction will be conducted by a vendor and/or the unit head in a class setting. Each class member will be given a word processing manual and a quick reference guide three to four weeks before the class meeting. The user-friendly manuals can be purchased or written in house or by vendors.

The people attending will have read their manuals before attending the class. The class presentation will be conducted with each employee having the use of new hardware, operating systems, and word processing software.

The people attending the class will be encouraged to make use of the classroom, and computer lab. They can contact the lab help desk at any time it is staffed. If need be, the work group will have overtime funds available to cover needed training for the hourly employees.

S5.3.6 Work Group Word Processing Budget

The work group word processing operation will have its own budget. The department may have monies budgeted for vendor services or purchasing. Their budget may be an itemized or a lump-sum budget. The items needed to be concerned with are:

A. Hardware

After a new hardware system is installed, capital asset acquisitions may be for upgrades or an expanded number of workstations. This is best budgeted as a lump sum for totally new systems or yearly capital asset acquisitions.

B. Software

As new word processing software it should be budgeted as one item lump-sum budget. It is difficult to forsee the cost of yearly upgrading. If a lump-sum budget is used, the money planned for an upgrade should be a line item to prevent monies budgeted for software upgrades and not used to be withheld.

C. Supplies

Supplies are recommended to be a department lump-sum budget. Company lump-sum supply budgets can be abused.

D. IT assistance

This can be in the form of help desk assistance or other IT services. Company policy will prevail as to the way this is handled.

4. DESK-TOP PUBLISHING

S5.4 DESK-TOP PUBLISHING

Desk-top publishing is a system employing computers, hardware support components, and software to produce camera-ready documents for printing. Desk-top publishing permits the combination of text, line drawings, graphics, and photographs on the same page. The page(s) is ready for the camera to produce offset plates for printing, which can be in the form of letterheads, newsletters, operation manuals, advertising material, brochures, etc.

The requirements for desk-top publishing are so unique that many of its components will not be on the approved lists. The status of all hardware and software will be reported to the IT asset manager. Also, help desk support will be minimal at the most. The number of employees using desk-top publishing in a firm is so few that information systems can justify a minimum of effort to control and standardize it. The main interests are that any desk-top publishing software used is acquired legally, that both hardware and software are recorded on the assets lists, and that the firm's desk-top publishing systems are not used for personal gain or illegal or immoral publication. Items that are not on the asset database will be corrected and the department head will be put on notice. Any acts of personal gain or illegal or immoral activities are grounds for immediate discharge. The area will be subject to random inventorying of all hardware and software in use by an IT unit.

S5.4.1 Desk-Top Publishing Operation Rules and Procedures

The following rules and procedures apply to the operation of all stand-alone microcomputers within the company. This is also to be complied within the operation of desk-top publishing systems:

- All software on the computer systems will be licensed.
- All secondary storage devices will have only licensed software.
- No food or beverages are to be placed on or near the hardware or software.

- No smoking is permitted near the hardware or software.
- A clean, cool, and dry working environment is recommended for the computer.
- The computer disks and reading heads must be at least two feet from telephones. Other magnetic devices should be kept away from the computer, disks, and tapes.
- All computers and peripheral equipment must be plugged into a surge protection unit.
- Key systems will have UPS devices.
- Non-computer electric devices should not be plugged into the surge protection outlet or into the same wall plug with the surge protection device.
- Only grounded electrical outlets are to be used.
- No illegal copying of software is permitted.
- No personal word processing or desk-top publishing is permitted.
- No personal hardware, software, or disks are allowed on the premises.
- Disk labeling will be done before they are applied to the disks.
- Disks will be kept in their containers.
- Confidential disks are stored in a locked container.
- The operator will make the computer inaccessible when he/she is absent from the area.
- No company hardware or software may be taken from the unit area without written consent of the unit head.

The unit head will be held fully responsible that the desk-top publishing operation rules and procedures are followed at all times. The unit head can contact any IT unit for assistance about the rules and procedures or any other thing that assistance may be provided. The desk-top publishing operation rules and procedures also apply to any freestanding desk-top or lap-top computer used by the unit.

S5.4.2 System Components

Desk-top publishing represents a system of technology; the technology includes both hardware and software components. A skilled employee with sufficient computer skills and desk-top publishing training is also a very important key item. Computers and related peripherals represent the major hardware components. Software packages or integrated software packages represent the software components.

A. Hardware

This starts with the microcomputer, which may not be the system of choice for the rest of the company. Skills applied to desk-top publishing are not as easy to convert to other computer platforms.

Comment:

With the skilled employee being such a major factor, his/her selection can overrule the standard for the rest of the company. This is a matter of artistic skills overruling other technical skills of the firm, but with worthwhile results. This presents no problem, since desk-top publishing can do without the help desk assistance, let alone most all of other IT technology assistance.

1. Monitor

The other hardware item that may have attraction will be the monitor, which will be a vertical design to display a whole page at a time. It will also have a WYSIWYG (what you see is what you get) screen. This sort of display is required for proportion and style of the image that it prints.

2. Scanners

There are several types of page scanners, both in color and black and white.

- Text scanner, converts text to computer code.

- Image scanner, copies the image to memory.

- Scanners that can do both.

Other scanners are text-line scanners. They scan a line of text at time. There are scanners that scan photo slides or negatives. These can scan both color and black and white.

3. Printers

There is a wide selection of printers available, in both color and black and white. The size output can compete with engineering drawings. The quality is so good it competes with photography. There are several types of printers.

- Ink jet printers.
- Laser jet printers.
- Dye-sublimation printers.

B. Software

The software available overlaps word processing. The high end of word processing software overlaps the low-end desk-top software. There is software available for both PC and Macintosh. Some software makers have desk-top publishing available for both hardware systems.

The software selection will dictate the hardware requirements. Professional-level systems can require:

- Large size of memory.
- Extensive hard drive storage.
- Tape backup.
- CD drives that can write or read.
- Large high-resolution monitors.
- High-resolution flat bed scanners.
- High-resolution film scanners.
- High-resolution printers.
- Electronic typesetter interfaces.

S5.4.3 User Training

When trained people cannot be recruited, training will be required. Continuous training will also be needed. The training will be limited to small groups or individual training. Training is available in the following forms:

- Interactive video.
- CD-ROM.
- Self-study courses.
- Technical college courses.
- OJT (for people who already have shown good word processing skills).

S5.4.4 Supplies

The desk-top publishing supplies will rely on the company computer supplies and their own inventory. The unit will have a lump-sum supply budget. Inventory items should provide for a usage of control by the desk-top publishing area management.

S5.4.5 Budget

The unit is so different from the mainstream company operations that it should not be part of a company lump-sum budget program. To have an itemized department budget is unrealistic because of rapidly changing technology.

The budget for the desk-top publishing should be a department lump-sum budget. The details for arriving at the capital expense and supply items will be listed. This information is needed for forming the lump-sum budget request for capital expense and supply items. When the budget is submitted, a copy with detailed information will be sent to the head of information systems for his/her audit.

5. GRAPHIC ARTS PROCESSING

S5.5 Graphic Arts Processing Systems

While word processing and desk-top publishing can perform some graphic arts tasks, their major function is not devoted to graphic arts processing. While hardware requirements for desk-top publishing are greater than word processing, graphic arts processing system requirements are greater than that of desk-top publishing. The hardware needs of graphic arts processing systems call for more primary and secondary memory and peripheral devices. There can be several different applications found within a company, with each computer configuration being different. A sample of end-user applications would be: CAD/CAM, video editing, photographic reproduction, commercial art, AV productions, photographic or art retrieval library, 3D animation, etc.

The requirements for graphic arts processing are so unique that many of its components will not be on the approved lists. The status of all hardware and software will be reported to the IT asset manager. Also, help desk support will be vendor provided. The number of users utilizing graphic arts processing in a firm is so few that information systems can justify a minimum of effort to control and standardize it. The main interests are that any graphic arts processing software used is acquired legally, that both hardware and software are recorded on the assets lists, and that the firm's graphic arts processing systems are not used for personal gain or illegal or immoral publication. Items that are not on the asset database will be corrected and the department head will be put on notice. Any acts of personal gain or illegal or immoral activities are grounds for immediate discharge. The area will be subject to random inventorying of all hardware and software in use by an IT unit.

S5.5.1 Graphic Arts Operation Rules and Procedures

The following rules and procedures apply to the operation of all graphic arts computers within the company:

- All software on the computer systems will be licensed.
- All secondary storage devices will only have licensed software.
- No food or beverages are to be placed on or near the hardware or software.
- No smoking is permitted near the hardware or software.
- A clean, cool, and dry working environment is recommended.
- The computer disks and reading heads must be at least two feet from telephones. Other magnetic devices should be kept away from the computer, disks, and tapes.
- All computers and peripheral equipment must be plugged into a surge protection unit.
- The CPU will have a UPS device.
- Non-computer electric devices should not be plugged into the surge protection outlet, UPS, or the same wall plug with the surge protection or UPS device.
- Only grounded electrical outlets are to be used.
- No illegal copying of software is permitted.
- No personal hardware, software, or disks are allowed on the premises.
- Disk labeling will be done before they are applied to the disks.
- Disks will be kept in their disk containers.
- Confidential disks are stored in a locked container.
- The operator will make the computer inaccessible when he/she is absent from the area.
- No company hardware or software may be taken from the unit area without written consent of the unit head.

The unit head will be held fully responsible that the graphic arts operation rules and procedures are followed at all times. The unit head can contact any IT unit for assistance about the rules and procedures or any other thing that assistance may be available. The unit head may delegate some or most of the responsibility to the lead operator. The operation rules and procedures also apply to any freestanding desk-top or lap-top computer used by the unit.

The lead operator will be the systems administrator and will be responsible for operating and maintaining the computer system. The duties include the following:

- Maintain proper adjustments to the computer system.
- Keep the operating surfaces clean.
- Maintain the expendable items at the proper level (toner, ink cartridge, paper, etc.) in the computer system.
- Maintain a supply inventory.
- Perform preventive maintenance and maintain a preventive maintenance log. The log will list what was done and when it was done. Any problem will be noted in the log at the time it is discovered.
- Maintain operation procedures and vendor hardware and software update information.
- Be the vendor contact person for the computer system's hardware, software, supplies, and training.

S5.5.2 Graphic Arts Legal Implications

Graphic arts systems can have some legal implications because of the nature of the tasks involved. The involvement of generating original graphic art and the use of copyrighted material should be the concern of the department head.

The items of concern that could be addressed are:

A. Model release

A model release is required when a person is identifiable in a photograph or work of art that is used by a company. The model release is a signed document giving permission, by the recognizable person(s), to use the image. If the person is not an adult, the parent or guardian must sign the release. It would be wise to compensate the person for signing the document, even if it is only one dollar. The release will require a signature of a witness. Model release forms can be purchased or made on a word processor.

B. Property release

If a photograph or work of art is used by a company that can identify a property, a property release will be required. This most often is real property such as a farm, home, or building. The property release will be signed by the owner of the property. It would be wise to compensate the person for signing the document, even if it is only one dollar. The release will require a signature of a witness. Property release forms can be purchased or generated on a word processor.

C. Copyright

Copyright protection can be provided to a company if the employee producing the item does it within the scope of his/her employment. The cost of applying for copyright is very nominal and the procedure is exceedingly simple. For further information or application forms, write to:

Information and Publications Section, LM-45

Copyright Office

Library of Congress

Washington, D.C. 20559

Items that are copyrightable works and copyright forms that are available include the following categories:

- Literary works.
- Musical works, including any accompanying words.
- Dramatic works, including any accompanying music.
- Pantomimes and choreographic works.
- Pictorial, graphic, and sculptural works.
- Motion pictures and other audio-visual works.
- Sound recordings.

When an item is created or produced, it should have posted the word "copyrighted," the date, and the name of the owner of the copyright. This should be placed on the item; on a photograph, it can be on the back. Using another party's copyrighted material without permission is illegal. Any unapproved use of copyrighted material makes the company liable. A copyright search can be conducted by the Copyright Office for a nominal fee if there is a concern about the copyright. For more information, contact the Information and Publications Section, LM-45 of the Copyright Office.

D. Patent

A patent is a very involved process that requires the attention of a patent attorney. There can be areas that employ graphic arts processing that would need assistance in this area. If this be the case, there will be existing patent procedures to follow. The head of the department employing the graphic arts system will set up the procedure to follow. The company will have a patent attorney that can be called on for assistance with generating documents for patent assistance.

S5.5.3 Graphic Arts System Components

Graphic arts system components is technology that has been put together for a given task. The technology is made up of both computer hardware and software components. A skilled operator with sufficient computer skills and the graphic arts training is the key item in the operation of the system. This person will be the systems administrator and will have the responsibility for maintaining the operation rules and procedures. The computer and its related peripherals represent the major hardware system. Software packages or integrated software packages represent the software component.

A. Hardware

This starts with the computer, which may not be the system of choice for the rest of the company. Skills applied to graphic arts systems are not as easy to convert to other computer platforms. Computers used for graphic arts, as other computer systems, are comprised of a CPU and input/output devices. The CPU will have attached to it the following:

1. Monitor

The monitor will be a large display screen. It will also have a WYSIWYG (what you see is what you get) screen. This sort of display is required for proportion and style of the image that it may print.

2. Scanners

There are several types of page scanners, both in color and black and white.

- Text scanner, converts text to computer code.
- Image scanner, copies the image to memory.
- Scanners that can do both.

3. Printers

There is a wide selection of printers available in both color and black and white. The size of the output can be the size of engineering drawings or even larger. The quality is so good it competes with photography. There are several types of printers available.

- Ink jet printers.
- Laser jet printers.
- Dye-sublimation printers.

B. Software

The software purchased or leased is available for many applications. The software selection will dictate the hardware requirements.

- Large size of memory.
- Extensive hard drive storage.
- Tape backup.
- CD drives that can write or read.
- Large high-resolution monitors.
- High-resolution flat bed scanners.
- High-resolution film scanners.
- High-resolution printers that may print very large documents.

S5.5.4 User Training

Training time and funding should be provided because of the ongoing need. Candidates selected to operate the system should be tested by human resources to determine that they have the skills required. Even skilled job candidates will be tested before they are hired. This can provide a warning sign and a test validation. Vendor and individual training programs are available. Individual training programs may be available in the following forms:

- Interactive video.
- CD ROMS.
- Self-study courses.
- OJT (on-the-job training).

S5.5.5 Graphic Arts Purchasing

The budget for the graphic arts computer system should be part of the department budget. The details for arriving at the capital expense and supply items will be listed. This information is needed for forming the department budget request for capital expense and supply items. When the budget is submitted, a copy of the graphic arts computer system information will be sent to the head of information systems. This information is needed for the computer hardware and software inventory files.

The purchasing process will be tied to the provided budget. Purchase requisitions will be used for buying hardware, software, and supply items. The computer systems administrator will provide the purchase information needed, in writing, to the department head. The department head will issue a purchase requisition and send it to the purchasing department. The department's copy of the requisition will be sent to the systems administrator and filed.

SUPPLEMENTAL ADDITIONS TO CHAPTER 5

5. GRAPHIC ARTS PROCESSING

S5.5 GRAPHICS ARTS PROCESSING SYSTEMS

S5.5.1 Graphic Arts Operation Rules and Procedures

S5.5.2 Graphic Arts Legal Implications

S5.5.3 Graphic Arts System Components

S5.5.4 User Training

S5.5.5 Graphic Arts Purchasing

Chapter 6
Ancillary Support Systems

1. POLICY

S6.1 Corporate Position

The information systems unit has provided central computer operations for the firm. To this was added the responsibilities of LAN, WAN, and voice corporate communications. The control and standardization responsibilities of end-user freestanding and work group microcomputers responsibility has also been given to information systems. The remaining natural area left that would be an inherent extension of the information systems unit's responsibility would be corporate ancillary service devices. This policy mandates the endorsement and support of top management of the organization.

Ancillary service devices are information processing apparatuses used by the company to conduct day-to-day business office operations. Traditionally, these devices are used in office areas and other areas of the company that require the processing of information for customer service or products. To have these devices standardized and controlled by information systems should reduce their total cost of operations and improve the overall service to the company. This may be accomplished at a local operating firm or at multiple sites a company may have throughout the country.

S6.1.1 Scope

The devices can be freestanding used in work groups or systems that cross work group boundaries. The scope of this area of information systems corporate responsibility can cover, but is not limited to, the following company-owned, rented, leased, or loaned ancillary service devices:

- Facsimile machines.
- Copy machines.
- Offset lithography.
- Micrographic systems.
- Wireless networks.
- Digital audio-visual equipment.
- Multimedia microcomputer systems.
- Non-linear video editing systems.
- Digital photo editing systems.
- Video duplication machines.
- Compressed speech computer systems.
- In-house video communications systems.
- Library CD information systems.
- Other related devices.

S6.1.2 Policy Objectives

The policy objectives are standardization, data logging, controlling, and inventorying these devices. The objective is to also optimize the utilization of these devices. This responsibility will also include the maintenance, the provision for procedural operating instructions, operator training, and equipment placement for optimum utilization. The supplies will be purchased at the best cost for company-wide control and standards utilization. Purchasing will work in concert with the information systems to obtain uniform products and supplies at the best price.

2. ANCILLARY EQUIPMENT INVENTORY

S6.2 INVENTORY OF ANCILLARY SUPPORT EQUIPMENT

The information systems unit head will assign the ancillary support systems inventory responsibility to the IT asset manager. If there is not an inventory or equipment system in place, the IT asset manager will establish one.

S6.2.1 Tagging Ancillary Support Equipment

Before the tagging of equipment begins, there will have to be a coding method devised. Computer hardware is tagged upon receipt by a sequential numbering system. The ancillary support systems will employ a different form of coding. A two-number prefix will be used, followed by a space and a sequential number on the tag. The prefix number will identify a type of ancillary support equipment.

After the inventory system is in place, the tagging will be done upon receipt by an agent of the asset manager. The equipment and packing slip will be compared with a copy of the purchase order to confirm that what was received was what was ordered. Supply items received will be checked with the packing slip and a copy of the purchase order. If the purchase is done by a blanket purchase order, the quantity received each time will be added to the total received to date and the quantity compared with the original blanket ordered quantity.

It is recommended that a bar-coded tag be used, along with a visually identified number posted on the tag, or a line scanner be used to ensure that the correct identification number is read. New hardware items received will have tags made and attached to the item. After the tag is secured to the equipment, it will be used as its identification number (during inventory checks, when it is moved to a new location, repaired, or disposed).

S6.2.2 Ancillary Support Equipment Inventory

A computer inventory system will be maintained by each type of ancillary support equipment. The following file record information will be maintained by each unit of hardware:

- Tag number, prefix, and sequential number.
- Date of purchase.
- Original cost.
- Manufacturer's code number.
- Vendor purchased or leased from.
- Purchase, lease, or free-trial code identification.
- Last date of preventative maintenance service.
- Last date of maintenance service.
- Last date of warranty service.
- Maintenance code.

A telephone number will be provided for end-users who may need maintenance. This number can be a IT service unit's telephone number doing the preventative or repair maintenance. Each vendor can perform: warranty service or even preventative maintenance or repair service.

Annual reports will be run by type of equipment, department assigned, department total, and grand total by type of equipment. The amount of usage will also be reported when such records can be provided. When equipment is acquired, moved, or disposed of, the information will be used to update the information database files.

3. ANCILLARY EQUIPMENT MAINTENANCE

S6.3 MAINTENANCE OF ANCILLARY SUPPORT EQUIPMENT

The information systems unit head will assign the ancillary equipment maintenance support to the IT service unit. The IT service unit head will compare maintenance service with vendor and in-house service for quality and cost. The service may be a form of hybrid mix of vendors and in-house service. The maintenance service should be reviewed annually because of the changing technology, availability of in-house and vendor service personnel, and the needs of the company.

> *Comment:*
> **Maintenance is orchestrated as a whole, but each device item will require a thorough study so that its best source of maintenance may be found. The in-house IT service unit head will examine each type of device that requires maintenance attention. As his/her staff resources permit, the device that lends the best return for the attention of an IT service unit's staff should be considered first. An IT service unit person may find the hardware of a multimedia computer system or wireless network not out of his/her realm. But offset lithography would be off limits. Vendor selection will also be based as a per equipment analysis as to who can provide the best service at realistic costs.**

S6.3.1 In-House Maintenance Control

The IT service unit that performs in-house maintenance will perform whatever ancillary equipment repairs and preventive maintenance that they can perform. Cost and in-house availability will be a determining factor as to who will perform what service. A service telephone number will be available for people needing service. This may be called the service desk. The service desk can assist the person, by telephone, with a machine problem. If the problem cannot be resolved over the telephone, the service desk will ask the person calling to place an out-of-order sign on the machine. They will inform the person calling that they will be called back. The service desk person will than contact an in-house service person or the vendor that has the contract to service the machine.

The vendor contacted will be for a warranty or repair service call. The service desk will have that information. The person who contacted the service desk will be informed when they may expect the service person to arrive, and asked to write the information on the out-of-order sign that is posted on the inoperative machine.

In smaller operations, the help desk and the service desk may be combined into the same job. These smaller operations may also have the IT computer services unit people perform some of the ancillary support equipment maintenance. There is also the value of having well-trained key operators. It broadens the scope of their job, and it provides for a level of care that will not require a skilled technician's attention. The extra training is well worth the investment. With this, smaller operations may not require a full-time help desk.

S6.3.2 Service Budgeting

The budgeting for in-house maintenance control and the service desk will come from the IT service unit's lump-sum budget. Although the item purchased may come from a department's budget, the IT service support cost may or may not be charged to the department. This charge will depend on the company's accounting policy.

All service maintenance done by the IT service unit will be reported on a daily service log. The completed work log sheets will be turned in daily to the IT service unit's head. The log report will contain the following information:

- Service person's name.
- Machine number serviced.
- Time spent on the service call.
- Type of call: service, preventive maintenance, or operator problem.
- Any replacement parts that were used.

Departments that purchase their own equipment with their own budget will require funds with which to obtain their own maintenance service. The departments will have to request funds for this maintenance service in their budgets. Some items that are leased may come with a provided service agreement.

All service performed by the in-house IT service unit or vendor will be reported by the IT service unit. The IT service people will provide their daily report to the IT service unit head. The vendor service will be recorded by the service desk. The vendor code number and machine number will be reported. The vendor's service document will be turned over to the help desk. Each day the service report is given to the unit head along with the vendor's service document—a copy will be made for the IT unit head and the original copy sent to the department head. A request for vendor service may come one of the following forms:

- Time and parts.
- Blanket maintenance contract.
- Warranty service call.

S6.3.3 Maintenance Service Report

Vendor maintenance will be reported by machine types each vendor has a contract to repair. The kind of vendor maintenance service reported will be shown as: warranty, preventive, or service maintenance. Time and replacement parts service charges will be listed.

The monthly maintenance service reports will list the machines and locations that were serviced. The report will provide the following information:

- What type of equipment was serviced.
- Who performed the service.
- The estimated cost for the service.
- The kind of in-house service performed.
- The kind of vendor service performed.
- What kind of service was performed.
- What kind of service was performed on the machine the last time it received a service call. When the last service call date was and what the current service call date is.
- A total monthly expense by machine type and a monthly grand total—there will be a year-to-date cost by machine type and a year-to-date grand total.

A second report (IT and Vendor Maintenance Cost Report) will be printed with information by vendor and the IT service unit. The report will list who provided what service to which machines. The report lists the subtotal cost for the month. Year-to-date costs will be listed by the service provider and a grand total year-to-date sum.

S6.3.4 *Vendor Maintenance Contracting*

The IT unit head, the asset manager, and a purchasing department representative will work together to solicit vendor contract bids. The same purchasing department representative should be used from year to year. It would be very beneficial if the same purchasing agent would also be responsible for ancillary supplies and computer supplies.

After IT has identified what items they cannot do or will not be able to service because of not having the required people, a list will be compiled of the equipment that will require vendor's maintenance bids. A form letter will be used listing all the items for which bids are requested. Vendors can provide an offer for any one item, any number, or the entire lot of items listed.

The list of vendors to contact can come from the IT service unit's head, the IT asset manager, and the purchasing department's representative. It will be the purchasing department's representative's responsibility to check each vendor before they will be sent the letter. The purchasing agent can use information his/her department may already have. Contacts with other firm's purchasing departments may be a source of information along with the firm's D and B rating.

When composing the request for bids letter as much information as can be provided will be given. A vendor company contact person will be provided in the letter. Any site visits will be arranged through the company's contact person. The letter will furnish the name and telephone number of the contact person, and the last day that the bids will be received. The following information will be furnished in the vendor letter or attachment to the letter:

- A list of unit types that the bid calls for servicing.
- The number of units for each unit type.
- The age and condition of each.
- Units that are under current warranties, and when those warranties expire.

If a particular vendor's bid is selected, would they be willing to provide a help desk telephone number? This would allow for company employees to contact them for information or a service call. Will there be a charge for this service if it is available?

Vendor selection will be based on several variables. Each variable will be weighted before the request for bid letters are dispatched. Vendor analysis will be based on this matrix. See Chapter 15.5.3—Vendor Selection—of the main volume, *Information Systems Policies and Procedures Manual*, for information about setting up a weighted matrix. Short-term contracts may be considered for yet unproven vendors. Before any contract is signed, contact the firm's legal representative, who will have the last word before it is signed by the firm's authorized representative.

S6.3.5 *Outsourcing Legal Ramifications*

Outsourcing different applications from companies has provided some mixed results, some good and some bad.

Comment:

There have been a lot of disappointments with outsourcing. Some of the vendors providing outsourcing and consulting services in general have been small upstarts. However, some can afford full-page ads in *The Wall Street Journal*. Vendors of this kind have been known to play the game of bait and switch. They send in their first string to get the contract signed, after which their trainees get their marching orders. They show up with the current buzzwords, smart suits, and lap-top computers.

In a case in Michigan, the trainees proved interesting. One made the comment that she received a low score on her MBA acceptance exam. One claimed to have an MBA, but would not say from which school. Another did not know that random time sampling was needed to do work sampling studies. The money the firm paid could have afforded many full-page ads in *The Wall Street Journal*.

The IRS has some defined rules to follow to have a person classified as an employee. IRC 530 of the Revenue Act of 1978 provides relief from some consequences of misclassification of employees as independent contractors. There are 20 guidelines presented in Rev. Rule 87-41, along with other IRS data. Some of the key guidelines of Rev. Rule 87-41 are:

A. Working on the employer's premises

   Especially when the work could be done elsewhere. This is indicative of an employer/employee relationship.

B. Method of payment

   Payment by the hour, week, or month generally is indicative of an employer/employee relationship. Payment by the job generally indicates that the person is an independent contractor. A lump sum may be computed by the number of hours required to do a job at a certain rate per hour.

C. Furnishing tools and/or materials

   An independent contractor ordinarily furnishes his/her own tools and materials.

D. Working for more than one firm

   The service provider's ability to work for more than one service recipient at the same time is indicative of an independent contractor.

E. Service available to the general public

   The fact that a service provider makes his/her services available to the general public is indicative of an independent contractor. A business telephone listing would be supportive of this guideline.

F. Business investment

   The investment by a service provider in facilities is a factor that tends to indicate an independent contractor. The investment must be significant and essential. The investment must be essential to the contractor. The investment by the service provider in facilities are adequate to perform the services contracted for indicates the status of an independent contractor.

   There may be other legal ramifications with labor unions and the contract. In this case, a good labor relations attorney may be a wise investment. If programming outsourcing results are being used in classified software development for the government, it could be a major problem. Outsourcing to parts of the world that use prison labor can also be problem. Outsourcing to be able to discharge employees over the age of 40 years also could spell trouble with the EEOC.

4. ANCILLARY OPERATION PROCEDURES

S6.4 MACHINE OPERATIONS

Ancillary machines cover a wide range of applications and complexities. The total investment is not always known by most companies.

> **Comment:**
> **Some pragmatic people had the foresight to contemplate that a lot of these ancillary machines would someday work together as a total office system. A paramount software maker did some early forecasting—they were in the thinking stage or a bit further along on this idea. Then one noted hardware manufacturer was planning to accommodate this thinking into its future machines. Because their efforts have been centered on more pressing things, this has been put on the back burner for now.**

Meanwhile, most ancillary machines operate without a central sense of direction. Without the orchestration and guidance of information systems, their costs will continue to grow while their efficiency will diminish. A major part of controlling this operation are the ancillary operation procedures set forth by an IT unit of information systems.

S6.4.1 Posted Machine Operations

The less complex operating ancillary machines will require only a simple set of posted operation instructions. If possible, the operating instructions should be placed on or near the machine. Lettering size should be bold enough to be seen and read in a matter of a minute or less.

The instructions should refer to a smaller size type of troubleshooting instructions. At the end of the instructions, a contact person—not the operator—should be identified if there is a problem with the machine. This could be the area key operator. If no one is listed or is just not available, the service desk phone number will be posted.

S6.4.2 Key Machine Operator

This is a person who is responsible for turning on the machine in the morning and turning it off before closing down for the day. His/her name will be posted as the key operator to be contacted if the machine needs attention or operator assistance. When turning on the machine in the morning, it should be checked for its running condition and that it is supplied with its needed usable material.

The key machine operator should be able to operate and perform minor machine adjustments. He/she will know how to replenish its expendable stock items, and perform standard housekeeping and preventative maintenance procedures. The key operator will be able to be walked through some of the malfunctions by the service desk or a maintenance person over the telephone. At the service desk will be a key operator's location book with the key operator's name, telephone number, and location listed. A second listing will be by location with the key operator's name and telephone number listed. This will be used to contact another key operator that is close by the unit for assistance when a unit's key operator is not available.

S6.4.3 Machine Operator Procedures

These are the operating procedures furnished to key operators and stand-alone ancillary machine operators. The operator procedure manuals will be furnished by the IT service unit or the systems and procedures unit. The manuals will provide operator instructions, minor maintenance instruction, and procedures for troubleshooting. Minor preventive maintenance procedures will be provided.

The procedure manuals will contain any manufacturers furnished material that is helpful to clarify the machines operation. The illustrations used by the manufacturer could be beneficial to the operator. Close-up and wide-view photographs would be helpful if included in the operator procedure manuals.

A prototype manual will be developed and tested before it is placed into service. An unskilled person will be used for the test. This should be done with more than one subject. The brightest person in the area and any experienced operator should be avoided for debugging the procedure manual.

S6.4.4 Supply Requisitions

The standard supply requisitions that the firm has in place will be used. If the form is outdated or there is no form, one will be designed by the IT systems and procedures unit.

A central supply location should be placed to limit the travel time involved. This will allow for unnecessary travel for the person seeking supplies. The supply center could also function as supply distribution location for the end-user computer operations supplies. Supplies can be delivered by interoffice mail. Large items may require another delivery system.

A requisition system will be employed to obtain supplies. The requisition will be approved by the key operator or unit head after all the items are listed with their respective quantities. A line will by drawn across the lines not used by the person before signing the requisition. Depending on the company accounting practice, the supplies will be charged to the unit receiving them or come from a lump-sum company budget. Spot checks on usage that are employing a lump-sum budget is recommended. The loss on supply items can be costly to a company. The supply area will be locked when unattended. Supplies stored in operating units will be locked at the end of the day or locked at all times if the view to the area is blocked from view.

S6.4.5 Service Desk Assistance

Help desks, along with service desks, cannot solve all user problems. It will require other assistance to cover the user's special needs. Some operations such as turn-key systems will be better off with a vendor-supplied service. Vendor help and service desks for special systems can provide much better service than in-house service. If the company is willing to provide for an in-house service desk and support it, there are still vendor services that can provide better assistance. They will do it better, and the equipment will be up and running faster.

The asset manager will publish an approved ancillary acquisition list for new ancillary purchases. This will cover what is in-house, currently operating and found on the ancillary inventory property list, but not on the approved ancillary acquisition list. Ancillary inventory property list is company property, identified and tagged. The approved ancillary acquisition list is a list of items that the IT service unit can repair or for which the service desk has a vendor contact. The service desk will also have the ancillary inventory property list and the source of service for each item. Some items may have been company property before the service desk assistance program was established.

Some items either have long life spans and seldom need to be replaced or the item is no longer manufactured—it can be replaced only with used equipment. The help desk will have a special number to call to have the item serviced. In cases of this kind, it is in the best interest of the company to have the key operator trained to do most of the repairs and preventative maintenance. The vendor service person will be contacted only if the problem is beyond the scope of the key operator or one is not available. Some of the items may not use the English measuring system and may require special tools to repair the equipment, or the manufacturer may be the only one that makes the tool.

The service desk does not have to be covered at the company site any more than the help desk. This is why so many vendor help desks are not found at company sites. This may be more difficult having the vendor provide full-service desk coverage. If coverage is needed other than normal working hours, service desk personnel can be on call at their homes for specific time periods. This can also apply to help desk personnel. In smaller firms these two jobs can be combined into one. There would be one number to call in the event of a problem. There is also the possibility that the problem may be related to both the help desk and the service desk. The help and service desk person should be able to have at home the current information that he/she has at their desk at work. It would be desirable to have it installed in a notebook computer.

5. MICROGRAPHICS

S6.5 DOCUMENT ARCHIVING

The computer age has provided the technology that allows for data image capturing, storage, rapid retrieval, and output. The output can be on a monitor or as hard copy. The hard copy can be smaller, equal in size, or even larger than the original. Vital records that require permanent storage and off-site backup storage start to run into problems as they age. Current computer secondary storage media will not reach the age of 20 years before it starts to deteriorate. Most, if not all, of today's computer secondary storage readers will not be able to read the information that was put on secondary storage devices 20 years ago. Data recorded on 5¼″ and 8″ floppy disks 10 years ago will not be able to locate an I/O device in most companies today that can read the information. That should not be a major problem, because the data will soon be unreadable. The shelf life of secondary storage media today is less than 20 years.

Microfilm of documents recorded over 50 years ago is still viable today. The microfilm images are still as readable as the day they were recorded and read on current microfilm viewers. Microfilm-recorded images have been known to have outlived the original documents. The composition of the paper document and its storage conditions will have a profound effect with its aging process. Firms today are rediscovering micrographics.

Comment:

Kodak has been very active with digital imaging. They have not put all their eggs in one basket. They still advertise nationally their microfilm products. They have also advertised that they certify life expectancy a <u>minimum</u> of 500 years. Can any of your secondary storage devices beat that? No one product is a solution to all problems, any more then penicillin was thought as a cure all when it first came out. At one point, I expected it to be a cure for flat feet. Computer document archiving systems have yet to be as good and safe as micrographics for one or more years.

Contact them for more information at 1-800-243-8811 or visit them on www.Kodak.com/go/businessimaging. There are still microfilm systems out there. If they would only come out with some new buzz words or acronyms, we would hear more about them.

S6.5.1 Forms of Micrographics

There are several forms of micrographics available. This allows for a wider applications of micrographics. The forms have changed little over the years because, in part, of their simplicity and dependability. The systems and procedures need much less updating than computer systems. There are some disadvantages of microfilm such as there are no national standardization as found with the computer high- and low-density $3^1/2''$ floppy disk. Micrographics cannot compete with computer random retrieval systems. Archival data will in most cases not require fast random retrieval. This is a question of tradeoffs.

A. Microfilm reels

Microfilm can be in a positive or negative reel film. This film can be had in black and white or color. Available sizes are 16 mm and 35 mm.

Sample applications are:

- Newspaper archival, employing 35-mm reel film and large-screen viewers.

- Canceled check 16-mm microfilming is done by banks. With lockbox systems, the bank gets the check for deposit and the bank customer receives a reel of microfilm. This deposits the checks even before the reel of film is received by the customer. If need be, the checks are filmed by two cameras at a time so the bank has a copy for its use and a backup.

- Medical records can be put on two reels of 16-mm film. One reel is for archival data and backup. The other reel is put into microfiche jackets, which will be placed into the patients medical records chart. This reduces the chart size. The microfiche is easy to read, and it is simple to make a hard copy.

B. Microfiche

COM (computer output microfilm) is a marriage of computer technology and micrographics. The output is in a microfiche format. It can also be produced by other methods and used interchangeably with microfiche jackets. Microfiche viewers are simple to use and much less expensive than a computer monitor. They are inexpensive handheld viewers that are used by service repair people looking at drawings or parts lists. They provide for a simple data information system for many users with a minimum need for storage space and an inexpensive viewer and distribution cost.

Comment:
Education libraries that provide college catalog information can provide it as microfilmed information. A single drawer can provide the space needed for a microfiche file of all the college catalogs in the United States. Hard copy can be made from the microfiche. This reduces the cost and space needed for maintaining a college catalog reference shelf.

C. Aperture card

The aperture card is the size of the former tabulating card. It employs a 35-mm microfilm placed on the card. It is primarily used for limited applications that require engineering drawings. The 35-mm microfilm can produce top-quality drawings in several sizes.

S6.5.2 Micrographic Processing Procedure Methods

If there is no microfilm processing system in place, a system will have to be devised. A project leader, preferable a systems analyst or comparable person, will be assigned the task of developing a microfilm feasibility study. The objective will be defined by management. The project leader will collect the management information and proceed with a task analysis.

To perform a task analysis, the following information will be required:

- The source of the input data to the micrographic system.
- The size of the documents involved.
- The current volume of the documents on file by size.
- The condition of the documents.
- The volume of new documents (by size) that will be added to the file each month.

To determine what micrographic format will be best suited for the system, the following information will be required:

- The expected micrographic output volume monthly.
- The expected number of microfilm references monthly.
- The expected number of hard copies needed monthly.
- The size of the hard copies that will be needed.
- The requirements for an off-site backup.
- The requirements for storage files.

From the collected data and the task analysis, enough information will be available to develop a request for micrographic hardware vendor bids. A letter will be sent to microfilm hardware vendors requesting bid proposals. The yellow pages can be a source for microfilm hardware vendors. The vendors will be informed that the project leader will be the company contact person.

The hardware vendor will work with the project leader and the information provided to determine the service level requirements, and what projected growth is expected over the next five years. The vendors will present a proposal as to what the hardware needs are and of the projected costs. The projected costs will cover capital investment, operating supply costs by year, and the expected number of people required to operate the system. The annual people cost will be based on the total expected hours per year, times the dollars per hour wages, plus fringe benefits. The project leader will forward the information to management with a cover letter expressing an objective opinion of each proposal.

To ensure that the maximum result will be obtained from the expense incurred, an outsourcing possibility will be studied. Microfilm service vendors will be contacted for competitive bids. A request for bid letters will be sent to prospective vendors. The yellow pages can be a good source for finding providers of microfilm services. For a vendor to provide the total service will require the following information:

- Project contact person.
- When the bids are expected.
- Condition of the documents. Samples of the documents to be microfilmed should be enclosed, if possible, with the request for a bid letter. The condition and colors of the documents will determine the quality of the image on microfilm. Documents that are printed on red paper present a serious problem.
- What volume can be expected.
- The turn around time that is expected.
- Scheduled service dates.

A. Total vendor service

A total vendor service is to outsource the entire micrographic process. The contract will state that the documents to be microfilmed are never to leave the premises. The project leader will be the contact person and a source for any additional information required. The proposed procedure will be as follows by the micrographics service vendor and the company:

- The vendor will arrive at a scheduled time and date.
- The documents will be available at the location provided for the vendor. Any special document preparation required for the processing and returning the documents back to the original form will be done by company personnel.
- The documents will be controlled with a before-and-after document count by the unit responsible for the documents. This count number will be recorded for later use.

- The location provided for the vendor will be used during the time the copying of the documents with a microfilm camera. The room should be at a comfortable temperature and have an accessible electrical outlet to meet the vendor's needs.
- The documents will copied onto microfilm.
- The microfilm will be processed by the vendor.
- The results will be processed and returned to the company in the form that was contracted. This can be negative or positive microfilm. The format can be 16- or 35-mm film, microfiche, or aperture card.
- When the microfilm is received by the company, the unit responsible for the documents will count the number of documents on microfilm. This count will be compared with the document count made during the time the documents were copied onto microfilm. If the counts do not agree, the error will have to be resolved.
- The microfilm will be placed into the designated files.
- The original documents will be returned to their original locations, placed in a holding storage for one year, or destroyed.
- When accounts payable receives the invoice for the microfilming service, it will send a copy to the file unit's manager for approval.
- The file unit's manager will confirm that the invoice is correct. The invoice will be signed and dated. A copy will be made for the file and the invoice returned to accounts payable.

B. Partial vendor service

Partial vendor service is used when the volume does not justify in-house film processing. The exposed film is sent to a microfilm processing vendor. In the case there is a need for aperture cards or microfiche, this can be part of the microfilm processing service. Microfilm processing vendors will be contacted and requested to provide a written quotation for the service. Vendors will be provided the following information:

- Project contact person.
- When the bids are expected.
- What volume can be expected.
- Turnaround time expected.

- Scheduled service dates.
- Type of microfilm processing.

The following micrographic production procedure will be followed:

- The unit responsible for the retention, or otherwise specified, will photocopy the documents. The process will employ one of the two kinds of cameras available or both: the planetary camera or rotary camera. The proposed microfilming procedures will be as follows:

  - Original documents will be collected for batch processing.
  - The photocopying process will be done.
  - The batch of original documents will be counted and placed into a holding container. The batch count will be posted and dated on a slip of paper and placed on top of the documents. Any of the documents may be retrieved for use while in the holding container; they will be required to be returned. A sign-out procedure will be required for taking any of the documents. The signout document will be held in the document holding container.
  - The exposed microfilm will be sent to the microfilm processing vendor.
  - The film will be processed and returned to the company in the form that was contracted by the microfilm processing vendor. This can be a negative or positive microfilm. The format can be 16- or 35-mm film, microfiche, or aperture card. The processed results will be sent to the company's records retention unit.
  - A designated person will receive the items from the microfilm processing vendor.
  - The completed films will be checked for quality and item count. If any documents were not photographed or are of unacceptable quality, the original will be held for the next batch processing.
  - The microfilm will be placed into the designated files.
  - The original documents will be returned to their original locations, placed in a holding storage for one year, or destroyed.
  - When accounts payable receives the invoice for the microfilm processing service, it will send a copy to the file unit's manager for approval.

- The file unit's manager will confirm that the invoice is correct. The invoice will be signed and dated. A copy will be made for the file, and the invoice returned to accounts payable.

C. Total in-house processing

- The unit responsible for the retention, or otherwise specified, will photocopy the documents. The process will employ one of the two kinds of cameras available or both: the planetary camera or rotary camera. The proposed microfilming procedures will be as follows:
- Original documents will be collected for batch processing.
- The photocopying process will be done.
- The exposed microfilm will be processed.
- The film will be processed into the format required: 16- or 35-mm film, microfiche, or aperture card.
- The processed results will be checked for quality and item count. If any documents were not photographed or are of unacceptable quality, the original will be held for the next batch processing.
- The original documents will be returned to their original locations, placed in a holding storage for one year, or destroyed.

S6.5.3 System Selection

From the information received, the vendors will compute and submit proposals. The proposals will provide estimates for annual costs for total vendor processing or partial vendor service. This will be given to the project leader. The project leader will review the proposals and add to it the estimated annual company cost. The company cost will be: capital investment of end-user hardware, supply costs, personnel costs, and any vendor service costs. The project leader will finalize the study and submit a report with recommendations. This report with attached vendor and company cost information will be submitted to management. A week or two after the report submission, the project leader will make a formal presentation to management and field any questions that need to be resolved.

The micrographic production system will depend on the volume and the control that management wants. The total process can be done in house or be outsourced. Vendors can also provide part of the process. The cost incurred by the proposed system can in part be offset by the cost of procedures no longer required. The final decision will be required by management, whether it be the company's data management head or a management group decision.

S6.5.4 Micrographics Operation Procedure

The micrographics operation procedures cannot consist of one procedure that fits all types of operations for all companies that can employ a wide selection of hardware system configurations. This would require a good size manual. But, there are some basic operations that are common to most micrographic policies and procedures.

A. Policies

Critical documents will be stored in an archival environment in a fireproof safe. Reels of the microfilm copies will be stored off site in an archival environment that is in a fireproof safe. The condition of both items will be checked annually. Appropriate measures will be taken if there is any signs of deterioration.

Critical documents are any of the following:

- Charters or deed titles.
- Copyright documents.
- Patent documents.
- Any other required permanent records.

Important documents retention requirements are based on legal requirements. The retention time limits will be decided by the firm's legal counsel. The original documents will be held in a fireproof safe. They will be disposed of at the end of their term limits. The disposal process will make the information unreadable. The microfilm copies will be stored off site in a fireproof safe. Samples of some of the documents are:

- Personal property titles.
- Tax records.
- Vendor contracts.
- Any other important records.

The microfilm will be stored for one year after the original documents have been destroyed. After one year the microfilm will be destroyed. Microfilm when no longer needed will be destroyed.

B. Procedures

Procedures that are common to all microfilm applications are:

- Disposal of all original documents will make the information unreadable.
- Microfilm no longer needed will be destroyed.
- Original documents will not be destroyed until the microfilm replacing the documents has been confirmed to be of good quality.
- A key operator is responsible for maintaining the procedure manuals, file storage areas, inventory supplies, general housekeeping, preventive maintenance, etc.
- Current operating instructions will be attached to each micrographics machine.
- Hard copy produced from microfilm when no longer needed will be made unreadable.

S6.5.5 Micrographics Training

Vendors will provide training for the key operator and backup key operator of the micrographics equipment and the film processing system. Vendors will provide end-user machine instructions. The key operator will be available for assistance and operator training of end-users. Vendors may be able to provide self-instruction videos for individual training.

6. TRAINING

S6.6 OPERATOR AND SERVICE TECHNICIAN TRAINING

The provision for training will cover a wide area of needs. The technology skill levels required for each service item will be one or more levels. Vendor-contracted ancillary service will not require as many levels of skills as an in-house service program. The service desk will have the levels of skill that are available for each item listed in the ancillary inventory property list. Depending on the nature of the problem, a skill level will be determined to resolve the problem. The item listed will have posted to it the persons who can perform a given level of skill. A person with a higher level of skill can perform a lower level of skill task. But a lower-level skilled person should not perform a higher-level skill task. The training will certify a level at which the service person can perform a task.

The training provided will be for certain skill levels. This training will be for vendor service and company-serviced equipment.

S6.6.1 Operator Training

The operator should learn the basic operation of the machine to produce the desired results. The more complex the machine, the more there will be to learn. The job of putting paper into a copy machine would be considered a task level that would be expected of an operator. The job of video editing is much more complex, but it also is an operator's job. Operator training will be provided in more than one form:

A. New machine operator training

When a new ancillary machine is to be used by operators, the training will be conducted in class. The vendor or the key operator will conduct the classes. The vendor should provide any of their handouts. The company instructor will provide any handouts that may be needed. A video or slide presentation would be helpful along with any hands-on training.

A list of the people attending the meeting will be taken. Anyone missing the class will be notified that they missed it and should attend the next class offered. If the classes are over, they will take the individual training provided to new employees later.

B. New employee training

Anyone missing the class will take the self-paced individual training. New employees that have no experience with the equipment will receive the self-paced individual training. They will be credited with receiving the instruction for the new equipment. Part of the instruction will be provided by the operator as OJT instruction.

S6.6.2 Key Operator Training

The key operator training will be given for all the machines in his/her job area that would need the attention of a key operator. The training can be from more than one source. The IT service unit will hold classes for key operators or OJT instruction for the machines that they maintain. The key operators will receive key operator manuals from the IT service unit.

Vendor training programs will be provided at the company site or at the vendors place of instruction. The vendors will provide manuals. The IT unit will also proved key operator's procedure manuals. Some sort of certificate will be provided by the vendor showing the person is now a certified key operator for the given machine.

The key operator should be able to provide OJT to new machine operators. They should be able to clean the machine, make adjustments to its operation, and perform some light preventative maintenance. They will be the key contact person in the area for operators, service desk, vendor service people, and the IT service personnel.

S6.6.3 IT Service Unit Training

Each IT service person will have a list of equipment that they can service for their own records, along with the service desk and the IT unit head.

Training will come from one of the following sources:

- OJT.
- A self-paced learning program provided by the vendor.
- Attending vendor's classes.
- Viewing VCR tapes for the equipment.
- Taking a correspondence course from the vendor or a private correspondence program.

S6.6.4 Service Desk Training

Effective service desk people are often individuals who have some experience as an IT service person. Their training can come from the areas where the IT service person receives his/her training—as the key operator and from operator training. It would help a new service desk operator to work with an experienced worker, which would be a form of OJT learning. On days when there is not a heavy load, they may try their skills at manning the service desk.

Service desk personnel can be expected to work overtime and be on call at their homes. The unit will have one or two lap-top computers that service people can take home with them when they are on call.

They are expected to have no less knowledge than a key operator about each machine and a general knowledge about vendor-maintained machines. They should have enough knowledge to assist an operator and communicate with a service person that works for the company or vendor. They should be able to assign service people to be used most effectively and best serve the company's needs. They can reduce maintenance costs with the proper assignments and the ability to walk operators through problems.

7. ANCILLARY DEVICE ACQUISITIONS

S6.7 ANCILLARY DEVICES AND SUPPLY ACQUISITION PROCEDURES

The budgeting can come from a corporate lump-sum budget or department budgets or both.

S6.7.1 Budgeting Procedures

Each department will submit their expected needs for the following year's budget. This will be based on the last year's budget plus any inflation, replacement of old equipment, and new needs. It is supported by the utilization of the current equipment and forecasted usage for the next budget year.

Budgets will be needed for the department's use of supplies and replacement of current equipment. Departments that have their own hardware for their one-of-a-kind use will require a budget for the maintenance of the equipment.

The information systems IT service unit will need a budget for their operation. They will need a budget for capital expenses that benefit the whole company plus a replacement parts budget. Also, a vendor service budget may be required.

S6.7.2 Requisition Procedures

Items that have been budgeted can have a requisition issued. The requisition will go to the IT asset manager to confirm that it meets standards or will require a standards waiver.

The requisition will be approved and sent on to the budget department by the IT asset manager so they can adjust their records and then be sent on to the purchasing department.

S6.7.3 Purchasing Procedures

Purchasing will receive the approved purchase requisition. If needed, they will take care of the competitive bids for the item. After the purchase order has been sent to the vendor, a copy will be sent to the receiving department and accounts payable.

S6.7.4 Receiving Procedures

The agent for the asset manager or a special order item representative will inspect the item for their approval. After it is approved, a receiving notice will be sent to accounts payable.

The asset manager's agent will affix a tag to the machine and record the information. The information will be sent to the asset manager.

SUPPLEMENTAL ADDITIONS TO CHAPTER 6

5. MICROGRAPHICS

   S6.5   DOCUMENT ARCHIVING

   S6.5.1 Forms of Micrographics

   S6.5.2 Micrographic Processing Procedure Methods

   S6.5.3 System Selection

   S6.5.4 Micrographics Operation Procedures

   S6.5.5 Micrographics Training

6. TRAINING

   S6.6   OPERATOR AND SERVICE TECHNICIAN TRAINING

   S6.6.1 Operator Training

   S6.6.2 Key Operator Training

   S6.6.3 IT Service Unit Training

   S6.6.4 Service Desk Training

7. ANCILLARY DEVICE ACQUISITIONS

   S6.7   ANCILLARY DEVICES AND SUPPLY ACQUISITION PROCEDURES

   S6.7.1 Budgeting Procedures

   S6.7.2 Requisition Procedures

   S6.7.3 Purchasing Procedures

   S6.7.4 Receiving Procedures

Chapter 7
COMPUTER SECURITY, AUDIT, AND CONTROL

1. POLICY

S7.1 CORPORATE CONTROL POLICY

There must be a centralized source for corporate audit and control of computer information technology. If the company has an in-house audit unit, it should be involved with all corporate computer security, audit, and controls. If the company has no plans for such a unit, the outside accounting firm will be required to provide the service. This should be a major concern of the CFO and the CEO. The auditing people will report to the CFO. The efforts for security and control will be a joint effort of information systems, auditing, and the CFO. Any unresolved disputes will be corrected by the CEO.

S7.1.1 Policy Scopes

Computer security requires controls and audit trails to support its endeavor. Good audit trails require controls and security. Controls are useless without the support of the audit trail and security. These three scope items are interdependent. The policy covers all items of any monetary value.

Security does not cover only financial interests of the firm. Information itself—if stolen—may not result in a reduction of net worth, and it can be a commodity that can be sold. This is a form of white-collar crime that is seldom followed up with severe jail terms. Some firms do not want to be embarrassed that such a thing could happen in their company, so they will not even file charges. Security, control, and audits cover all levels of company employees. No one is immune to their scope of coverage.

Comment:

Private ownership has no immunity to theft. What an owner steals is what he/she does not have to pay tax on. He/she may be aware of the statute of limitations, but there are none for tax fraud.

The other misconception is that all working family members are honest. If one believes that, they are sure to get a good deal on buying a bridge in Brooklyn.

S7.1.2 Merit of Controls

Controls can be overextended beyond their monetary merit. Monetary merit is one thing, but the firm's reputation and future security can be at stake. Each control must be examined as to its merit. There can be controls, security, and audit trails built into a system as a by-product of other procedures or operations at a minimum of effort or cost, and at times no additional cost. This practice is supported as a policy and should be applied when ever possible.

S7.1.3 External Access

External access from stand-alone and work group computers will have policy constraints. The policy covers the following accesses: LAN, WAN, e-mail, and internet. A company-sponsored web page will comply with the policy. The policy is that no illegal, immoral, or improper dialog will be permitted at any time by a company employee in any form with these accesses.

The company has an obligation to monitor these activities. The company will not condone any improper activity. Any employee found to conduct any improper activity will be appropriately dealt with. If it occurs too often, the employee will be discharged and the standard IT procedures will be followed for discharging employees.

Immoral acts will not be condoned by the company. Any employee found to conduct immoral activity will be appropriately dealt with. This is a more serious violation than that of improper activity. When it occurs, it can lead to having the employee discharged. The human resources department will be utilized for assistance with this type of conduct. The standard IT procedures will be followed for discharging employees.

Illegal acts are grounds for discharge; the employee will be discharged and the standard IT procedures will be followed for discharging employees. Depending on the nature of the illegal act, the human resources department will be responsible for contacting the authorities.

The human resources department will be required to approve the procedures before they are published. Any subsequent changes to this policy area will require their approval before it is enacted. The approvals will be given in writing. Copies of the approvals and any disapprovals will be filed in a secured place.

2. HARDWARE SECURITY

S7.2 PROTECTION FROM NATURAL AND HUMAN DISASTERS

The days have long passed when firms showcased their computer systems. Today, security is a major concern of corporate data processing centers—and for very good reasons.

> **Comment:**
> **There was a utility in Wisconsin years ago that provided a view from their lobby through a large window of their computer operations. By pushing a button next to the window, the onlookers were informed over a speaker what each major hardware unit was and what each person's job was by the color of his/her jacket.**

Today, computer systems are likely to be the target of protestors, disgruntled workers, or even rioters. The decentralization of computer systems, work group systems, and stand-alone systems has increased the difficulty of protecting the computers and their information contents.

S7.2.1 Natural and Man-Made Disasters

Natural disasters are often defined as acts of God. These environmental disasters are virtually impossible to predict, let alone avoid. Some parts of the country are more prone to one type of disaster than another. There are also micro-environmental problems that are not confined to any one region. These micro-environments can come from acts of God or man. When the locations of critical computer center sites and network file servers are involved, both the region and the micro-environment should be the first concerns.

A. Earthquakes

Earthquakes are more prone to occur in known areas. Even if there is no damage to the computer facilities, there will most likely be power outage for up to several days. The computer center should be located in the most earthquake-safe location of the firm's sites. Large cities present a serious problem, which can be helped by doing the following:

- Avoid top and bottom floor locations.
- Avoid rooms with windows, or as far away as possible. If windows are in the room, use plastic or shatterproof glass.
- Avoid placing any objects that may cause damage to the computer system if it is too close to it.
- Place fireproof safes used for storing backup data and software in a different room than the computer.
- Have larger than normally needed UPS systems to carry all the current needed by the system. Have posted procedures to turn off any hardware that is not essential to the system operation. Laser printers are known to be heavy users of power. If backup generators are needed to run the system until local power is available, have enough power to furnish lights and the air conditioner.
- Have a cellular phone charged and ready.

B. Hurricanes

Hurricanes, like earthquakes, are prone to occur in particular areas. Hurricanes provide some warning time before they strike. Some last-minute things can be done to be prepared for a hurricane:

- Avoid top and bottom floor locations.
- Avoid rooms with windows, or as far away as possible. If windows are in the room, use plastic or shatterproof glass.
- Place fireproof/waterproof safes used for storing backup data and software in a different room than the computer.
- Have normally needed UPS systems. If backup generators are needed to run the system until local power is available, have enough power to furnish lights and the air conditioner.

- Have a battery-operated radio for hurricane advisory information.
- Have a cellular phone charged and ready.

C. Tornado

Tornados, like hurricanes and earthquakes, are known to occur in some areas and not others. To prepare, follow these suggestions:

- Avoid rooms with windows, or as far away as possible. If windows are in the room, use plastic or shatterproof glass.
- Avoid placing any objects that may cause damage to the computer system too close.
- Place fireproof safes used for storing backup data and software in a different room than the computer.
- Have normally needed UPS systems. If backup generators are needed to run the system until local power is available, have enough power to furnish lights and the air conditioner.
- Have a battery-operated radio for weather advisory information.
- Have a cellular phone charged and ready.
- There should be a safe place for employees to stay until the severe weather warning is over.
- The computer system should be turned off when the warning sounds. If time permits, backup disks and/or tapes should be locked in the safe.

D. Floods

Computer centers should not be located on any flood plain. The flood plains have been identified by the government. Insurance is also a problem to obtain when the area is a known flood plain.

Comment:

There is an insurance company in the tornado belt that has a large fireproof, and by all appearances bombproof, walk-in vault joining its computer center. In a matter of seconds, the staff can get in the vault and be safe from harm, along with the already-there backup files and programs.

E. Water damage

There are man-made constructions that can damage computer centers that are difficult to foresee. These can result from plugged storm sewers, broken water mains, or roof leakage. Computer operations that are not manned 24 hours a day and seven days a week may want to consider a water detection device that will turn off the system and notify a commercial alarm company. The company should be provided a priority list of names and telephone numbers to call to notify someone in case of a problem.

F. Power failure

A UPS system should be plugged into the essential file servers and main computer systems. The other devices may only need surge protectors. There should be an automatic computer backup and shutdown within the UPS system. Computer systems that are not manned 24 hours a day and seven days a week should consider the value of having a power failure detection device that will notify a commercial alarm company. The company should be provided a priority list of names and telephone numbers to call in case of a power failure.

G. Fire

The computer areas should have fireproof access doors and nonflammable walls, ceiling and floors. There should be automatic fire extinguishers that are turned on after a 30-second alarm is sounded if workers are present. If workers are not present, the fire extinguisher should go off immediately. The value of having a smoke detection device that will notify a commercial alarm company should be considered. The company should be provided a priority list of names and telephone numbers to call to notify someone of the event.

S7.2.2 Human Intrusion

The first consideration is the basic physical requirements and location for security. The human-factor intrusion considerations should be given to the following items.

A. Computer site location

The computer operations building should be located away from the perimeter of the company grounds. It should not be in a building with a lot of people traffic. The ground floor should not have any windows. If windows are needed, they should be made of bulletproof glass. Another precaution would be a second window on the outer side that is also bulletproof and made of small panes of steel that can act as bars. This combination is not unattractive. An upper-floor location without outside walls would be a better solution.

> **Comment:**
>
> **One Ohio firm had its computer center on the main floor. A public sidewalk went past the window. It was the only place that it could be located and the employees enjoyed the view. When the information systems manager was asked about the risk the window provided, he said "the window is made of double-plated bulletproof glass."**

B. Entryway

The doors should be of strong fireproof steel with secure locks. Locks that require a plastic card that identifies the person coupled with a key pad asking for the current password is a solution. A double set of doors is a better controlled entryway. The first door is opened when the person is recognized by an observer. This can be visual recognition with the proper ID presented. After the person passes through the first door, it is locked. After the first door is locked, the second door is opened.

> **Comment:**
>
> **A Midwest firm has a building with elevators. The elevator will not stop on the floor where the computer center is located.**

C. Rest area

A small area should be set aside for rest rooms and a place to eat within the computer complex. Tables and chairs will be provided along with a refrigerator, microwave, trash container, a sink for water access, and a radio for news and weather reports. No food or beverages are to be consumed outside this area.

D. Secondary electrical power supply

The computer complex will have its own secondary electrical power supply for lights, computer hardware, and air conditioning operations. There should be enough fuel to run the generators for three days. Other units support work group file servers, online key people, etc.

E. Other considerations

All available devices are not required for a security system. The following are items that are available depending on the micro-environmental needs:

- Armed guards.
- Disaster-recovery procedures.
- Remote network file backup site.
- Commercially available computer backup systems.
- Television surveillance systems.
- Remote cameras recording on digital tape sequenced time exposures.
- Public address system.
- Indoor temperature alarm systems, when the temperature gets beyond a high or low reading.
- Automatic-dial fire or police telephones.
- Do not allow maintenance and CEs in the area without IT operation personnel present.
- Do not post signs to make the site conspicuous.
- Do not allow non-computer center personnel to bring in any packages or briefcases that are not inspected before they enter the computer center.
- Conduct frequent drills of backup systems.
- Conduct emergency drills more than once a year.
- Have portable fire extinguishers throughout the computer complex.
- Have all fire extinguishers checked once a year.
- No smoking in any computer areas.
- Have no water or drainage pipes running, inside or outside, along the ceiling, walls, or floors.
- Provide for a backup heating and cooling system for the computer center only.

- Locate the computer center in a low-traffic area.
- No parking is allowed next to the building.
- Avoid locating the computer site in a high-crime area or in the path of any radar scanning.
- No computer hardware shall be brought into or taken out of the computer area without the approval of the operations supervisor.

3. SOFTWARE AND DATA SECURITY

S7.3 SOFTWARE AND DATABASE SECURITY CONTROLS

Hardware security is pointless without the controls of the software that drives the computer systems. Database controls are required for their integrity and provide information for audit trails used for auditing the information processing systems. The security of software and data is as equally important as the hardware if not more important. Software and data can be moved to hardware at other locations and the processing can continue. Even the best hardware is useless without software or data. Many of the hardware security and controls also furnish a safety net for the software and data. The nature of these stored bits on tape and disks requires additional security and control that hardware security and control cannot provide.

S7.3.1 Software Security and Controls

Software security and controls are becoming more complex because of necessity. This necessity is driven by the vulnerability for more numerous methods of breaching software and data security. Therefore, software must have controls developed to provide security and must be used at all times.

Software and data endangerment comes from more than one source. The sources can be internal or external.

A. Human data entry

Human error is by far the most common, and it is internally generated. This cannot be totally eliminated but can be reduced by the following:

- Identification size. The longer the stream of numbers, the greater the chance for error. At one time, IBM felt it so important that they published a manual on the subject for customers.

- Less errors are incurred when the numbers are grouped in three or four number sets. The US government issues a social security number comprised of a nine-number code. It is grouped as a three-number set, a two-number set, and a four-number set.
- Check digit card-punching machines were once available to denote a number error or the transposing of numbers. Check digits should be used by computers systems as part of the input edit programming routine.
- Alpha characters can also assist miscoding and provide a larger selection than one number with a range of zero to nine.
- Have the coding identify something as part of the code.
- More firms are going to the telephone number as a code identifying the customer.

Comment:
Military equipment was issued numbers in sequence for a unified method for saving the taxpayer's money. A requisition for a 250-watt light bulb got an Army base a 23-ton battleship anchor.

B. Programming errors

Programming errors are the second largest source of software problems. Programs so large that groups of programmers are needed is a growing predicament—especially in the area of operating systems.

Some software is designed with built-in program protections. Other software protects systems data by editing the input. Security that uses programs to provide software protection is a good avenue of software security.

There are things that can be done to reduce this error rate.

1. Naming conventions

A list of names is provided by the project leader or lead programmer. The names used for given item elements are identified by a data dictionary. The data dictionary defines:

- The title of the data element.

- The size of the data element (now four is used for the year).
- Is the data element alpha, numeric, or alpha-numeric?
- What is the level of security? This is most helpful when defining what goes into what level of the database security. The data or database manager must define how many levels of security there are, and what the criteria are to be in each level.
- A program used list. These are programs that use the data element. The data elements are defined as input or output data.
- Authority list. This a list of: who can access the data, who can change the data value, and who can have the authority to remove the data element value.

2. Program debugging

This means going back to the program after several days and walking through it in detail. Today's structured or modular programming makes it a lot easier to perform this task. Set up test data to ensure that the data coming out is what it should be for the data going into the program. Call on end-users for test data material. Make use of the software compiler, which has a tracing utility program.

One person should be responsible for major test data. This should be the person most familiar with the intended operating system. Past data will identify uninspected input data. The expected results should be predetermined.

Any software that is being written or updated that affects monetary transactions and items of monetary value will be subject to computer auditors' reviews for the required controls. The auditors should have their test data confirm that the program meets the audit control needs. The auditors will run a program test before software is presented to operations for their acceptance. The auditors will be present when the program is first run by operations, and then again tested after the computer center's operation is completed.

3. Systems testing

The programming is far from being complete until the total operating system is a flawless operation. The testing should start with very simple test data. With precomputed results, monitor- or printer-formatted results should compare with the actual ones run.

As each level of testing is completed, more complex test data are used. The reason for this approach is that when too many programming errors appear, the correction process itself generates more errors. In some cases, it has been known to be so bad that the whole programming process had to be restarted.

Comment:

A teaching hospital in Northwest Ohio turned over a patient's account to a collection agency for ten dollars. The patient had paid over twelve hundred dollars to the hospital already, and wondered what the ten dollars was for and why they did not try to collect from him first? He wrote the CEO of the hospital about the problem. After a couple of months, he received a letter from the hospital controller with a check for ten dollars. The patient overpaid his bill by ten dollars. The programmer wrote the program so that after 90 days any number in the amount-due field was turned over to the collection agency. He/she was not old enough to have worked on an IBM 402. The 402 carried a credit ID by printing a CR in a one-character print field.

C. Other software problems

A smaller amount of software problems are lumped together. They consist of an occasional hardware problem and unauthorized accessing of software or data on the system. See Chapter 5.5—"Data Security"—in the manual for more information. There are some systems management guidelines that would help address the access problem, including:

- Authorized access to the system should be controlled at all times.
- Access method approved by the IS auditors.
- Bypassing security procedures should be restricted.
- Purchased security software should be installed by IT security personnel.
- The attempted security breach should sound an alarm with IT security. If possible, the access should be traced.

- All new software, regardless of the source, will be tested for any form of virus before it is loaded onto the system.
- Once a program has been written, tested, and received by computer operations, it is the sole property of operations, and no access to the program code is available online to the programmer.
- Any downloaded data that are not from a company source will be screened for virus.
- The maintenance of software security is an ongoing process.
- Do not rely on one line of defense for software security.

S7.3.2 Information Transmission

LANs, WANs, direct telephone dial-in, and the Internet have become information highways for data and software transmissions. There are needs for the encryption of transmitted data. Also, viruses have been known to be passed along these highways.

A. Guidelines to follow

There are some guidelines for pursuing the use of encryption. Access to a computer system that is capable of communicating can be a victim of another computer in any part of the world. The more transmitted information becomes a valuable commodity, the more it should be protected. There are computer hackers out there who are looking for challenges and the only reward they hope to obtain is to access a well-defended system. Therefore, it should be a policy for top management to not brag publicly about how impregnable their computer system is. It only offers a challenge for the uncounted number of hackers who would be willing to stay up nights to prove the company VIP was wrong.

B. Cost analysis

The cost must be compared to the benefit of the security system. The costs include the reduction of the system's rate of transmission, the cost of the system, time required for an IT person to police the system and protect the encryption key, etc.

C. Installation procedure

There is a sequence of events for introducing cryptography to information systems IT operation's unit:

- Select what must be protected.
- What is the quantity of the data and software to be protected?

- Between what communication locations will data be transmitted?
- What will be the communication media?
- Conduct a study of what is available. If time is pressing, contact the consultant that the vendor's customer may have used.
- Select a system.
- Test the system. To debug the system, enlist the aid of a known consultant.
- Configure the system.
- Convert to the system—after some testing has been done, move up to higher-level security.
- Have the system monitored by the information systems security person.

D. Security post-installation operations

After the security system has been installed, there are some concerns to maintaining the security system. The following concerns and recommendations should be addressed with the security system:

- Have the list of items approved for protection. Have the list continuously updated. Remove any items that are not needed.
- Have the physical levels of security defined.
- The system should be monitored during classified information transmission.
- Change the key often and at random intervals.
- Encrypt the data both in transmission and storage.
- Keep the unencrypted backup in a locked, fireproof safe. Two people will be required to access the safe, one with the key and the other with the combination. Every year, have the lock rekeyed or the combination changed.
- Segment messages being sent.
- Have regular security checks run on all employees who have access to any part of the security system. The reports will be sent to the audit and control head. He/she will make a copy of the reports for the information systems head in a double-sealed envelope.
- Keys or passwords are stored in a file safe in an encrypted format.
- Track data transmission to ensure that it is not being taped.
- A separate key will be assigned to each data resource that requires security.

- Keys should be changed randomly and frequently.
- Records of keys' users will be maintained.

4. DATABASE SECURITY

S7.4 DATABASE MANAGEMENT SECURITY

The information systems organization will contain an IT database unit. Depending on the organization structure, there may be a corporate data administrator at the same organizational level as the IS unit head. With this form of organization, the IT database unit will report to both the IS head and the corporate data administrator. The IT database unit will be part of the corporate data administrator's scope of responsibility. His/her interest is the total corporate data resource. He/she will devise the policies that govern the database operating procedures. The corporate data administrator will police his/her policies throughout the organization including the database applications that apply to IS operations. The following procedures are for operations that do not have a corporate data administrator. If there is one, he/she should review them for their approval.

S7.4.1 Requirements for Database Security

Database security is concerned with data safety and a protected operation of its database holdings. This concern is with normal operations and intrusions. These operations can come from within the company site or from external sources. Customers may be permitted to look at the inventory status of finished goods so that they can fulfill their own customers' needs. While the database is to serve its clients' needs, it has to assure the client that the available data are valid. These procedures are for the security of that data.

Any database system is vulnerable to misuse or security violations. The misuse of the database is mostly done by end-users, both at the company level and at the end-user work group data server level. At times, a programmer can misuse the database. That is why the programmer must follow procedures when working with a database for testing.

A. Database users

Users of the database will have levels of access to data their workstation, time window, and access password will allow. This is part of the database security system. The password will allow access to a given number of database files. The password will also identify which record's elements can:

- Be seen only.
- Be changed by permitted access to given data elements.
- Be removed.

B. Programmer's database access

Under normal use of the database, the programmer's user access will be the same as any other user of the database. The programmer may need to see more. The need to change or remove data by the programmer would normally be very restricted.

Programmers are required to get permission from the database head to off-load a part of the database. This off-loaded data will never be returned to the database. In cases of an emergency and under the direct supervision of the head of the IT database unit, database information can be uploaded into the system.

C. Safeguarding the database

To safeguard the system's database, certain precautions must be built into policies and/or procedures. The following are samples of the precautions:

- UPS backup for the system's computer and secondary data storage devices.
- Memory protection.
- Access control.
- Data encryption.
- Data storage redundancy.
- Application of software security controls.
- Provide audit trail of transactions.
- Continuous and random audits by the audit unit.
- Password protection.
- Security background checks of operating and database employees.
- Continuous monitoring for unusual activity that can come from within the firm or from an outside source.
- The database unit maintains a current database dictionary.
- Random testing for database accuracy.

Comment:

Spot inventory checks will reveal database accuracy. Beware of minus quantities of goods in stock recorded in the database. The database should flag any time a minus occurs in the quantity field, unless minus numbers can be expected.

A spot-check of a hospital's database revealed that there were empty beds, single-occupied beds, and some double-occupied beds. The control totals were correct, but not the patients' bed location data.

D. Data dictionary

The database unit will maintain data dictionaries. The information is essential for programming and controlling user access. As the need arises for new record file elements because of the development of new programs, the IT database unit will work closely with the program project leader. Naming conventions used by the programmers must agree with what is in use and new ones developed will require approval of the IT database unit.

The data dictionary contains the database schema, data conversion algorithms, and data element attributes. The data element characteristics found within a record will be identified and described. The data dictionary defines:

- The title of the data element.
- The size of the data element (now four is used for the year).
- Is the data element alpha, numeric, or alpha-numeric?
- What level of security will it be? The data or database manager must define how many levels of security there are and what criteria are required for each level.
- A program used list. These are programs that use the data element. The data elements are defined as input, output, or generated data elements.

- Authority list. This a list of: who can access the data, who can change the data value, and who has the authority to remove the data element value. The user ID and password to access the data will identify at what level the user can operate.

E. Database management system

The DBMS (database management system) is the software that is used to organize and access the database.

The interfacing between the user and the database is accomplished by logical and physical access paths. The schemas and subschemas are used to describe the database and its internal relationships. There is more than one type of database available. Each type is marketed and has advantages over the other depending on the application.

F. IT database unit responsibilities

The IT database unit is to work in concert with the IT programming unit in the development of naming conventions for new database elements. If there is a corporate data administrator, the IT database unit head will seek its policy guidance from him/her. The IT database head will report to the information systems head.

The unit's head supervises the IT database unit and is responsible for seeking annual budgeting for the operation of the unit, development of new technology, and maintenance of the database management systems operation. Operation duties of the IT database unit will be:

- Maintain the data dictionary.
- Safeguarding the database.
- Maintaining database management systems.
- Establish access control procedures.
- Maintain change logs. This is to document all changes made to the system, containing both new and old values.
- Monitor the structural integrity of the database system. Spot checking quantity value elements to ensure they are correct.
- User authentication is checked for correctness on a regular basis, to ensure that access no longer required has been removed.
- User cutoff. This procedure must be developed so that a user access can be denied at a moments notice from any IS management person or corporate security.

5. IS AUDITING

S7.5 AUDITING THE IT ENVIRONMENT

Most cases of computer fraud were discovered by accident before the advent of the concept of auditing corporate information systems. Most firms did not want the fraud to embarrass top management of the company. The computer fraud cases that were reported by the news media were only the tip of the iceberg. The hidden dangers of inefficient operations most often exceeded the cost of employee theft. Unsound operating procedures cost many firms more than their reported earnings. Inasmuch as most processing of information is by computers today, there is a need for auditing the process to avoid honest and dishonest losses. Most organizations have reached a point where they are computer dependent—this dependency has now gravitated from mainframe computer centers to the microcomputers found throughout the company.

The regulatory agencies throughout all levels of government have increased the types of information that firms must now collect, process, report, and store. Some of the reporting is now in the form of computer input data, and in the format that is specified. The changes of custody of data have shifted from hard copy to computer files and databases. The hard copy data documents that were audited by visual auditing have now become hidden in files and databases. The built-in safeguards that were included the manual procedures are now required of computer operations and data files.

New specialists that are a hybrid of accounting and information systems have come into demand. Computer programming skills are also a plus for this new specialist hybrid auditor. Management has the ultimate responsibility for involving auditors in the IT operations of the firm.

S7.5.1 Management Responsibility

Financial statements are issued with the management's endorsement that the information is genuine. These statements are generated by procedures that management has set down for their creation. Management must engage auditors to assist in meeting their mission that the controls incorporated in the computer accounting systems are valid. These auditors may be from the firm's external auditors or from their internal organization. Management should seek assistance for their concern of the reliability of computer accounting systems in a number of areas along with:

- Examining the conformity of internally generated computer financial statements with known established standards.

- Reviewing computer-generated reports with those that were done manually. Examine the validity of the information. Review current and future computer systems for their audit trails, reliability, and their built-in audit controls.

- Verifying that all IT controls are actually being employed by the accounting related systems.

- Auditing verification of capital assets, cash, in-process and finished goods inventory, supplies, etc.

Auditors are available in two forms—internal and external. There are advantages to the employment of both.

A. Internal IS auditors

Internal auditing is not a mandatory requirement for firms. Larger national firms have internal audit units. In growing numbers, firms have their own information systems auditing units, which is an internal control function for monitoring and confirming systems development programs are following audit policies. There is a concern of top management with the reliability of computer operations and the reports that are generated by the computers systems throughout the company.

Internal IS auditors have extended their activities into areas that have not existed before. They have extended their scope into areas that now require computer skills to perform their duties. The responsibilities that management requires of IS auditors is a much broader scope than what would be expected of external auditors. The IS auditors are concerned that everyday practices of IT operations, programming, and systems development are following audit policies. It is the responsibility of the internal IS auditors to monitor and test the systems that control the firm's resources and generate the reports for the management of the firm. The internal IS auditors will simplify the work required by the external auditors when they examine the firm's accounting practices.

B. External auditors

Annual reports are certified only by an external auditor. The internal auditors active in the management practices as part of the firm's operation cannot independently certify the annual report. This can be done only by an independent public accounting firm.

The external auditor evaluates the reliability of IT controls. The principal objective of its evaluation is to minimize the amount of detail auditing and confirmation of the validity of the IT financial reports. External auditors can make cost-effective analysis for systems development. They must confirm that the internal IS auditors were involved with the design, construction, and testing of new or revised systems. A testing criteria can be established that will apply to program software before it is declared operational and will satisfy the external auditor.

Audit firms enlist the services of qualified IT auditing specialists if they do not have their own staff. Audit firms have found it an increasing necessity to have their own IT auditors. These auditors will provide their expertise to the external auditing firm. They can also provide for a billable consulting service to their clients. This service can be for clients that do not have internal IT auditors or even ones that do have their own IT auditors.

After a careful study of the accounting practices, both manual and computer systems, the external auditors can legally certify the annual financial statement of the firm. The external auditors can certify other reports as needed, and provide on-call IT audit services as needed. The external auditors work for and represent the company. This is not the same situation as what is expected of government auditors.

C. Internal/external IT auditors

The firm can more easily do without the service of the internal IT auditor. The external auditor is a must if only to confirm the annual financial statement. There are advantages of having the two. The advantages are:

1. Money saved

    The work that the internal auditor provides is less than the hourly charge of an external IT auditor. The savings would be extended into the time it would take an external IT auditor to perform a task. This added time would be required because of the external IT auditor's lack of knowledge of the firm.

2. Availability

    The internal IT auditor has less time conflicts because he/she is a company employee. He/she serves only one employer. He/she could be available at a moment's notice. This is very important when an emergency occurs and his/her authority or service is required.

3. Company knowledge

   This company knowledge will also pay dividends in the form of the auditor's time and company employee's time saved. This time saved would be costs incurred with an external auditor.

4. Auditors' relationships

   The internal and external IT auditors can develop a working relationship. This relationship can pay dividends in the time saved by both parties. It can enhance the communications between the company and its auditors.

5. External IT auditors assistance

   The external IT auditor can be of assistance as an information source. They may be able to open doors at companies that could provide:

   - Solutions to the same problem.
   - Observations of operating systems.
   - Report formats.
   - Verification of vendor's hardware quality.
   - Verification of quality of brands of software.
   - IT auditing technology information.

6. Audit the internal IT auditors

   Management can be assured that a qualified IT auditor is looking over the shoulder of the internal IT auditor. If problems arise over an IT audit problem, the external IT auditor can clarify the problem and defend the internal IT auditor's actions. This can help avoid any collusion with the internal IT auditor and a second party for any improper acts. This should be an ongoing process to insure management that the internal IT auditor is doing all the correct things. It would be even better to have more than one external IT auditor work with the internal IT auditor. This would reduce the risk of any collusion between the internal IT auditor and the external IT auditor.

S7.5.2 IT Audit Functions

IT auditing is the process of performing audits within computer operations. This has been done with the principal computer operating system but now can be expanded to computer work groups and even freestanding computers. The auditing function can be divided into two main areas: operation procedure auditing and the financial audit.

A. Operation procedure IT audit

Operational procedure IT auditing is relatively new and has no legal, certifying, or licensing authorities. The bulk of operating procedure IT auditing is done by the internal IT auditors. With larger and more complex operations, the IT auditors can be counted in the dozens. With enough IT auditors, there can be specialization for different operation areas. Smaller firms may rely on one or two IT auditors. Firms that have no IT auditors should seek assistance from their CPA firm. If the CPA firm cannot provide assistance, they should provide a source for this kind of service. Today, there are more occasions for misuse of the firm's resources and outright theft with computers than ever before. Policies and procedures should be well documented and provided to each unit that has a part in the procedure process.

1. Information sources

There are some federal information processing standards that relate to information system. The standards are available from the National Technical Information Service, U.S. Department of Commerce, Springfield, VA 22161. The Federal Reserve district offices provide information to Federal Reserve banks. Information from them can be helpful to financial institutions. Different states publish IT standards manuals—a good source to contact would be the state's Department of Finance. Local colleges may also provide courses on the subject.

2. New and revised systems

When the IT systems unit is working on new or revised systems projects—actually, before they are undertaken—an IT auditor should be assigned as part of the project team. It is better to find an audit problem in its development stage than when the project is finished.

When the project starts, the IT auditor will have a file folder in which he/she will collect the following items:

- A copy of the document requesting the project and any attachments with it.

- Systems flowchart(s) and detailed subsystem(s) flowcharts.

- Sample input documents and/or digital input formats.
- A copy of the data dictionary.
- Descriptions of the hardware to be used.
- The location(s) of all the hardware.
- Data control procedures.
- What kind of UPS system will be used?
- Copies of the backup, recovery, and restart procedures.
- What software language will be used and what will its source be?
- Manual operating procedures.
- System operating procedures.
- Description of the physical security controls.
- Samples of test data used.

3. New and revised software

   When new or revised programs are in the process of being developed, the detailed flowcharts and other program information (e.g., report formats) should be made available to the IT auditor for his/her sign-off approval. The IT auditor will study the documentation to develop test data for the programs. This process also applies to turn-key systems software.

4. IT audit tests

   When an accounting system includes adequate controls that are applied consistently throughout the system process, there is a greater assurance that the correct controls are in place. The IT auditor will be present when the system is running with the test data provided by the IT auditor. The IT auditor will provide the data and oversee the process until the reports are generated for his/her approval.

5. Plant IT audit control traps

   This is when the IT auditor plants a trap to see if it will produce the expected results. An example would be to place an order for an item with a credit card number and leave off the expiration date. Another example would be to have an employee's fake time card placed in the system or a former employee's card. Then see what happens. There are many options for this kind of testing of the controls of a program or system.

Comment:

An IT auditor had his son planted as an IT audit control trap. The son was rated as being turned over to a collection agency by the auditor's mail order firm. The auditor was surprised that his son received an approved credit promotional mailing. An investigation followed, and to everyone's amazement, the warehouse was filling only bad credit–rated customer orders. It was caused by a programming error that was never checked. The company is no longer in business.

B. Financial IT audit

Financial auditing covers all procedures involved with producing financial statements. There are basic accounting rules that govern auditing. The scope of an audit covers all hardware and procedures used in the processing of financial data. Within the accounting profession there two major groups of standards that have been developed that affect the format of the financial statements for publicly held firms. They are the generally accepted auditing standards (GAAS) and the generally accepted accounting principles (GAAP). The CPA firm that the company employs has very little, if any, bearing on the IT auditing. Internal auditors are not required to follow the general accepted auditing standards in the process of their audits.

Computer financial controls became a major concern some time after the introduction of the third generation of computers. Therefore, there has not been enough time to develop internal IT audit standards. It is suggested the internal IT auditors seek guidance from the firm's CPA auditors. Communicating with the same standards will facilitate better information flow.

There are other standards. The two noted are for publicly held firms, which does not even cover a majority of institutions (e.g., sole proprietary firms, partnerships, nonprofit organization, and all the levels of government). The GAO (Government Accounting Office) has made inroads in this area. The basic thrust is that the financial IT audits will be under the guidance of the internal auditor head.

S7.5.3 Computer Control Objectives

The audit trail has been management's control guidebook. The computer systems can still follow the same concept. In some cases, it will provide management with financial information it could not afford or justify with manual forms of audit trails and manual systems. There is the consideration of the term *reasonable assurance.* This means that there is justifiable, but not absolute, confidence that the data is being protected and that the financial records are reliable. There are the IT controls that provide reasonable assurance that there exists a framework to maintain accuracy, completeness, and the reliability of the data.

The basic objectives of IT auditing are only a few items that encompass a vast amount of responsibility. The IT auditor's objectives are:

A. Fraud

   This covers monetary fraud or theft, information or material theft, and unauthorized use or sales of service. Fraud is committed mostly by people outside the company. It covers the misuse of credit cards—invasion of network systems to receive goods that are not paid for. The computer systems require better access controls to reduce this type of theft.

B. Embezzlement is the outright theft of company funds by all employee levels—from the CEO, CFO, and controllers to the hourly workers.

Comment:

A large mail order firm had an employee fraud problem with the output side of the computer. As orders were processed through the system, one copy of the shipping label and packing list was sent to the warehouse for shipping. The computer operator would substitute the name and address of the original document with one of his relatives. The items were shipped parcel post with no audit trail. The person placing the order would get a dunning notice later for non-payment.

Each year, top management makes the news when companies prosecute their embezzlers. No one knows the number of cases that did not make the news because the firm did not want the information to get out. The expected number of embezzlement cases that are never discovered far exceed the ones that are known.

> **Comment:**
>
> **The Wall Street Journal carried an article on March 26, 1996, page C1, titled "For Many Executives, Ethics Appear to Be a Write-off." It noted a study of 400 people (85% men) "that 47% of the top executives, 41% of the controllers, and 76% of the graduate-level business students they surveyed were willing to commit fraud by understating write-offs that cut into their companies profits." The study was by four business school professors and was printed in the February issue of the Journal of Business Ethics.**

One major problem with embezzlement is that it is often done by managers, who are the guardians of the firm's assets. This places the internal IT auditor at risk. He/she may be fired by some trumped up charges to protect the guilty. One thing that may help is to take advantage of the relationship with the CPA firm's IT auditor. Enlisting his/her advice may be helpful to the firm and to one's career.

C. Faulty systems design

This is the reason the internal IT auditor becomes involved with the design of new systems. See section 7.5.2—IT Audit Functions—and subsection A-2—New and Revised Systems—for more information. This addresses the developing system issue, but contributes almost nothing to the faulty system or why the system is being revised. The internal IT auditor can be of help with the problems that relate to his/her area of responsibility.

For current operating systems that are faulty, there can be several solutions. The solution choice depends on the severity of the problem and the quantity and quality of the systems staff. This is a management problem. The route to systems for too many is the promotion of a good programmer into a systems analyst. The company loses a good programmer and gains a poor systems analyst.

The route for the internal IT auditor is to inform his/her supervisor of the problem. This should be in the form of a memo, so it will be on file.

> ***Comment:***
>
> **An ASM (Association of Systems Management) survey conducted in 1985 showed that 26% of the systems people did not perform any computer programming before becoming an analyst. The estimate now indicates that more than 50% of the analysts were programmers with little or no training in the areas the analyst should receive.**

D. Faulty programming

Faulty programs are obvious with the proper controls in place. Faulty programs have been known to put companies out of business. This issue should be brought to the attention of the IT programming unit head. If it is a turn-key software problem the vendor will be required to be contacted. If the problem cannot be resolved by the vendor, an alternate processing method should be found. An interim manual procedure may be the solution until a new computer software is found.

E. Disaster problem

Disaster due to nature or man has to be reckoned with. Redundancy is a solution to resolve this problem, but not the only one. The internal IT auditor is responsible for providing policies and procedures to prevent this from happening. If need be, the CPA IT auditor may be officially contacted for advice and guidance with the policy and procedure problem. See section 7.2.1—Natural and Man-Made Disasters—for the procedures of this problem.

If the backup software and data are at another location in the same town, all could be lost in a major disaster. Three locations should be considered—especially with document-scanned data such as:

- The corporate charter.
- Titles to property.
- Patents.
- Copyrights.
- Bonds and other securities.

Microfilm is still an ideal way to back up hard copy. Microfilm that was made before World War II is still readable with today's hardware. It is almost impossible to find hardware that will read a computer tape or disk from the late 1950s. In addition, computer tapes do not last that long in digital form. For archival storage, microfilm is still the best and safest way to store documents long term.

For digital backup, always have two hardware units that can still read the data in file. The life span of digital data is longer than the life expectancy of the hardware. That is the reason to always have two units that read the data that is still stored. One data storage disk or tape life cycle can count on no less than two hardware life cycles because of rapid developments in hardware technology. Have two older reading units that will interface with a current system or have only one reading unit and a reciprocal agreement with another firm in the same general area of the country. Being in a nearby building is not as secure as being on the other side of the state.

6. IT AUDIT CONTROLS

S7.6 IT OPERATION AUDIT CONTROLS

With so many computer systems not working when they are installed, it is a relief to have a system operating with or without any form of controls. When time permits, the audit controls will have to be corrected or even installed. Often, there is no regard that it is critical to the success of the operating system until some months later. It is like a farmer who finally is able to get the tractor running to plow the field—he will get the brake problem fixed after the plowing is done. This is the same kind of thinking that often happens in the computer field.

The fact that there are no unified and accepted standards in the computer profession does not help the matter. There are independently operating groups that are trying to establish uniform criteria. The accounting profession—through their IT audit responsibilities—will more likely resolve the problem; necessity is the mother of invention. The internal auditor should seek guidance from their CPA firm and/or professional organization. The government may be of help as they have in the banking and IRS arenas. The major need is not faster computers, but a unified standard with which they will operate.

S7.6.1 Computer Reliability and Control

The internal IT auditor should develop a manual, with the CFO's blessing and support. The CPA IT auditor can be of help with guidance and any needed arm twisting to get the message across to the CFO of the importance of an internal IT audit guide manual. Before issuing such a document, it should be reviewed and approved by the CPA firm's IT auditors—they can make suggestions and get the CPA firm's stamp of approval. This will give it credence for top management support. The manual should not be too large to read and be understood by lay personnel. It is only a guide so that the IT units will have all of their oars in the water at the same time.

The IT auditor's manual will also save the internal IT auditor's time of repeating the same thing over and over again. It will save project teams the time of redoing systems design. Programmers will be guided as what to look for before the program is written and not after the IT auditor's test bombs the program or the software system.

It must be understood that no one control is reliable enough to resolve the firm's IT control. That is why the world's best-made car is so expensive and reliable; for one thing, it has three separate and independent braking systems because of the value placed on stopping. The reliability of controls can be accomplished by some redundancy. The factory may be going full blast and customers are happy, but the company can still go under because the computer system does not have the needed controls, unless management is more concerned with the net profit than gross sales.

> **Comment:**
> **A Midwest company did not know if it made or lost money for the year until seven months into the new year. Controls were not a major concern of their system.**

A. Controls

When controls are properly installed, they should provide assurance that standards will be met. This is confirmed when the IT auditor's test is run with the test data. Control can be the by-product of other operations. As an example, when workers are paid for piece work, take their total and compare it with the total production count.

Comment:

An Indiana firm, no longer in business, discovered that this comparison came out to be more than a million dollars a year. Another firm, in Michigan, discovered that this came to $2,800,000 a year.

With data entry now being done at workstations, the source of data can reduce input errors that happened with work group operators. Numbers can still be transposed or the wrong key pressed. With a central source for data entry, they also proved that the data will be verified. There are also batch and control totals to police the input. This is not available when a worker is also the operator. There should be control balances after each day's work or running totals to monitor. A lot of data entry editing controls are required with today's systems. Audit trails must be there to trace back to the source of the error.

Control functions come in three basic forms.

1. Preventive IT controls

   This is often done by redundancy of manual operation. An example would be data entry and data verification. Computer controls of this kind include editing input data, verifying batch counts, verifying quantity, etc.

2. Detection controls

   This can be manual or computer controlled. Verifying the signature on the back of a credit card is a manual control. After the machine reads the credit card number, the computer control permits the purchase or flags a credit overlimit.

3. Corrective controls

   This control is most often found in the IT operations area or workstation attached to the database. Measures often allow for the correction of items that were flagged by the detection control. An example of this would be a person's being over his/her credit limit for a purchase. The current balance is carried interactively to show the amount charged up to that point. The customer has a refund coming from a sizable purchase that was returned. The return credit processing is a done by a batch process system and will update all the accounts later that night. Corrective controls would allow the purchase by updating the current interactive account balance.

B. Reliability

Reliability is a gauge of the controls that are in place and working. Redundancy and comparison controls are all important to the reliability of the audit process. Data can be available from the database to compare or balance a control function. Controls are appropriate at key processing points. The internal IT auditor requires reliability of a system. To get it, he/she may have also play the role of the devil's advocate. The IT auditor's manual should stress items of concern for providing the controls to assure reliability:

1. Input editing

Input data to the system will be edited. Any abnormal data or missing data should rejected. The rejected data should be in a file and identified why the input was rejected. This will require a control person to review the input data and confirm what is correct.

2. Output controls

The computer has all kinds of opportunities with the resource information in the system. The output controls are both manual and computer generated. When writing payroll checks, the total number of checks should not exceed the number of people on the payroll. A manual system of check control is to keep track of the beginning and ending check numbers.

3. Adequate segregation of duties

The person should only do part of a process when the operation requires it. The worker doing piece work and getting paid by the number of items produced should not be the one to enter the data into the system. Nor should the person writing a requisition be writing the purchase order and acknowledging the amount received.

To reduce opportunity for theft, relatives may be segregated. An example would be a wife's approving her husband's expense account.

C. Application controls

Each application system does not require the same generic form of control. The internal IT auditor is concerned with the same basic area of controls, but not necessarily in the same fashion for each area. The areas of concern are:

1. Input controls

   The control of input will vary with its source. Method consideration for input controls are for:

   - Outside hard copy raw data.
   - Inside hard copy raw data.
   - Data entry from online LAN sources.
   - Bar code and manual data entry.
   - Scanned data input.
   - Captured data input from an outside source. This will require downloading to a freestanding system to screen for any virus.
   - Data received from IT transaction files.
   - Data from backup files.
   - Data from interactive databases.

2. Software controls

   Are IT-developed software, contracted software, and purchased turn-key systems providing the controls outlined in the IT auditor's control manual?

3. Output controls

   Output controls rely on both the computer system and manual procedures. Some of the output concerns cover:

   - The correct number of documents being produced.
   - Are the documents being received by the correct people?
   - Are access controls in place so that the correct online output is going to the correct source?
   - Are control counts being maintained on control documents?
   - Verification of modem access is being confirmed to ensure that the output is going to the correct party.
   - All unneeded output is properly disposed of and verification of the process.

4. Transmission controls

   The transmission control policies and procedures are being used for new systems and programming development and systems maintenance.

5. Personnel security

   All IT personnel and employees accessing the computer systems will require one of three levels of security clearance. The security level will be built into the password. In some cases, an employee may have need for more than one password. This will be determined by the size and complexity of the firm and the number of computer systems installed. The IT database unit will be assigned the task of providing passwords, and assigning the security level to the employees. They will verify that the criteria for the security level will be met. All IT personnel will require a password and a security clearance. The three levels and their security clearance requirements are:

   a. First level

      This is the lowest security level given to a person. This allows for the access of a given workstation within a given time window. The password will find in the data dictionary the allowable access to the database. The password will allow certain data input to be received.

      To qualify for this level, a retail credit check will be required along with a review of the person's personnel file.

   b. Second level

      This an upgrade from the first level. All IT personnel are required to have this level of security. Other people that would also need this level would be accounting personnel, work group leaders, and company security. The security clearance required for this level will be an extended background check through their high school years, and any military service. This would be the military equivalent of secret clearance. A battery of tests will be given to determine the personality of the person.

      These people will also receive passwords that will determine what they may access and what they may do with the information that is accessed. Their password will be changed at random times, no less than four times a year. These people will be bonded for no less than $250,000 each.

   c. Third level

      This is the highest level that can be given. This level has access to any and all files of data. Their access will be monitored as any other access is monitored. Their password will be changed weekly. The size of this group will be limited to the following personnel:

- The head of IS.
- The head of IT computer operations.
- All the internal IT auditors.
- The head of the IT database unit.
- The data administrator.
- The head of company security.

This level of security is the military security clearance equivalent of top secret. To receive this clearance, a background check will be run on each person and their immediate family. A complete background check will be done after the person has passed the battery of personnel tests. Each of these people will be bonded for no less than $1,000,000.

7. PC AUDITING

S7.7 PC SYSTEMS AUDITING

The internal IT auditor's major concern are the computers that are used for the firm's financial record keeping. These computers may be in the following forms: stand-alone desk-top, work group, and lap-top or notebook machines. With telecommunications ability, any of these machines may have the access and capabilities of changing financial data.

The IT asset manager will be of assistance to the internal IT auditor. He/she should be able to identify the end-users and locations of the computer hardware. The internal IT auditor can also be provided with a list of software that these computers should have. The IT asset manager and the internal IT auditors may be able to assist each other in the performance of their respective areas of responsibilities.

S7.7.1 IT Asset Management and IT Audit Coordination

There is a lot to be gained in the firm's behalf when the two areas coordinate their activities. The IT asset manager will provide the internal IT auditor with hardware and software asset listings. These listings will provide the type of each computer hardware system, its location, its listed software, and the person who is responsible for its operation. The list will be for all mainframe, mini-, and PCs. The listings and their revisions will be provided to the internal IT auditing staff on a continous bases. The internal IT auditors will be able to access the hardware and software databases at any time from their assigned microcomputers with their password.

The internal IT auditors will notify the IT asset manager of any computer that is not found in the location that it is reported to be in. Lap-top and notebook microcomputers will not have to meet this requirement. Laptop and notebook computers are not exempt from the internal IT auditors scrutiny. Any software found on any computer that is not on the software database list will also be reported to the IT asset manager. Any unauthorized data housed in the computer will be dealt with accordingly.

S7.7.2 Database Management and IT Audit Coordination

The internal IT auditors are concerned with the access of the IT databases by end-users of freestanding microcomputers. Any work group computer systems that have a gateway to access the IT database will also be the concern of the internal IT auditors and the database manager.

The IT database unit will provide the internal IT audit unit with copies of the data dictionaries and the schema and subschema. The internal IT audit unit will be informed of any pending changes that are to be made to the data dictionary and schema or subschema. From this information, the internal IT auditors will determine who may have access to which data elements. The type of access will also be determined by each data element. The kinds of access are: read only, read and change, and the ability to remove data elements. Each data element will have its security level identified. The internal IT auditors will also determine which passwords will be allowed to look at what information that is in the database.

Data dictionaries that do not apply to financial controls will be the responsibility of the IT database manager. A copy of these data dictionaries will be furnished to the internal IT unit.

Any disputes that arise over the access control of databases between the IT database manager and the head of the internal IT unit will be resolved by the data director. If there is no data director, the dispute will be resolved by the CFO. The company's CPA firm may be required to assist with the final decision.

There are other databases other than the IT databases in the company. The IT database manager may have concern of what is out there. Unless the other databases interact with his/her databases, there is little to be said by the IT database manager. He/she may be asked for advice or even direction by these other database operations. If there is a company data administrator, he/she will have the authority to be involved and control any of these databases. The internal IT auditors will keep the IT database manager informed of what information they may have need. The other databases are:

A. Stand-alone databases

   Personal databases that are residing in freestanding microcomputers and are not under the control of the IT database manager will still be accessible to the internal IT auditors, and whatever information needed will be documented. The existence of such databases and their contents will be reported by the internal IT auditors to the IT database manager and the data administrator.

B. Work group databases

   If the company has a data director, he/she will be consulted by the auditor before contacting the unit that has a work group system. The data administrator should be provided with a list of what type of data is handled by the work group system. If the company does not have a data administrator, the IT operations head may be of help if the work group has access to the IT database. The access may be via a gateway on their system. The person to contact next, whether or not the IT operations head has been of any help, is the IT asset manager. The asset manager will provide whatever hardware and software information there is about the work group computer system. The next step is to evaluate the information and than contact the work group head for an appointment to visit him/her.

   Work groups that have computer file servers will have databases or files. This data may be checked with the unit head. The unit head will provide file or database hard copy information to the internal IT auditor. If the files or database contains information that is of a financial nature, the unit head will provide whatever information the internal IT auditor will request. The internal IT auditor may not see the same professional database documentation that is found in the IT operations. If the unit head is uncooperative, the auditor will go to his/her superior who will contact the CFO about the problem.

S7.7.3 *Auditing New Systems and Programming Assignments*

When new or revised systems and/or programming is planned, the internal IT auditor unit will be provided a calendar of scheduled projects. The projects can be undertaken by information systems or end-user work groups. Information systems can be working on:

- Their own projects.
- Work group projects.
- Stand-alone computer projects.

Information systems may perform their own work or use contract systems analysts and/or programmers. They may have requests for bids (RFBs) for a total system packages or purchase turn-key systems.

Work groups may use the IS resources or perform their own projects. They may have requests for bids (RFBs) for systems and/or programming projects, or purchase turn-key systems. Any contract systems and/or programming will be done through IS. This assures end-users of quality work, proper monitoring, and uniform professional practices.

The internal IT auditors will select which systems or programming projects will require their attention. When a project that uses financial and/or asset data of the company is completed, it will require the internal IT auditor assigned to the project to examine it in detail. The project may be for IS, a stand-alone computer, or an end-user work group. The work may be done by IT personnel, end-user work groups, or vendors. Whoever performed the work will be required to have an internal IT auditor sign for its approval. The vendor may not be paid or a program may not be turned over for use until it receives the auditor's signed approval.

If the system application is a manual operation that uses financial and/or asset data of the company, it will require approval of a internal IT auditor before it is implemented. Before any programming that uses financial and/or asset data of the company can start, the system module for the program must be completed and approved by the internal IT auditor.

Software that uses financial and/or asset data of the company will require program flow or logic charts, input and output data elements to be defined, and any monitor screen displays or hard copy output layouts to be furnished to the auditor. The programmer will furnish whatever information the auditor may need. The auditor will be required to examine the source coding and program documentation, the data access controls, and the operations manual(s). The internal IT auditor will provide whatever test data may be required. The auditor will have to sign his/her approval before the program(s) are used with real files or database.

Turn-key systems that use financial and/or asset data of the company will require the internal IT auditors approval before the purchase or lease can be made. Any free-trial approval of any turn-key system cannot use any file or database that is under the control of the firm's IT, freestanding, or end-user computer system.

When systems and/or programs that use financial and/or asset data of the company are revised, they will be required to be certified as complying with the IT audit standards of the company. No revised system and/or program(s) will be put into service without an IT audit certification. To receive certification, the revisions will be subject to the same examination and testing by the internal IT auditors as for new projects. All revision documentation will be filed with the original documentation binder in the IT audit unit. All revised projects will be noted in the system or program logs maintained by the internal IT audit unit. The log will record the following information:

- The user of the system and/or program: IT, end-user, or freestanding system.
- The system and/or program titles.
- Who made the change(s)?
- What part of the system and/or program was changed?
- What were the changes?
- What date was the change information given to the IT audit unit?
- The date the changes were certified.
- Who certified the changes?

S7.7.4 Auditing IT Communications

Computers use varying forms of communications. The internal IT auditors have a vested interest with the transmission of financial and/or asset data of the company. These concerns have a level of legitimacy. The internal IT auditors are not expected to design or control this area of IT responsibility. They will be required to be assured that the controls are in place and working. The major forms of company data communications are:

A. Local area networks

Local area networks (LAN) are used primarily by work group microcomputer systems, and IT local area network systems. Work group computer systems employ a PC file server and attached PCs and/or work stations. The only major difference from PCs is that work stations usually do not have secondary access I/O devices such as: floppy drives, zip drives, jazz drives, or CD drives.

IT LAN servers use a main computer that contains files and/or database(s). The main computer can be a mainframe, mini-, or a PC. The units attached to the main computer can be: terminals (keyboard and monitor), workstations, or PCs.

Linkage between the computers is a system connection called hardwiring. Using simple telephone wire is called a twisted-pair network wiring system. Fiber optics has extended the boundaries of LAN systems and has reduced the ability to tap into the communication lines. It has an added feature when becoming wet—it will not short out as does the twisted pair. The drawback is that it cost somewhat more than using twisted pair wiring, although in many cases it has been worth the investment. For shorter LAN communications, wireless communication systems are available. They provide the simplicity of mobility of desktop microcomputers without having to do any rewiring. They do have a major drawback and that is that unauthorized taping of communications can be easily done. This system is not recommended for the transmission of financial and/or asset data of the company.

B. Wide area networks

The use of this form of transmission does not have the same level of LAN transmission security. Therefore, the transmission of financial and/or asset data of the company will require encryption. The company may lease line service or employee dial-up service for less often used transmissions. WANs can employ one or more of several transmission devices at a time. The transmission route for WAN communication can be over:

- Tested pair of wires.
- Fiberoptics.
- Coaxial cable.
- Satellite transmission.
- Microwave transmission.

C. Gateways

Gateways are devices that allow one LAN system to access another LAN system and/or a WAN system. Gateways will also allow one WAN system to access another WAN system. These are the communication systems employed by a company that are also a major concern to the internal IT auditors.

D. Modems

Modems that are installed in desk-top, lap-top, or notebook micro-computers can access computer systems that have a modem attached to their main server. Modems need a telephone service to be used. This is often employed when there is a distance problem with LAN network communications. Modem communications by telephone can be used by employees from their home or while traveling to access in-house computer systems from most anywhere in the world. This can be a serious concern for the internal IT auditor. There will be strict security controls maintained by IT security for this type of data transmission. The transmission of financial and/or asset data of the company will require encryption when modems are employed.

E. Internet

The Internet has provided for another source of WAN and some LAN communications. The major problem here is that anyone in the world can access the connected computer. This is also a major concern of the internal IT auditors. There will be strict security controls maintained by IT security for this type of data transmission. The transmission of financial and/or asset data of the company via the Internet will require encryption.

F. Data communication systems IT auditing

The auditor's concerns are focused on the ability to provide for an audit trail and to recognize areas of risks that occur with the transmission of financial and/or asset data of the company. The communication risks are identified as passive wire tapping or active wire tapping.

1. Passive wiretapping

   Passive wiretapping involves the illegal copying of data and may involve the copying of designs of new equipment, trade secrets, strategic planning material, along with financial and/or asset data of the company, etc.

   IT security will require the prevention of this data being downloaded by an intruder. There are options to prevent this from happening:

   • Using fiberoptics or coaxial cables transmission.

   • Employing encryption.

   • Intermixing different data transmissions.

2. Active wiretapping

This form of wiretapping can be discovered immediately or at a later time. This form of wiretapping can provide for a much greater security risk than the passive type. It is also much more complex. There are a whole host of options depending on the level of security needed and the communication media. It is suggested that the internal IT auditor meet with the IT security head for a multilevel security system. If the company does not have a communications security person of the caliber needed, the company's CPA firm could be contacted. Their IT audit unit may provide assistance for this service or recommend a vendor.

The internal IT auditor should discuss with the head of IT security the operational procedure controls needed. If information systems does not have a person of the caliber needed, the internal IT auditor should seek help from the company's CPA firm's IT auditors. The following items should be of concern of the firm's communication system:

1. Employee security checks

That all people should have the security checks for their level of communication responsibility.

2. Company security policy

The company should maintain an up-to-date security policy plan, have it in place and be administered and monitored.

3. Employee education

Employees should be educated as to the value of security to the company and their jobs. They should be free to provide the internal IT auditor with any information and not have the source revealed.

4. Documentation

Operation security consists of the following:

- Operation manuals.
- Current procedure manuals.
- Posted instruction information.

5. Systems logs

This may be maintained by a manual log. When needed, a computer operations log system is much better for continuous monitoring.

6. Real-time validation and editing

    Computer software is commercially available for this purpose.

7. Monitor any program changes

    The real documented system software should be compared with the operating system software at random times to ensure that the software in operation is what should be running.

To review the current communication status, the IT audit head should have a meeting discussing the issues that may concern them. The internal IT auditor and the IT affected unit heads should meet at regularly scheduled times. The number of meetings should be determined by the need, but no less than once a year. What will be reviewed may consist any of the following subjects:

• Network access controls.

• Data integrity.

• Any noticed changes to the log pattern.

• Will there be a need for any other item added to or deleted from the log?

• Has the data integrity been maintained?

• Are the network access systems working without any problems?

• Are there any problems with audit trails being maintained?

• Are system and software modifications being monitored?

• Is the password system being maintained properly?

• Are data dictionaries up to date?

• Any future plans for communication changes.

• Status of restart and recovery procedures.

S7.7.5 Auditing Stand-Alone Computer Operations

The stand-alone computer operations will most often have little or no IT audit attention required. The internal IT audit unit will have software and hardware information provided by the IT asset manager. The location of each unit will also be provided. This information may warrant the attention of the internal IT auditor. As an example, the scrap control department may have a PC with a modem and have database and spreadsheet software. This could be a stand-alone problem that would flag the attention of the internal IT audit unit.

All units may be checked along with IT asset manager's help, to identify what there is in the stand-alone desk-top, lap-top, or even notebook computers. The IT auditor is as concerned with the hardware and software property of the company as the IT asset manager. This is when they may be of help to each other.

The standard hardware, software, and data security should be maintained. Proper backup procedures are being followed, and no password is attached to any unit. Units that command the attention of the IT auditors are the ones that have financial and/or assist information. These units will be provided to the auditors as needed. The unit should follow all the procedures that are required of their IT operating and security procedures, along with procedures provided by the IT auditors.

If the stand-alone PC has access to computer systems via modem, what does it access? What is its password? Does it ever access the Internet? These are the types of things with which the IT auditor should be concerned. To simplify the process, the internal IT audit unit should have a checklist form to ask questions and document information. The form will be for your company's needs at that location. The form could be preprinted by the IT asset manager, listing the computer location, the hardware and software authorized, and the name of the user. The rest of the form would contain the standard questions the auditor would ask and a place to write the information. The form will not need to be limited to one page, but it should be the standard size of copy paper. The IT auditor should also access the computer to confirm what software and data are on the hard drive.

S7.7.6 Auditing Work Group Computer Operations

Work group systems will attract more attention to the internal IT auditor. The IT asset manager should be able to provide a computer printout of the hardware and software configuration that makes up the work group system.

The first thing the internal IT auditor will do is confirm that the hardware configuration at the site agrees with the report provided by the IT asset manager. The second item will be the confirmation of what software there is installed on the system. The site could call for a normal audit or for an involved study of the computer system. This will depend on the third item of concern—what files and/or databases there are at this location.

The work group system will have an IT audit study in accordance with the value the auditors place on the work group's priority security level. The items will be studied in accordance with the group's priority security level for the system.

A. Physical location

Is the site location adequate for the level of security that will be required? Is the location easily monitored by the security organization?

B. Physical security

The area will be secured when not in use. Is the file server in an area that provides more security than the rest of the system? Are there fire and intruder alarms? The alarm system should be monitored around the clock, and list of key people to be called in the event that an alarm goes off. The main microcomputer will have a UPS backup system. All other computer hardware will have power surge protection devices. Electric outlets for computer hardware will not be used for other devices.

C. Backup procedures

A fireproof safe should be available and used for data and software security. If need be, a second location will house a second set of software and data backup.

D. Operation log

A manual operation log will be maintained as to when backups were performed, when preventive maintenance was done, and when the main computer system was turned off or on. The operation log will be kept by the work group's key operator.

E. Input controls

What are the sources of the input? Each source of input will have its own input control procedures. There will be procedures to cover for virus protection from the input sources as needed.

F. Output control

Output controls are required for controlled documents. This will be in the form of manual and computer procedures. The location the report is sent to and/or the uploaded data sent will be recorded in the data operation log.

G. Separation of duties

Procedures will call for the separation of duties to avoid a conflict of interest. The separation of responsibilities will help ensure the integrity of the system.

H. The source of the system design

The following information is required about the work group system:

- How long has the work group been at its current site?
- Who developed the system?
- Who programmed it?
- When was its installation date?
- Who does the software maintenance?
- Who is the key operator?
- What kind of training is available for operators?
- Who has copies of the system and programming documentation? Where are they kept?
- What records are available of software maintenance?
- When was the last visit by an IT auditor recorded?

I. Operation documentation

What is the state of the following items:

- Key operator manual.
- Operator's manuals.
- The current unit's policy and procedure manual.
- Vendor documentation.
- Service manuals.

J. Planned changes

What if any planned computer changes are there in the near future? Are there any planned software upgrades? What is the life expectancy of the current system?

8. EXTERNAL ACCESS

S7.8 PC EXTERNAL ACCESS

The use of company hardware and/or software for personal use beyond the limits of a employee's assigned computer for their use is forbidden. To gain external access with a computer not assigned to an employee that is not for company business is forbidden. The use of personnel software for external access with portable computers assigned to an employee is forbidden.

S7.8.1 LAN Access Restrictions

LAN communications will be recorded for data backup and security. This information is available for computer failure and recovery procedures. The information is subject to review by the security and audit units. Any security and audit violations will be resolved by the respective units. Any unauthorized Internet or e-mail access via gateways is considered a breach of security. Any such breach of security will be recorded and dealt with by IT security management.

Any employee found to have conducted any improper activity will be notified in writing by their supervisor. The second time this occurs, the employee will receive a written notification and will be interviewed by their supervisor. A written report will be placed in the employee's personnel file. After a second report is placed in the employee's personnel file within a year of the last report, a meeting will be scheduled with the employee, their supervisor, and a member of the human resources department. A prepared form will be provided by the human resources/IT department which will be signed by the employee. This form is to put the employee on notice that if, within a year, a similar occurrence is repeated, the employee will be discharged. A copy of the form, also signed by the supervisor and the human resources agent, will be given to the employee. If this occurs again, the employee will be discharged and the standard IT procedures will be followed for discharging employees.

Any employee found to have conducted an immoral or an EEOC violation will be notified in writing by their supervisor. The first time this occurs, the employee will be interviewed by their supervisor and a member of the human resources department. A prepared letter will be provided by the human resources/IT department which will be signed by the employee. This letter is to put the employee on notice that the next time it is detected, he/she will be discharged. A copy of the letter will be given to the employee and a copy placed in their personnel file. If this occurs again, within a year, the employee will be discharged. If this employee has four occurrences of this practice over the course of their IT employment, they will be discharged. The standard IT procedures will be followed for discharging employees.

Illegal acts are grounds for discharge. The employee will have a meeting with their supervisor and the head of human resources. If the evidence supports the judgement that the employee be discharged, they will be discharged at that time. The standard IT procedures will be followed for discharging employees. If the employee is not to be discharged, the employee will be asked to step out of the office while the IT supervisor and the head of human resources resolve the issue. The employee will be called back in the office and be informed of the resolution.

S7.8.2 Internet Access Restrictions

Internet and e-mail activities will be monitored. This will be an informed policy. The company is held responsible for its employees actions and therefore has the amenable right to monitor the conduct of its employees. Employees with access to the Internet and/or e-mail will utilize this access for company transactions only.

Any downloading of data or program software from this access that is not authorized constitutes an improper act. Any employee found to have conducted any improper Internet and/or e-mail activity will be notified in writing by their supervisor. The second time this occurs, the employee will receive a written notification and will be interviewed by their supervisor. A written report will be placed in the employee's personnel file. After a second report is placed in the employee's personnel file within a year of the last report, a meeting will be scheduled with the employee, their supervisor, and a member of the human resources department. A prepared form will be provided by the human resources/IT department which will be signed by the employee. This form is to put the employee on notice that if, within a year, a similar occurrence is repeated, the employee will be discharged. A copy of the form, also signed by the supervisor and the human resources agent, will be given to the employee. If this occurs again, the employee will be discharged, and the standard IT procedures will be followed for discharging employees.

The employee requires permission to utilize the Internet or e-mail access. If the employee has unauthorized software to access the Internet or e-mail and has completed a external access procedure, he/she will be in violation of company policy. This rule also applies to portable computers that employees may take home. The first time this occurs, the employee will be interviewed by their supervisor. A prepared letter will be provided by an IT department manager which will be signed by the employee. This letter is to put the employee on notice that the next time it is detected, he/she will be discharged. A copy of the letter will be given to the employee and a copy placed in their personnel file. If this occurs again, within a year, the employee will be discharged. If this employee has four occurrences of this practice over the course of their IT employment, they will be discharged. The standard IT procedures will be followed for discharging employees.

Illegal acts are grounds for discharge. The employee will have a meeting with their supervisor and the head of human resources. If the evidence supports the requirement that the employee be discharged, they will be discharged at that time. The standard IT procedures will be followed for discharging employees. If the employee is not to be discharged, the employee will be asked to step out of the office while the IT supervisor and the head of human resources resolve the issue. The employee will be called back in the office and be informed of the resolution.

S7.8.3 Company Web Pages

Company web pages and their design will require the approval of the head of IT. There can be more than one web page. After a web page is in service, any screen changes will be cleared through one source appointed by the head of IT. The web page will only be used for the firm's business. Any infractions, such as unauthorized changes or activities, will not be tolerated and can be grounds for reprimand or dismissal.

Any interactive web page that allows input from the web will require close monitoring. There should be a firewall restricting input access to the microcomputer used. The computer used for the web page will be a stand-alone system and should not be attached to a LAN.

SUPPLEMENTAL ADDITIONS TO CHAPTER 7

S7.1.3 External Access

8. EXTERNAL ACCESS

S7.8 MICROCOMPUTER EXTERNAL ACCESS

S7.8.1 LAN Access Restrictions

S7.8.2 Internet Access Restrictions

S7.8.3 Company Web Pages

Chapter 8
IS HUMAN RESOURCE RETENTION

1. POLICY

S8.1 IS PERSONNEL POLICIES

The information systems operation requires the best available IT personnel to undertake projects, run operations, and perform other responsibilities. To accomplish these tasks, a company must be competitive with regard to hiring and retaining IT personnel. Management must provide policy support to make this happen.

> **Comment:**
>
> In 1997, *Computerworld* published "100 Best Places to Work in IS," a good resource for assisting with the development of IS personnel policies. Copies may be obtained ($3 each) from libraries, which can get reprints from Copyright Clearance Center, 27 Congress Street, Salem, MA 01970. 35-mm microfilm copies can be purchased directly from University Microfilm, Periodical Entry Dept., 300 Zeeb Road, Ann Arbor, MI 48106.

S8.1.1 IT Supplemental Personnel Policies

The information systems department will be provided with supplemental personnel policies that will permit it to compete in their area of the country for IT personnel. The recommended items that may be considered are:

A. Career guidance

When a person is being considered to join the IS organization, his/her future goals must be determined. His/her goals may change with time, but there must be a start. If the person fits within the firm's planned needs for five years, he/she will be considered to continue with the other hiring criteria screening. After the person has been hired and has completed his/her probation period, he/she will be given assistance with his/her career planning.

B. Education and training

After a person has joined the information systems organization, he/she will be provided with indoctrination education and technical training required for the position. There will be a lending library within the IT training unit that will have available: video tapes, CDs, self-teaching materials, books, magazines, and other text material. This material is to be used on the employee's own time. There will be unit circulation copies of magazines and other printed material that may be read on the job. After he/she has completed his/her pro-bationary period, new employees will have a company education re-imbursement opportunity. Education and training will be at three levels.

1. Job-related skills training

   Training for job-related requirements will be on the company's time and paid by the company. One of these courses will be a speed-reading course.

2. Personnel enrichment technical training

   Training for future technical considerations will be company paid, with half of the time on the company's time and half on the em-ployee's time.

3. Employee career education

   This will be on the employee's own time, but company reim-bursed at a graduated scale depending on grades received for each accredited course.

C. Salary

Salaries will be competitive with respect to the location of the com-pany. The same job in different cost-of-living areas may reflect salary differences. The salaries will be in the upper third for the region.

D. Working-at-home policy

Salaried employees may work at their home up to one half of the year. It will be up to the IT unit supervisor to determine the procedure involved.

E. Other work time arrangements

Flex time is permitted, with core time of no less than four hours per day. The core hours will be determined by the head of IS. Operation employees may work a compressed work week at the discretion of the IT operations units.

F. Benefits

The average benefits—including spousal and family benefits—must be in the upper third compared to the same positions within the region.

G. Sabbatical

After every five years of full-time service, employees will be allowed a one-year sabbatical. No salary will be drawn, but all benefits will be maintained. Sabbaticals will be approved for education, public volunteer works, or special stay-at-home endeavors.

H. IS personnel evaluation policy

The first evaluation will be at the midpoint of the probation period. The second one will be at the end of the probation period. The first evaluation will be two way. The employee will receive a unit/company evaluation form to complete, provided by his/her superior's own supervisor. The supervisor will have a standard IT evaluation form to review with the employee. The second evaluation will repeat the first, plus two or more co-workers will be asked to complete an evaluation form. If the person is a supervisor, all his/her employees will evaluate the supervisor. Two of the supervisor's co-workers that have the most interaction with the supervisor will be selected to evaluate him/her.

The second evaluation policy will be a model for all subsequent evaluations conducted. The next evaluation will be in six months, and after that on an annual basis. If there is a need by the employee for an evaluation, it will be granted within two weeks. No employee-granted evaluation may be conducted more than once a year. The results of the evaluation are finalized within five working days and the results presented to the employee and placed in his/her personnel file.

I. Monthly lunches

There will be a monthly luncheon where each employee is invited to attend. This will be a two-hour get-together paid for by the company. There will be an annual IS get-together. This will be conducted on a

Saturday, and all IS personnel not on duty are invited. The IS head will have an annual budget for these events.

S8.1.2 IS Communications

There will be a monthly IS newsletter published by the IS organization. The newsletter will be sent to all IS personnel, work group key operators, internal IT auditors and CPA IT auditors, all senior management, and anyone requesting a subscription. The newsletter will disseminate IS information such as:

- People who complete a course.
- Notices of class schedules.
- New promotions or job changes.
- New projects to be scheduled.
- Any personal news, unit news, etc.
- Work group news.
- Internal IT auditor news.
- Vendor news.
- Any company news of interest to the readers.
- A response letter from the IS head to questions that were placed in the suggestion box.

Comment:

The suggested policies and procedures in this book try to stay within the National EEOC constraints. There are state and local authorities that have their own equivalent of the National EEOC regulations. These regulations can also change. Therefore, if there is any concern about an innovative policy or procedure, it would be wise to consult the closest authority for a conformation ruling in writing. They are used to seeing employer violations and most likely would welcome an employer that wants to be fair and an upright leader of human rights. The system has its network of finding out who are the good people and who are the ones that are not reliable.

2. MANAGEMENT

S8.2 IT MANAGEMENT

One of the major problems facing IS management today is hiring and maintaining good employees. IS management can buy the best hardware and software and still have problems without good "peopleware." Good IT employees are the result of good IS management—and management needs more than just the job title. It takes good management to retain good employees, and bad employees likely will not leave unless they can find other bad IT management to hire them. Without a trained and contributing IT workforce, the CIO officer, IS director, or whatever the title, is in trouble. One easy solution for this level of management is to outsource the problem.

When foreign competition arrived in America, the companies first affected did not have a corner on the management market. Firms that were put out of business more often than not had poor management at the helm. Poor top managers tend to hire heads of IS that are mirror images of themselves. In this way, ineffective top management replicates poor IS management. The other problem is that good technicians are often promoted into supervisory positions based solely on their technical skills. This

> *Comment:*
>
> **A Michigan director of information systems had serious problems with his IS operation. He was looking for a systems manager. A candidate was being interviewed by the IS head and other management people. The IS head asked the candidate if he would be willing to come in at any hour of the day to work with inoperative programs that they were trying to run. The candidate replied that this would not be part of the job description of a systems manager. The information systems director responded by standing up and screaming that this is what he had been doing.**
>
> **Then there is a story about an Ohio CEO who was looking for a head of IS. When the candidates were interviewed, he/she sat in a chair that faced the CEO, whose desk was on a platform with spotlights pointed at the CEO.**

problem occurs in other areas—many hospitals, for example, have the same problems. It is a universal problem. Some firms have attempted to re-solve the issue with company-paid training. The promoted IT person often gets the job because of their technical skills and they know it, so it is still very important to them.

S8.2.1 IS Management Two-Way Communication

The IS head must educate and inform top management of the impor-tance of information systems operation and its people policy to the com-pany. There are ways of doing this, including the following:

- Enlist the assistance of the CPA accounting firm's IT auditing people. They can communicate to their superior any special needs or information to come from that direction.

- Put top management on the distribution list of the IS newsletter. There can be some soft-sell editorializing on the behalf of the IS organization. The newsletter can also report the success of train-ing and education programs provided as well as the status of IT operations to the industrial norm, which can flag good points of lower turnover, absenteeism, and down time compared to the norm for the same type of industry.

- Remember who is the head of IS and what skills are required to determine resources and the calendar time requirements needed to complete a project on time and within budget. One has to earn the reputation of completing projects on time and within budget, if provided the required support from top management.

- The IS head must act and communicate like other management professionals—not as technicians. This is especially important in the presence of other management people.

- Send clippings, with handwritten notes attached, to top manage-ment about published IT activities in their professional areas.

Downward communication occurs between IT management and tech-nical people. The IS head must still act and communicate as a manager, but he/she should also use his/her IT knowledge and vocabulary skills. IS is such a vast and complex area that no one person can master all facets of the profession. The IS head is concerned with his/her specialty of IT man-agement. Formal written communication, letters, announcements, and memos should be professional looking. Formal meetings with IT staff and/or vendors should be relaxed and somewhat formal.

The IS head will practice MBA (Management By walking Around) management style. He/she will informally stay in contact with all employees. This may mean saying hello to the second- and third-shift operations people or having a cup of coffee with a group of employees. The IS head will attend every annual outing and any invited monthly lunches. Rotate the lunches to avoid showing favoritism. The information systems newsletter will carry any response from the head of IS to questions placed in the IS suggestion box. The newsletter may carry a short column by the IS head as needed.

S8.2.2 Management Self-Improvement

The IS head should practice continuous self-improvement. This sets an example for the next level of IS management. The IS/IT management will find the time to do much more when properly trained. When taken, the training should never have anyone reporting to another attending the same program at the same time. Some suggestions to get more out of the same time and effort include:

A. Time management courses

The management will learn how to be better organized and use time more effectively.

B. Speed reading

An effective manager should be able to read 1,000 words a minute or better. Repeat the course if need be. The company should provide speed-reading courses. It is sometimes helpful to take a second course later from another source. There are also self-instruction speed-reading courses marketed. Another way to get more from your reading is to look at the table of contents and skip items that do not apply to the manager's interest. When you have to go someplace that requires waiting, take along things to read.

C. Management education

Take credit and non-credit courses for honing management skills. This can be supplemented with audio tapes (while driving or riding as a passenger) and videos. The IS head should spend more than half of his/her education time with materials other than IT technical education. The next level of IS management should spend 25 to 35% of their time with non-technical education.

D. Management IT technical training

Management's IT technical training should be geared to management- and supervisory-level education. There are quite a few technical books in print in addition to hundreds of periodicals in print. This is an effective way of obtaining technical education. There are some videos available that focus on microtechnical details. There are commercially available one- and two-day programs presented all over the country.

Comment:

CIO **is an excellent professional monthly publication for IT technical management and IS heads. Many people qualify to receive it free. Their address is CIO Communications Inc., 492 Old Connecticut Path, P.O. Box 9208, Framingham, MA 01701-9208. Subscriber Services (800) 788-4605, e-mail: denisep@cio.com. They have a web site: www.cio.com.**

Another recommended publication is *Computerworld.* **It is a weekly tabloid and an excellent source of what is happening in the IT world, along with management and technical articles. It is recommended for IT management, project managers, and senior systems personnel. Subscriptions are $48 per year and are available by calling (800) 343-6474. The web site can be reached at: www.computerworld.com.**

E. Trade shows

This is another source of IT technical information for IT management personnel. The latest and soon-to-be available hardware and software will be on display. There may also be vendor booths showcasing a variety of different services.

F. Networking

There is an informal source of networking with other IT management people. It is a two-way communication and more will be gained by both parties.

G. Employee feedback

Using the mosey-around management style will glean a lot of good feedback. Any information that is off the record will stay that way or it will stop any future information of that kind. Employee evaluation of their supervisors can be a good source of IT management evaluation. This will require careful handling of the feedback information received by senior IS management. Another source is questions or suggestions that may be dropped in suggestion boxes.

3. RECRUITING

S8.3 WHAT KIND OF PEOPLE?

The corporate culture and the people recruited should match. What would work for HP would not work at GM—the management and corporate culture are worlds apart. The people have to fit the firm. That might be a problem with keeping some firms from getting the best people. Those companies will deserve the people they can get. The recruiting of family members is not encouraged, because it can provide difficulties and create IT auditing problems.

S8.3.1 IT Talent Search

There are several sources for acquiring IT personnel. The first consideration to be made is what skills are required for the position. The sources will be determined by skill level required.

A. No IT skills required

There are several sources for people that have no IT skills. Education requirements are what high school graduates should have. These people may require some training after they are hired. The following list is in order of preference:

1. Company employee

Current company employees with proven work records.

2. High school graduate

Contact high school advisors for graduating or graduated students.

3. Local assistance

Contact heads of local minority organizations for candidates they would recommend.

4. Blind ad

Place a blind ad in the local newspapers.

B. Entry-level IT-trained candidate

These are people who have completed a two-year level IT degree program from an accredited institution. The following list is in order of preference:

1. IS employee

   IS organization employees's with proven work records.

2. Company employee

   Current company employees with proven work records.

3. Two-year IT graduate

   Contact college placement offices for students that have a grade point average of 3.0 or above and a 3.5 or above for their major. An official transcript of the student's grades and a résumé will be sent to the IS person assigned the recruiting task. IS will provide the advisors with a copy of the required format for the résumé. The résumés will be much easier to review and compare.

4. Blind ad

   Place a blind ad in the local newspapers requesting a letter. The letter should identify their credentials, which will be the same as the two-year degree applicant. After the letters have been received and reviewed, the ones that meet the criteria and have a passable typed letter will be sent an IT application form and self-addressed business-size envelope.

C. Entry-level college graduate

   These are people that have completed a four-year degree program from an accredited college. If an IT degree is required, it will be asked for; otherwise, a business degree or industrial engineering degree with two or more IT courses will qualify. A liberal arts degree and an IT minor will also be qualified. The following list is in order of preference:

1. IS employee

   IS organization employees with proven work records.

2. Company employee

   Current employees with proven work records.

3. Area colleges

   Contact college placement offices for students who have a grade point average of 3.0 or above and a 3.5 or above for any IT course work. An official transcript of the student's grades and a résumé will be sent to the IS person assigned the recruiting task. IS will provide the advisors with a copy of the required format instructions for the résumé. This will make the résumés easier to review and compare with others.

4. Internet recruiting

   Set up a web site to recruit entry-level employees.

5. Blind ad

   Place a blind ad in the local and regional newspapers requesting a letter. The letter should identify their credentials, which will be the same information as required by the two-year degree applicant. After the letters have been received and reviewed, the ones that meet the criteria and have a passable typed letter will be sent an IT application form and self-addressed business-size envelope.

D. Experienced IT skilled candidate

   This is when a special IT skilled person is required. The position should be well defined as far as what is expected. This is a risk of getting the right person for the position, and can be a very costly error to the firm. The following list is in order of preference:

1. IT promotion

   An IT internal promotion should be the very first consideration. IS organization employees with proven work records are an obvious choice. If the person falls short, he/she should not necessarily be ruled out. A person new to the company will have to be with the company for four to six months before he/she is productive. Then there is the likely factor that the new hire will not be around as long as the company person. When any plans are made for future hiring, preparations should be made for an internal selection. This will allow more time to groom the candidate for the position. With these two factors considered, it might be a much wiser choice for the internal selection.

2. Classified ad

   Advertise in *Computerworld* and be specific about requirements. This will not be a blind ad. Provide detailed information about the job, the company, the salary range and benefits, and the community. Approved applicants will receive an IT application form and cover letter. Others will receive a thank-you letter for applying.

   If the candidate is selected for an interview, all expenses will be paid by the company. If the candidate is selected to be hired, there will be a return visit with the spouse paid by the firm. The second visit will last two to three days. The first day, both the candidate and the spouse will be shown the area, and all meals will be paid for by the company. The escorted tour will include the highlights of the area and special interests such as golf, private clubs, tennis, boating, cultural opportunities, etc. The following day, the spouse will be given a tour of his/her interest. If the spouse will be seeking employment, he/she will meet a person from the personnel office, who will provide information and assistance with locating a job within a commuting distance from their possible home site location.

Also note in the ad that the firm will pay for all moving expenses and provide realtors' fee for selling their current home. There will be an expense account provided for local living expenses: lodging, restaurant meals, clothes maintenance, and furniture storage. The living expenses will be covered for four months or until they have purchased or rented a place to live. When their furniture is shipped, it will paid for by the company. There will be a move-in bonus (to pay for cleaning, new draperies, etc) of 3% of the starting salary. The spouse will be assisted in finding a local professional job, and if placement fees are required the company will pay one half of the fee. If the employee has children, the nursery care will be paid for while the spouse is seeking a job.

3. Search firm

There should be a partnership between the recruiting firm and the hiring company. Settle for one good search firm. Too often, a person will use more than one firm and more than one résumé copy will be received. A good placement firm should provide the right person. It may take anywhere from 90 to 120 days to come up with the right candidate. The company picks up the placement fee of 10 to 25% of the starting salary. If the placement firm recruits the same person placed within five years, the firm will never be used again. This notice will be sent to the firm in writing.

The interview and moving benefits program will be that of the placed ad procedure. The only difference will be that one-half of the placement fee will be withheld from the salary if the person leaves on their own within 18 months. If the person is fired, the company has the option to withhold any and all of the placement fee paid by the company.

8.3.2 Selection Process Procedure

The selection process procedure requires reference checking and a battery of psychological testing, followed by a healthy dose of interviewing. Properly selected employees require less training, respond better to guidance, and are a better fit for the position selected and the corporate culture. There are three major devices for confirming that the best candidate has been found for the position: certifying personnel histories, psychological testing, and interviews.

The IT résumé format and the IT application form are the preliminary search procedures. Both are designed to start comparing people that have reached this stage of the search procedure. The search is not completed until the right person has been selected and has been put on the company payroll. The following are the next tasks of the selection process procedure:

A. Candidate ranking

The IT application forms with the attached resumes will be ranked by a committee. The name and address will not show on the copies—an ID number will identify the person. A committee will rank the applicants independently of each other. The criteria for the ranking will be weighted and totaled for each applicant. The documents will be given

> ### Comment:
>
> **A person's name may identify the applicant's nationality and gender. The address may distinguish ethnic neighborhoods. This provides for an audit trail for an EEOC inspection.**

to the IT-assigned recruiting person. The rankings will be averaged and placed in order of the ranking scores.

The cutoff will have to meet a predetermined total IT application score. The score will be determined by the manager having the position to be filled and approved by his/her superior. The people that have not passed the cut-off point will have their applications placed in a file and held for one year. After that, they will be placed in an inactive file.

After the candidates have been selected, the ones that have passed will be sent a letter with a follow-up telephone call confirming their mutual interest in each other. A ranking list will be made by the IT-assigned recruiting person. The people that did not make the grade will be sent a form letter informing them of the decision. They will also be informed that their résumés will be held in an active file for future reference, and they will be thanked for applying for the position.

B. Reference checking

The degree of background checking of the candidate will be determined by the security level required for the position. If there is any possibility that the candidate may be considered for a promotion within three years, the promotion position's security level will be used. See Chapter 7, Computer Security, Audit, and Control, section 7.6.1 *Computer Reliability and Controls,* C. Application controls, 5. Personnel security. All candidates will have all but their last place of employment verified. The verification will consist of starting dates and job titles and ending dates and job titles. The current place of employment will be confirmed. The candidate will bring a copy of his/her last pay stub, or bank check deposit when coming for the psychological testing and the interviews. This verification will be done before the testing process starts.

C. Psychological testing

Unless the firm has a person authorized to buy copies of the tests listed in *Tests in Print* and knows which tests are the best for the position and match with the corporate culture, an outside testing psychologist with a PhD should be used. The psychologist should be able to screen potential employees and rank order them.

D. The interviews

After a candidate's psychological testing is finalized, the results will be faxed to the IT head or IT unit head. The candidate will have a folder that will at this point contain his/her:

- Job application letter.
- Résumé.
- IT application form.
- Reference checking results.
- Other background checking information.
- The candidate's psychological testing results.

The candidate will be picked up after the psychological testing and taken to lunch. After lunch, he/she will be taken on a tour of the company and IS department tour. After the tour, he/she will be interviewed. The copy of the candidates folder will be passed on to each interviewer to review. The interviewer will be provided with a list of structured questions to ask. There will be room on the form to list questions the interviewer may want to ask and take notes. The folder will be passed on to the next interviewer before the candidate arrives for their interview. Please refer to the main volume, Chapter 12—IS HUMAN RESOURCE MANAGEMENT, section 12.5, Employment Interview—for interviewing procedures. Each interviewer will finalize his/her notes. A form will be used for the traits needed for the job and the weighted value for each trait. The interviewer will tally the total points for each candidate and a copy of this information will be sent to the IS head or the IT unit head that is coordinating the process from this point.

S8.3.3 *The Final Selection*

The person coordinating the process will tally all the interviewer's points to come up with a total for each candidate. The results will be very confidential until all the candidates have been selected. The interviewing process will be called to a halt when the person coordinating the process feels there is a large enough qualifying pool to stop the interviewing process. The people not yet interviewed will be sent a letter informing them of the delay. The people interviewed will be sent a thank-you letter. Both types of letters will be sent by the person coordinating the process.

All the people who did the interviewing will convene for a meeting to discuss the candidates. Each candidate will be discussed in random order. There will be a recording made of the meeting for future reference and an EEOC audit trail. Minutes of each candidate's discussion will be typed and placed into their respective folder. A vote will be taken on the ranking of candidates, after which the person coordinating the process will reveal the average ranking of each candidate submitted by the interviewers. If there are the same rankings in both cases, the first-choice candidate will be selected, then the second and third choice.

The selected candidate will be called with the news. He/she will be asked for a return trip and to bring his/her spouse along, if there is one. The return trip will be arranged. The visit will last from two to three days; this will allow for tours of available housing and to meet the area's citizens at the local country club or other locations. Any information about the area and company will be supplied if requested. The good points about the area and company will be stressed. The person or couple will have a luncheon meeting with one or more of the company's senior management.

The spouse will meet with the company psychologist for a luncheon chat about job opportunities in the area or volunteer work. The spouse will be provided with job opportunity information if requested. He/she will be assisted with any job hunting if requested. Questions about schooling if there are any school-aged children will be supplied if requested. The spouse will be asked if he/she has any reservations about moving to the area. He/she will be informed about the high regard the company has for his/her spouse.

The company psychologist will telephone the person coordinating the process and provide an opinion about the spouse (e.g., whether he/she likes the area and will fit in with area and the corporate culture. Also, if he/she is a stable person and will not present the other spouse with any problems that would be a distraction). If there are any last-minute problems, the person will be sent off with the information that there will be a need for a meeting to make an offer in writing. Otherwise, a contract spelling out the details will be presented at the farewell dinner. If the person signs it, he/she is hired.

S8.3.4 The New Employee

The new employee will be greeted in the lobby and escorted to his/her office area. There will be coffee and rolls delivered, so all personnel in the area can greet the new person. Then he/she will be taken to the human resource department to complete paperwork and to watch an orientation video. The person will be presented a packet of company information that he/she may not have already received. He/she will be escorted back to his/her area. He/she will be invited to the department's monthly luncheon, after which he/she will meet with the IS head, followed by each IT unit head. After work, if he/she needs a lift home, someone will take them to his/her residence.

The next day, he/she will meet with his/her supervisor and discuss the planned activities. He/she will be asked if he/she would like to have a mentor. The supervisor cannot be a mentor. If the employee has no one in mind for a mentor, he/she will be assigned a mentor. Anyone selected as a mentor will be on a trial basis. After two months, he/she may select a new mentor.

The rest of the week will be meetings with all new people—the people will all be wearing name tags so the new person is not overwhelmed with new names. There will be a lot of information to read about IS policies and procedures, along with any vendor material. The person will not be left to shift on his/her own for coffee or lunch for the first week or two. He/she will be informed about the probation period. It will be over before he/she should sign for a new house. The probation period is for his/her and the company's benefit.

4. CAREER PLANNING AND RETENTION

S8.4 IT CAREER PLANNING

Money alone is not a solution for retaining IT employees. The IT person is attuned to the job market—he/she can read about which are the better companies to work for and what these firms have to offer. The people who are not good performers know they cannot find a better place to work, so they stay. However, these workers will most likely have a higher absenteeism. The turnover occurs with the employer's best people. The 80-20 rule applies here and indicates that 20% of the workers do 80% of the work. With a 10% turnover, the firm most likely is losing people who are doing 40% of the work.

> *Comment:*
>
> **Wayne County General Hospital between Ann Arbor and Detroit, Michigan, was a county teaching hospital. It had 2,700 employees, the bulk of which was the nursing staff. There was a study conducted a few years ago, before it closed, to find out what was wrong with nurse staffing that was causing a high turnover and absenteeism problem. The study revealed that the RNs had the high turnover and the LPNs had a lot of absenteeism.**
>
> **Absenteeism was so prevalent that people were taking time off work even when they had run out of vacation and sick time. The unpaid wages came to enough dollars a month that county budget people allowed the line-item nursing count be expanded and still be within budget and not re-duce nursing care levels.**
>
> **The county hospital was not a popular place to work. None of the top management had any administrative training and did not seem to want any. The union management was better educated in this area, including one union VP with**

an MBA. The problem was that the LPNs made a few hundred dollars a year less than the nurses and received the highest pay in the area. The registered nurses' pay was not competitive. They were more professional and felt obligated to come to work, until they found another job.

No one solution will change things overnight. This requires strategic management planning. Management must adjust its sails when the wind changes and steer a proactive course. The IT wind has changed, along with a changing nation. There are numerous stories of people trading high-paying jobs for a better life.

Comment:

The June 15th, 1998, issue of *Informationweek* noted on page 14, "Career Conundrum," that "about 40% of people working in IT would major in either education or another nontechnical subject if they could go back to college." This was from a survey from George Mason University and the Potomac Knowledgeway. The article went on to say "89% said they would stay with an employer that paid for their education."

The publication is one of the best-written IT magazines published today for IT management. Their subscription number is (800) 292-3642. They can be found at www.informationweek.com/educalhot/.

The reason Scott Adams' Dilbert cartoon is so popular is that truth is stranger than fiction. The characters mirror life where the readers work and often where they used to work. What IT people need and want is to have a place they look forward to coming to work. The following will present some ideas that have worked and are working.

Comment:

A family-controlled company in Indiana had three consulting firms come in one at a time. They all had the same solution to the problem: get rid of the management. Do you know the statistical probability of getting three honest consulting firms in a row?

Employee career planning and retention have a very high correlation. The more the firm cares about an employee's career, the more the same employee wants to stay with the firm. What it costs to help an IT employee is less than the 10% turnover rate it costs the company. Have your cost accountants look at it to justify it.

S8.4.1 IT Career Planning

One of the single most important items to young or middle-aged employees is their career. Career counseling is better done by a mentor or the IT training unit career advisor than a supervisor. The person can open up the way he/she really wants. Not all people want to go the management route—besides, not all IT people would be ready for management for some time if ever. Why not climb a technical ladder? Look at the costs for consultants in high-tech software, communications, database, etc. An IT person can develop and climb the technical ladder if that is what he/she wants.

The IT advisor will have to get management's and the employee's permission to look at his/her personnel folder. This will include performance reviews, psychological test scores, and education and training to date. With this information, the IT employee will have to face what he/she needs for planning his/her career. Not everyone wants to be a CIO, not even some of the CIOs. He/she should have a five-year goal and some later goal that he/she hopes to achieve before he/she retires.

A plan will specify what is needed to achieve that first goal. The last goal may provide a general direction, but it can change more than once during one's career. What has to be placed on one side of the balance scale is the first objective. This side of the scale will contain the requirements for the objective. The other side will contain the employee's assets toward meeting the requirement. If the scale does not balance, there are not enough met requirements to accomplish the first objective. So the next task is to list the items needed.

The items will be listed by the advisor along with the time needed to accomplish each task. The tasks that can be run in parallel will be noted. When all the tasks have been identified, a PERT chart will be drawn. A copy of the flowchart will be made for the employee. The original will be put in the employee's career planning folder and kept by the advisor. This will denote that the objective will require this minimum of calendar time. This does not allow for any slippage. Slippage can occur when a given class is needed and not available. When all the information is satisfied for the needs and laid out on the PERT chart, the objective date will be identified. For PERT chart information, see PERT charts—Chapter 14-29 in the main volume.

The listed required task items will be identified and when needed to be accomplished. The source for the task items can come from a whole host of sources:

- IT training classes.
- Company training classes.
- Non-credit short course available by vendors or local schools.
- Credit classes.
- Degree programs.
- Toastmasters for speaking improvement.
- Correspondence courses.
- Online or Internet IT course.
- Books to read.
- Videos and cassette tapes available from the IT training unit and local library.
- Printed handouts.
- Lectures to attend.
- Social skills development programs.
- Self-learning IT tutorials.
- Speed-reading instruction programs.

The employee will be furnished information on how to plot out a Gantt chart from the PERT chart. A Gantt chart will be made of his/her task items for a five-year time span. The five-year mark is a reasonable span to set one's sights on. See the main volume for Gantt chart, Chapter 19-29. The Gantt chart should be posted on the wall in his/her home so it is seen every day. One or two times a year, or as needed, he/she should visit the career planner to update progress or reset their goals. The career advisor will also receive a copy of the Gantt chart and update or review it with the IT employee.

After a goal has been met, the IT employee will be asked if he/she wants to set another goal—even if it is the ultimate goal. If there is a new goal, the process will be repeated. With the completion of the goal, the advisor will take the IT employee out for an extended lunch. The employee will be given a pen with his/her name and the year engraved on it. The lunch fee and cost of the pen will be paid out of the career planning budget. After the pen has been presented, a champagne toast will be made to the IT employee for a job well done.

S8.4.2 Retention Planning

To begin the planning phase, get a reprint of the February 9, 1998, copy of *Computerworld*. The article to read is "Retention Getters: The 25 Companies That Excel at IT Retention" (page 82).

> ***Comment:***
>
> **At the top of the list is Xerox, for which this writer worked as a systems analyst. One given assignment was to write a textbook on inventory control. This text was part of a training package of books on the various functional areas of the business to be given to the new hire sales force. The requirement of the book was that the reader could stop at any point and the information read would be usable. The systems analyst was given three months to write the book, given a liberal expense account, and told to go home and write. Xerox has spent time and effort to be at the top of the list, but being at the top was not their primary objective!**

The article listed IT organizations that had less than a 2% 1996 IT personnel turnover. Two items listed that all firms had flexible work hours and zero layoffs. The other items listed were astounding. The article is a required reading for any CIO or IT manager that wants to have a better operation. Some managers keep things in a turmoil and inform management that they are the only ones that can keep things under control as a method of job security.

A plan must be devised based on a cost study of what the current IT loss factors are. The labor costs should include the company-paid benefits. The loss factors can be:

- IT turnover.
- IT absenteeism.
- Feet dragging by programmers and systems people.
- Time wasted on not doing things right the first time.
- Overtime pay.
- Errors made by people operating computer equipment without proper manuals or no manuals.
- New system failure costs for the information systems department and the end-user.
- Costs because of late and/or poor maintenance.
- Costs of late systems installation.
- Costs because of poor reading skills of operational personnel.
- Costs because of poor or no documentation.
- Improper planning costs.
- Employee sabotage.

After the total cost is computed, there are still some unaccounted items. The cost will be compared to what a new IS personnel policy costs. Do not expect a 100% return on investment the first year. If top management does not buy it, outsource all of the IT units to a firm that can and will do what is really needed.

The proposed IT personnel policies are a good start. The next part is to be realistic on what resources and calendar time is required to do a project. Plug contingencies into problem areas and then add in a final contingency for the total. If you meet the deadline, the IT people will not be exhausted. Have a party and celebrate the completion of the project.

Training is what people want. The IT training unit should not be the IT elephant graveyard. Take a survey of what the IT people want the most. Allow for 10 items in rank order. Do not provide a list to be checked off—it is extra work but it will be worth it. Provide the instructions, which include using a word processor to list the items so that no one person can be identified. The lists will be placed into a sealed box that will not be opened until after everyone has presented their selection. Run the same survey with IT people who have left the company, if possible. The responses will be placed into a postage-paid return envelope.

Take the information and rank order the responses and do not be surprised what is discovered. Compare this with other job satisfaction surveys, such as the *Computerworld* surveys. Base an action plan on the responses. Look at the cost for each item. Start at the top of the list and accumulate the cost as the list works its way down. When an acceptable cost is reached, compare it with costs of what the operation costs are now. All the items need not be installed at the same time. Inform the IT people what is going on. One of the major complaints has been that management has kept them in the dark about information.

Money alone cannot solve the IT problems any more than all the money spent by government on social welfare programs. What may be expected are some of the following:

- Performance bonuses.
- Desire for flex time.
- Suggestion boxes.
- Educational and training opportunities.
- More money.
- Be more informed about management plans.
- Opportunity for promotions.
- A better working environment.
- Career planning opportunities.
- Family benefits.

5. EMPLOYEE COMPENSATION

S8.5 IT PAY

IT pay, in comparison to other jobs in the company, is considered high; however, it can be low for several reasons. One reason is that the IS head may not be making enough himself/herself and will not have someone reporting to them that makes more. Another reason is that some industries pay more than others, so people change to industries that pay more.

Pay is not the major concern for IT people. Depending on which survey one is looking at, the importance of salary may vary. A ballpark figure places it about fifth in necessities an IT person is looking for in a job. The pay in one firm may be high for the industry they are in, but they are frugal when it comes to company benefits.

S8.5.1 Determining IT Pay

There is a universal procedure for performing wage surveys. A consultant that does IT wage studies should be retained. This avoids the internal conflicts that can arise and have been known to occur with IT salary surveys. Consultants will render unbiased reports. They will also have the credibility to support their findings. It is helpful to also have the consultant collect data on cost-of-benefits packages.

Before calling on the consultant, have all the job descriptions well defined and titled properly. This will save time and money. Do not provide any current salary or benefit information. Part of what the consultants should provide the firm is comparable salaries for all the jobs within the IS organization. The organizational structure and staffing levels will be needed to assist with the IT management salaries. The consultant should have some idea as to the hardware complexity and total number of people working within IS. When presented with the results of their study, it will then be safe to reveal the internal pay and benefit scale of IS. The other reason for not providing the information at the start is to convince top management that the consultants did not know what the internal pay scale of IS was to effect the consultants end results. This information will help the consultants rectify any major pay difference in any of the job positions.

The next step is to determine what percentile level top management is willing to agree with. To be competitive, the pay scale should not be any lower than the upper third for the geographic region. This is what was recommended in IT supplemental personnel policies, and is a top management decision. It may not be resolved until the planning is done for the next budget year. If funds are available, problem areas may require attention now.

S8.5.2 IT Benefits Package

The consultant's report will provide the benefit amounts paid by other firms. The IT supplemental personnel policies recommended amount was the average benefits, spousal and family, to be within the upper third of the region. This is a top management decision. This may be more of a problem to correct than the salary issue, because benefit programs are geared to the company as a whole.

One solution is to outsource the IS operation and have them put into place an attractive salary and compensation package. The other approach would be for the company to put into place a "cafeteria"-style benefits program. The information systems unit could very easily have the larger dollar amount needed without any problems. The other solution would be to raise the salaries even more so that the two together would be what is needed.

The ultimate solution is to have a cafeteria plan. It would provide an equal amount of money for each employee at the same job level. Each employee would select what would be best for them. Selections that an employee may choose from include:

- Life insurance.
- Medical plan with options for dental and optical.
- Company-matching 401K plan.
- Stock purchase options.
- Subsidized child care.
- Profit-sharing.
- Paid membership to clubs or organizations.
- Extra vacation days.
- Tuition reimbursement.
- Paid book and publication subscriptions.

6. IT PERSONNEL DEVELOPMENT

S8.6 IT EDUCATION AND TRAINING

The information systems training unit will report to the head of information systems. The IT training unit will be a resource center for IT education, training, and personnel. It will also provide end-user training. The center will maintain a library of educational resources, and will assist IT personnel with employee development and career planning. The training unit will be staffed for night use of the library resources and class instruction.

S8.6.1 IT Library

The IT library will have publications, audio-visual material, and learning centers. The individual learning centers will provide for multimedia computers, video and slide viewing, speed-reading programs, and audio tapes. The material will be available to be used in the library or checked out.

Comment:

Capitol College in Laurel, MD, is now providing long-distance education. Interactive software known as Internet-based higher education community powers Capitol's on-line college. Degree programs online include MS degrees in Systems Management and Telecommunications Management. Fall 1998 will have an MS degree program in Electronic Commerce Management. Also available online are BS degree programs in: Software Engineering, Software and Internet Applications, and Computer Engineering. Capitol College is a fully accredited institution serving degree and non-credit programs on high technology and management instruction. More information is available from: ken@capitol-college.edu, hhtp://www.capitol-college.edu or (800) 950-1992. Because of the demand, there are more institutions offering long-distance learning in IT and management than ever before.

A. Video material

The videos may be checked out or watched in the library centers. The video selection will range from introductory to advanced subjects, and include self-paced program learning videos.

B. Books

There will be an extensive selection of books. Some more popular books will be checked out for one week while the rest will be for two or more weeks. For books that have been checked out, there will be a waiting list of first come first served. Any books returned late will be fined twenty-five cents per work day. This money will be put into an employee library fund for buying non-technical publications.

C. Magazine library

A wide selection of magazines, including *Computerweek* and *The Wall Street Journal* may be read in the library. There will be hobby magazines purchased from the employees' library fund. Magazines will be read in the IT library.

D. Programmed learning software

There will be a selection of programmed learning software to be used with the learning center or checked out for given time limits. The items will consist of the following:

- Computer-operated tutorials.
- Audio learning tapes.
- VCR learning tapes.
- CD learning disks.
- Speed-reading machines.
- Sound and slide programs.
- Printed programmed instruction books.
- Web-based training on the company servers.

E. Career planning information

A career resource library will be available and will contain:

- Scheduled IT classes and seminars.
- Local classes and seminars being offered.
- Available IT library self-learning packages.
- National IT and management seminars being offered.
- Local college catalogs, within an hour's drive of the company site.
- Local self-improvement clubs or organization contact persons.
- National correspondence school catalogs.

F. Copy machine

For business use, it is free. For private use, it is five cents a copy. The money will go into the employee fund.

S8.6.2 Conference and Classrooms

The IT personnel development center will have classrooms and conference rooms. These rooms will be available for IT instruction, IT meetings, end-user instruction, and available to the rest of the firm if not being used by the information systems.

A. Classrooms

The classrooms will be large enough for 20 students each and one larger room if needed. Supply items for the classrooms will be available from the library clerk. Each classroom will have the following teaching hardware:

- A standing lectern.
- White board.

- Overhead projector.
- VCR projector.
- Slide/digital projector.
- Student soft-seated chairs.
- Tables for two to three students per table.

B. Conference rooms

The conference rooms will each have one conference table and soft-backed chairs. The room will be provided with the following teaching hardware:

- A tabletop lectern.
- White board that has the ability to make handouts of what is on the board.
- Overhead projector.
- VCR projector.
- Slide/digital projector.
- Flip charts.

S8.6.3 Career Planning Assistance

The IT Education and Training Center will have offices for instructors and career guidance advisors, where meetings may take place with IT employees and their career advisors. Career advising is covered under section 8.4.1—IT Career Planning. The career planning people will be IT management people. They cannot work with any of their direct employees. These part-time career advisors will receive instruction in career advising before working with employees. Larger organizations may have full-time career planning instructors.

When a person joins the IS organization, he/she will be assigned a mentor for the first six months. When they have completed the first six months, they should be able to select the mentor of their choice and start planning a career path. The IT education and training unit will provide services for career guidance. A career guidance advisor will contact employees that have not had a first visit and inform them of the service. The employee will visit with the advisor to discuss the person's career objective and inform them of all the resources that are available. The rest of the process will follow the procedure as defined in section 8.4.1—IT Career Planning.

The new employee will be informed of local organizations that may

Comment:

A national study done in 1985 indicated that seven hours a week of reading alone were needed to keep up with new computer technology. Today, it could be more than twice that much for reading, as well as other forms of learning. That is why computer people feel that keeping up is so important. One company is reported to allow one full day a week for IT self-improvement.

be of interest to them, such as the local International Toastmaster group or ACM (Association for Computing Machinery). ACM can also be reached on the Internet at www.acm.org. Both organizations are worth investigating for career development and self-improvement.

S8.6.4 Other Resource Services

The IT Education and Training Center will provide IT employees with career development advice, training, and also be an IT information source. They will provide instruction to end-users of freestanding and work group computer systems. The other resources of the IT Education and Training will also be available to them.

Other company employees that have an interest in any of the course offerings—be it IT programs or other programs—are encouraged to attend. Employee family members may also attend any programs that are still open the day before the program starts.

Classes that are not IT related will be offered, when requested, for IT employees and their families as resources are available. The classes will have merit, such as self-improvement, health improvement, mental health improvement, financial planning, or family relations. The employee library fund resources may also be used for this type of programming.

7. EMPLOYEE BURNOUT

S8.7 IT EMPLOYEE BURNOUT

No employee should suffer from burnout. Any supervisor that is responsible for the pressure and time demands that results in any company employee's experiencing burnout is subject to a severe reprimand. The details for the reprimand will be placed in the supervisor's folder. This will also include project managers or leaders.

S8.7.1 Company Assistance

The management of information systems will do whatever is needed for the employee to recover from burnout. Any medical and therapy assistance will be paid for by the company. Information systems will also arrange for the company employee to have a week's vacation to recuperate. This will not be counted as employee vacation. Other company employees that are not IS people may be granted the same privilege if involved in IT projects, but not at the expense of IS.

At the signs of impending burnout, management may help with its prevention. The following are some suggestions that may ward off the problem:

- Encourage the person to take a seminar some place that will reduce the strain. Include a weekend "on the house" stayover for some fun time. He/she may include his/her family this weekend. No contact between company and employee will be allowed during this time.
- Periodically rotate IT tasks.
- Allow for telecommuting and more flexible work hours.
- Limit overtime.
- Limit on-call demands.
- Reassign work loads.
- Encourage feedback.
- Schedule social group activities for meeting project milestones.

S8.7.2 Signs of Burnout

IS management should be aware of any signs of impending burnout. Symptoms of burnout are:

- Extreme dissatisfaction with their work.
- Notice of heavy drinking during lunch or after work.
- Reduced productivity.
- Panic attacks.
- Use of drugs.
- Marital problems.

Comment:

There are several signs of good management: low employee turnover and absenteeism, no employee sabotage, good productivity, and a reliable employee suggestion system. American management's employee suggestion systems result is about 14 per 100 employee suggestions a year with a 24% acceptance rate. The Japanese management's employee suggestion system result is 1,241 per 100 employees per year with a 91% acceptance rate. There is no worker sabotage, and their turnover/absenteeism is within the 25 best USA IT companies.

Why is this? The Japanese place a higher value on industrial engineering and human resource jobs. Our IEs are the lowest paid of the engineering family, except for maybe the sanitation engineers. Our personnel departments used to require typing skills to get a job; then they were promoted into management. In some firms, it is still the company's elephant graveyard. The hot jobs in this country, outside of IT, are marketing and finance. The hot jobs in Japan are industrial engineering and human resource management, with a lot of value placed on training. Most of the good products are produced in Japan and we will use US marketing people—who could sell refrigerators to the Eskimos—to sell the products. The finance people are needed in this country to compute how bad a product can be before the lawsuit break-even point is reached. What wonders the bean counters can now do with their lap-top computers.

The solution may be having our hot marketing people sell the Japanese on hiring all our MBAs and we will throw in the bean counters for free! But that will force Scott Adams to learn Japanese and put a lot of attorneys out of work. Good marketing could sell the world on their needs. There must be something to that. The USA has 5% of the world's population but has cornered the market by having 70% of the world's lawyers.

- Problems with working with coworkers.
- Persistent eating, sleeping, and fatigue disorders.
- Noticeable signs of depression.

8. PRODUCTIVITY

S8.8 IT EMPLOYEE PRODUCTIVITY

The first consideration of worker productivity is what management is doing about it. The buck stops at the manager's desk. The US has some of the world's best and worst management. An MBA is not a sign that the person has management and leadership skills required for IT management. IT productivity requires management and leadership skills.

S8.8.1 IT Management Productivity

There are several signs of good management: low employee turnover and absenteeism, no employee sabotage, good productivity, and a reliable employee suggestion system. The signs may be good but must be confirmed. Some ways to confirm this in information systems are:

- Projects are finished when planned.
- Completed projects are finished within budget.
- End-users have faith in information system reports.
- Most IT job promotions are filled from within the company.

IT managers must be actively working outside of their offices. Do not depend on memos and the telephone to have a grasp of IT productivity. The following suggestions can help management actively promote IT production:

- Encourage participatory management.
- Ask what can be done about problems, and listen.
- Set new norms and goal.
- Utilize real quality circles.
- Employ time management.
- Delegate and follow-up.
- Learn when to say no.
- Set deadlines.

- Finish what is started.
- Do difficult jobs during the more productive time of day.
- Make a daily timetable.
- Do the unpleasant things first.
- Employee behavior due to weak supervisors.

Management will require feedback to gauge productivity results. One way is the question and sugestion box. Also, give praise to managers that deliver results. Do not keep them in the dark if they are meeting your goals, as they are doing the project, and not the month later.

S8.8.2 IT Employee Productivity

It is much more difficult to measure IT personnel's productivity than production jobs. Areas that are hard to monitor are systems and programming. Programmers are all too often measured on how hard and long they work, along with how many lines of code they write. The programmer not given credit all too often is the one that could do the same program in one tenth the time with half the lines of code and no test data errors. He/she will not get the credit or raise but will leave the firm.

To discover programmer productivity, survey other programmers as how they would rank their colleague's skills. This could be done at employee review time. The feedback could be informing. Other ways to get feedback are:

- End-users speak well of the help desk and other IT assistance by programs and systems.
- Utilize work simplification studies for programmers and systems people.
- Compare performance with other projects and tasks.
- Have all projects' work effort ranked as to each member's contribution to the project's completion.
- Have a programming contest. Identify your best programmers. This may also confirm management's suspicions.
- What course grades are received?
- Survey who is the most helpful and who people go to for help.
- Review of how systems conversions are made. Are the end-users happy about the assistance, training, help desk response, and the presence of project members during and after the conversion?

9. PROBLEM EMPLOYEES

S8.9 REMOVING PROBLEM IT EMPLOYEES

There will be times when an employee will have to be removed from his/her job. The person may also be a problem with other IT or end-user employees; therefore, the only solution is to remove him/her. This may be required from time to time. This procedure must be in place before the time comes to use it.

S8.9.1 Firing IT Employees

Firing an employee for reasons other than something such as stealing, sabotage, or physically assaulting a co-worker requires some documentation. The following should be practiced before terminating an employee:

- Provide honest feedback or areas that require improvement and document the information.

- Do not hope for things to improve—report them at the time of occurrence, and document the time and date of what was said.

- Present the information during evaluations, and have the employee sign that he/she has received the information.

- Be very clear about the standards set for the person's responsibility.

- Prepare for the termination quietly. Have all his/her access cut off at a given time for the computers. Have him/her return anything that he/she may have taken away from the company site.

- Inform the individual that he/she is a good employee but not suited for his/her job.

- Provide any assistance in planning his/her next career move. Consider using outplacement professionals for assistance with the transition process.

- Inform him/her that his/her personal items will be packed that night and sent to his/her home. Any property that belongs to the company (e.g., books or training material) is expected to be returned.

- Have the employee escorted to his/her car. If he/she does not have a car, a cab will be called and paid for by the company.

- Let the employee know as he/she is leaving that he/she can feel free to use the company as a reference.

10. IT MANAGEMENT COMPETENCIES

S8.10 IT MANAGEMENT COMPETENCY NEEDS

It is not enough to have technical knowledge, skills, and experience to be successful in an IT management position. As technology is becoming integrated with every aspect of a business, the business community is expecting IT management to solve business problems and to propose technology solutions that will reduce the complexity of the business processes, cut costs, and manage independent work activities. General management skills, rather than the traditional technical management skill set, help to make an effective IT manager.

S8.10.1 Seven Key Competencies

IT management is much more than implementing, supporting, and maintaining systems. It is working closely with the business line management and end-users to best understand their needs and requirements. It is working as a member of a cross-functional team to design new systems. Another factor that must be acknowledged is that change does not happen when a new system is implemented and new policies are established. IT management needs to be involved in influencing behavior change to support the new system. Where the IT function was once focused on knowing how to use machines, it is now focused on how people use information.

Below are seven key competencies that are needed for the successful IT manager.

A. Business knowledge

This competency involves having an overall knowledge of how business works. This includes understanding policies, practices, and trends affecting the industry and the organization. It also includes understanding who the current and future competitors are and the strategies and tactics that are making them successful. The IT manager should be able to discuss IT issues in the context of finance, sales, marketing, logistics, and distribution in order to evaluate the best business technology solutions for the organization. With this knowledge, the IT manager becomes a better business partner, who understands the issues, priorities, and concerns of their internal customers. This moves IT management from a functional focus to a big picture focus.

With the big picture view, the IT manager can enable the company to best benefit from technology as a business resource. Today E-commerce alone is changing how organizations do business. One example includes the emergence of Amazon.com who is challenging the methods of other booksellers such as *Borders* and *Barnes & Noble*.

B. Communication

If the IT manager is to be a true business partner in the organization, he/she will need to be able to communicate his/her knowledge and perspective related to technology and the business. This message will need to be communicated with the audience perspective in mind. Not all business partners are literate in IT terminology; therefore, choosing words wisely is important in getting a message across. A skilled communicator is able to express their thoughts in a way that is clear, concise, and appropriate to the audience.

Communications should be organized so that the main point of the message is clear. Messages that are too wordy, have grammatical or usage errors, and are disorganized are ineffective and present a poor image of the IT function.

Knowing when to communicate is as important as knowing how to communicate. When in doubt about communicating an issue, it is frequently better to inform the appropriate parties. Very rarely are internal customers complaining that an issue has been overcommunicated.

C. Customer focused

The first step in providing excellent customer service is knowing who the customers are and their needs and expectations. This information should be received first hand from the customer and not on what the IT manager believes the customers' needs are. Contact with the customer is not a one-time event, but rather involves regular communications to keep up to date on changing needs and expectations. Once customer information is gathered, decisions should be made with the customer perspective in mind.

IT management needs to be committed to providing exceptional customer service. IT management's role is to identify and remove any barriers to providing top-notch service. Some of these barriers include excessive paperwork, acceptance of the status quo, or front-line workers lacking the authority to make decisions. The IT manager's role is also to seek feedback from the customer. The IT manager needs to be willing to handle criticism, complaints, and special requests. These are all part of information gathering to improve customer service.

Some organizations have established "Service Level Agreements" with their internal customers. The goal of these types of agreements is to understand and measure the services IT provides to its internal customers. These are often established with a team of IT professionals and representatives from the business units to benchmark current service levels and to negotiate future needs and service levels.

D. Interpersonal skills

Strong interpersonal skills are needed to relate to people at all levels inside and outside the organization. These skills are critical in building effective teams and in meeting organizational goals and productivity levels. Interpersonal skills involve treating people fairly and with respect, being approachable, showing a personal interest in others, being positive in all interactions, using diplomacy and tact in volatile situations, and developing a more accepting view of others strengths and weaknesses.

The IT function can sometimes be seen as more interested in technology than people. To dispel this stereotype, it is important that IT management is visible in the organization and increases their sociability with those outside their own department.

E. Project management

A project is often defined as a problem with a defined schedule for a solution. From this definition, it becomes clear that project management is different from general management, which often involves managing ongoing activities that are generally repetitive in nature. Project management involves defining, planning, and meeting project objectives. These objectives often include performance levels, time commitments, and cost issues.

Effective project management skills are heavily reliant on the ability to organize resources and activities to get things done. Problem-solving skills are as important as organizational skills. Problem-solving skills are needed to simplify complex processes and identify opportunities for synergy and integration. A strong knowledge of the business and organizational culture helps identify the best solution when problem solving.

Because project management skills involve coordinating resources, with one of those resources being people, excellent interpersonal and communication skills are key. In many projects, the team members come from various functions in the organization, which means the project manager has no direct authorization over these individuals. Strong communication and interpersonal skills can be helpful in dealing with issues that may occur because of this situation.

F. Strategic outlook

With technology constantly changing, strategic thinking is a critical skill to any IT organization. A person skilled in having a strategic outlook is someone who can see ahead clearly to anticipate future trends and consequences and picture credible possibilities for the future success of the organization. The person with a strategic outlook displays a certain sense of curiosity, flexibility, and breadth of knowledge and interests. They are skilled in several types of thinking skills including critical, conceptual, creative, and intuitive thinking. The higher the role in the organization, the more strategically focused the individual needs to become to lead the business to success.

G. Team builder

Much of the work that occurs in the IT arena revolves around teams. Examples of when teams are established include implementing new financial software, developing a web site, or identifying business requirements for a new marketing system.

The person who effectively builds teamwork is skilled in establishing a common cause and shared mindset among the team members. This person also creates a strong sense of morale and team spirit which helps to support open dialog and open lines of communication between team members. The skilled team builder realizes that the best teams are made up of a variety of skills and abilities, and works on drawing out the best from each team member. The effective team builder recognizes that success and failure of the project is dependent on each team member fulfilling his/her role.

S8.10.2 Methods for Developing the Competencies

Once the key competencies have been identified, the IT organization needs to begin the task of assessing the skill level of its current and future management population. Various tools such as skill assessments, supervisor and peer observations, and feedback from customers can all be a part of assessing a person's skill level in the competencies. Once skill levels are assessed, the next step is to establish a development plan. There are very few individuals that fully demonstrate all of the skills mentioned above, but there are many people who can develop these skills if given the right tools. Just as technical skills need to be learned and practiced, so do the competencies listed above. Below are several methods to develop the skills discussed earlier.

A. Job rotation

Job rotation can involve anything from a complete job change for a period of time to taking a role as a project manager for a small assignment. It can include filling a position in the IT function or moving out into a business area to perform general management responsibilities for a period of time.

B. Memberships

Associations are valuable tools for gaining and sharing information about products, best practices, and the newest developments in technology. Associations exist at the national, regional, and local level and are geared for various positions in the IT industry from CIO to IT professional. Below is information on four IT trade associations.

- Society for Information Management

  Chicago

  Phone: 312-527-6734

  Fax: 312-245-1081

  Web Site: www.simnet.org

- Association of Information Technology Professionals

  Park Ridge, IL

  Phone: 847-825-8124

  Fax: 800-224-9371

  Web Site: www.aitp.org

- The Conference Board and the Information Management Center

  New York

  Phone: 212-339-0403

  Fax: 212-980-7014

  Web Site: www.conference-board.org

- The Information Management Forum

  Atlanta

Phone: 770-455-0070

Fax: 770-455-0082

Web Site: www.infomgmtforum.com

C. Mentoring

A mentor will often help a junior person identify areas for improvement, develop an action plan, provide feedback, and hold the person accountable for improving their performance and stretching their skill level. Mentors also seek out opportunities for the mentoree to attend or present at upper management meetings where the mentoree would not normally be invited. These events provide an excellent opportunity for the mentoree to gain exposure to upper management. Mentoring is an effective tool especially when it comes to maneuvering a company's culture and politics.

The mentor also gains from the mentoring relationship. The mentor further develops his/her management skills and is often recognized for the success of the person mentored.

Some mentoring programs are very formal and include policies, training for mentors, and a defined process for matching mentor and mentoree. Less formal programs rely on the mentor and mentoree making contact on their own to establish the relationship.

D. Reading

There are many magazines and books that address the IT world specifically; however, to understand general business issues and strategic thinking skills, magazines and books outside of the IT arena will need to be utilized. Some of these include *Forbes, Fortune, The Wall Street Journal, Harvard Business Review, Wired, Fast Company,* and *Strategy and Leadership,* a publication of the Strategic Leadership Forum.

E. Training

Both internal training programs of the organization and outside sources should be used. Many larger organizations have complete curriculums for developing the competencies discussed earlier. Numerous colleges and universities across the country have executive education programs that focus on management skills. Some of these include University of Pennsylvania Wharton School, Stanford Continuing Education Executive Programs, and University of Michigan Business School. Other training sources include the American Management Association, Center for Creative Leadership, and Arthur Anderson & Company.

11. CURRENT PERSONNEL CRISIS

S8.11 CURRENT PERSONNEL SHORTAGE

As every IT hiring manager knows, recruiting and retaining top talent in today's dot-com world is tougher than ever. According to a study commissioned by the Information Technology of America Association (ITAA), U.S. companies will seek to hire an additional 1.6 million IT technology workers in 2000, but they will be able to fill only half the positions because of a shortage of workers with the appropriate skills.

One reason for the shortage is a negative image of information professionals held by most people. The media portray IT professionals as geeky/nerdy individuals who wear bow ties, glasses, pocket protectors, pants that are too short, and lab coats. They are depicted as bald white males who are passive geniuses and work alone with their computers. Movies such as *Jurassic Park*, *The Nutty Professor,* and *Honey, I Shrunk the Kids* combined with disparaging representations of IT professionals on television have contributed to this unfavorable image. Even ads for IT workers have used terms such as "nerd" and have shown pictures of individuals with "taped" glasses. In addition, there are few highly visible role models for students and adults. This image problem makes it difficult to attract young people into training programs to prepare them for IT jobs and discourages older workers from the training necessary to move into IT positions. Older workers are also discouraged by the image of companies working computer personnel extremely long hours, and that companies prefer younger workers who are willing to sacrifice their personal life for their job.

A recent article in *The Wall Street Journal* described the plight of managers who are forced to pay new hires far more than they do loyal, long-standing employees, thereby running the risk of ticking off the more senior employees. Retention is a major issue, with turnover averaging 11 percent to 20 percent and, in some corporations, reaching the 50 percent mark. The problem is most severe in Silicon Valley, Boston, and New York, with turnover at 25 percent to 30 percent. Turnover this high is painful: The cost of replacing an IT worker is estimated at one and one-half to two times annual salary. Placement fees can take up 20 percent to 30 percent of that figure, sign-on bonuses for hot skills eat up another 10 percent to 20 percent, relocation costs take another cut, and the balance goes to other perks and incentives. IT salaries are a factor in staffing problems, with an average 20 percent annual increase. That compares average annual increases of 4 percent for non-IT salaries.

Exit interviews reveal that employees, while not immune to the effects of compensation and bonuses, are increasingly seeking workplace flexibility regarding telecommuting, flex time, sick time, and paid time off instead of vacations.

S8.11.1 Attracting Top Talent

To attract the IT talent needed to operate the business, companies are using more aggressive recruiting strategies. News about companies cash-rich from fresh venture capital and successful IPOs drive up salaries all over the country. Examples of some of the more creative employee perks include:

- Use of a company sports car—either for an employee of the month or for every employee.
- On-site dry cleaning.
- In-office massages.
- Corporate concierges to run personal errands.
- Stock options, hefty signing bonuses, and all the free sodas you can drink are now considered part of the standard employment package at many companies with a dependence on technology workers.

Many companies are looking to get noticed by potential employees by sponsoring happy hours, renting out movie theaters, sponsoring sporting events that attract younger people, and throwing open bar parties with bands. In exchange, the company requires a resume as the price of admission.

Comment:
The growth in the number of software developers will slow each year for the next couple of years, contributing to an already problematic worldwide IT skill shortage, according to market researcher International Data Corp. (IDC).

Employers are also spending more resources marketing and branding their company to communicate to potential employees that their company provides an exciting and challenging work environment. Radio and roadside billboards are increasingly used to reach their target employee market.

S8.11.2 Retaining Top Talent

It is critical that the top levels of the organization understand the role that IT plays within the company. The CEO and human resources director need to understand that when it comes to your IT personnel, the company has three options. Any one of the options is acceptable, but the company must make sure that it has made the optimal choice. The options are:

1. Keep employee salaries competitive with the marketplace to minimize unwanted attrition and maximize morale.

2. Keep employee salaries where they are and watch them drift up anyway as employees paid less than market rates leave and are replaced by new ones who are paid at market rates while they spend months becoming effective.

3. Keep employee salaries where they are, refuse to pay market rates for new hires in the twin interests of frugality and fairness, and instead pay premium prices for contractors to fill the empty positions for which you can't attract applicants.

The market will set the price for which you pay for these resources. The company must decide how they will choose to pay it and take the appropriate course of action.

Comment:

A recent McKinsey & Co. study estimates that global demand for offshore software development in the Asian region could be valued at as much as $180 billion by the year 2010.

Chapter 9
INTERNET AND E-MAIL

1. Policy

S9.1 PURPOSE OF THE INTERNET AND E-MAIL POLICY

The purpose of the Internet and e-mail policy is to formalize standards for how the company is connected to the outside world though the use of the Internet and e-mail. While the Internet provides access to a wealth of valuable information and facilitates communication, it also opens the potential for others to access the company's valuable proprietary information. Internet access and e-mail are valuable and costly corporate resources and must be used only to facilitate the business of the company. Irresponsible use of these resources reduces their availability for critical business operations, compromises corporate security and network integrity, and leaves the company open to potentially damaging litigation. This policy mandates the endorsement and support by the CEO/head of the organization.

S9.1.1 Scope

The Internet and e-mail policy covers all types of connections to the outside world thorough the Internet. The types of connections include:

- Individual computer using a POTS (plain old telephone service) connection through a modem.
- Workgroup server using a dedicated dialup POTS connection through a modem.
- Workgroup server using an ISDN, DSL, T1 or cable modem connection.

The policy also covers all activities performed while using the Internet, which includes but is not limited to browsing (viewing web pages), using e-mail, instant messaging, and transferring files using ftp (file transfer protocol).

S9.1.2 Policy Objectives

The objectives of this policy are to provide guidelines to ensure the secure, proper, and reliable use of the Internet. The policy objectives should be flexible enough to cover new methods of Internet connectivity as they become available.

The company's Internet and e-mail usage policy will be part of the new employee orientation process. Any new or existing employees must sign an acknowledgment that he or she has received a copy of this policy. The Internet and e-mail usage policy will also appear in the employee handbook. An online message that appears when the user logs onto e-mail or the Internet would also be helpful to remind employees of this policy. The company should also offer training sessions on Internet and e-mail usage.

2. Internet Access

Comment:

An analysis of a survey of more than 9,000 MSNBC.com readers found that one in five men and one in eight women admitted using their work computers as their primary lifeline to access sexually explicit material online. And other studies have revealed that 70 percent of e-porn traffic occurs between 9 A.M. and 5 P.M. on weekdays.

S9.2 METHODS OF INTERNET ACCESS

There are several methods by which a connection to the Internet can be made from an individual workstation. Each individual workstation might have its own connection to an Internet service provider (ISP), or it might be connected through the workgroup or corporate LAN. The connection itself can be on-demand or continuously connected to the Internet. Each method has its own set of advantages and disadvantages.

S9.2.1 Individual Access

The technically simplest method to connect to the Internet is for each individual PC to connect directly to an ISP using a modem and a POTS line. The user's PC connects to the local ISP using Dial-up Networking (if using Microsoft Windows) and uses a browser to view content on the World-Wide Web.

The IT technical support unit will develop the procedure for connecting to the Internet through individual PCs. The procedure will be distributed to users requiring individual Internet access. The IT technical-support unit will also determine the browser software to be used and may need to install the browser on the user's PC if it did not come preinstalled.

An advantage of using this method is that there is less direct exposure of the LAN to the outside world if any existing LAN connection is unplugged. Another is that the user's PC is exposed for only the time he or she is connected. This gives hackers less opportunity to gain access to the user's PC. Personal firewall software should be used as a form of protection while connected to the Internet.

A disadvantage of individual connections to the Internet is that no centralized monitoring or control is possible. Usage standards cannot easily be enforced, and virus protection is left up to the user. Speed is also severely limited when using a modem and POTS line. Any time you have a connection to the Internet the machine with which you are connecting to it and any subsequent machine behind it are subject to unauthorized access.

When using the Internet via an individual connection, the following procedures must be followed:

- Personal firewall software must be installed and active.
- Any LAN connections must be unplugged.
- Virus-scanning software must be installed and active.

Comment:

Examples of personal firewall software include ZoneAlarm and WinProxy. ZoneAlarm for Zone Labs costs less than $20; see their website at www.zonelabs.com for the latest information. WinProxy 3.0 from Ositis is a personal firewall and proxy product. They can be reached at www.winproxy.com.

S9.2.2 Corporate/Networked Internet Access

In most cases employees will have access to the Internet and e-mail from their workstations through the corporate or workgroup LAN. The LAN will be connected to the Internet through a router and/or proxy server; this can act as a firewall to protect the LAN from unauthorized access. The user's PC uses a browser to view content on the World-Wide Web.

The IT technical support unit will develop the procedure for connecting to the Internet through the corporate or workgroup LAN. The procedure will be distributed to users requiring Internet access. The IT technical support unit will also determine the browser software to be used and may need to install the browser on the user's PC if it did not come preinstalled.

An advantage of using this method is that Internet usage can be centrally monitored and controlled. Also, a centralized firewall (either software or hardware) can be used to protect the LAN from unauthorized access. Virus software can be centrally installed and kept up-to-date.

A disadvantage of Internet access through the corporate or workgroup LAN is that there is a single point of failure protecting the LAN from the outside world. The connection is normally up 24x7, which gives hackers more opportunity to test your protection. Any time you have a connection to the Internet the machine with which you are connecting to it and any subsequent machine behind it are subject to unauthorized access.

When using the Internet via the corporate or workgroup LAN, the following procedures must be followed:

- Firewall software or hardware must be installed at the point of connection to the Internet.
- Virus-scanning software must be installed. All download files and e-mails must be scanned for viruses.
- The IT technical support unit will generate a weekly report. The report will show the most frequently visited websites and total time connected to the Internet for each user.

Comment:

Losses related to Distributed Denial of Service (DDOS) attacks in early 2000 that shut down several popular websites could easily come to more than $1.2 billion, according to a report from the Yankee Group.

3. Internet Security

S9.3 INTERNET SECURITY POLICY

The information systems unit head will assign the responsibility for Internet security to the IT manager. Internet security policies are critical for protecting corporate system while connected to the Internet. The IT unit responsible for the corporate Internet connection will develop and enforce security procedures to protect corporate systems while connected to the Internet.

A connection to the Internet not only connects a computer to systems all over the world, but also with all computers it may be connected to over a LAN. The Internet was not designed to be very secure, as open access for research purposes was a major consideration of the Internet when it was created. Other factors that make an Internet connection a possible security problem include:

- Vulnerable TCP/IP services—a number of the TCP/IP services are not secure and can be compromised by knowledgeable intruders; services used in the local area networking environment for improving network management are especially vulnerable.

- Ease of spying and spoofing—the majority of Internet traffic is unencrypted; e-mail, passwords, and file transfers can be monitored and captured using readily available software. Intruders can then reuse passwords to break into systems.

- Lack of policy—many sites are configured unintentionally for wide-open Internet access without regard for the potential for abuse from the Internet; many sites permit more TCP/IP services than they require for their operations and do not attempt to limit access to information about their computers that could prove valuable to intruders.

- Complexity of configuration—host security access controls are often complex to configure and monitor; controls that are accidentally misconfigured often result in unauthorized access.

S9.3.1 Firewall Usage

A firewall is a system that provides security to a network. A firewall includes a number of items such as policy, network arrangement, and technical controls and procedures. The firewall protects the network from probing by unauthorized users and allows only authorized access to the system.

Management must first define the type and level of security desired for the Internet connection for the protection of information resources within the organization. Issues to consider include:

- Dial-in policy.
- SLIP and PPP connections.
- Which Internet services the organization plans to use (telnet, ftp, etc.).
- Assumptions about security versus usability (when does a service become too risky to use).
- Access to internal resources from the Internet.
- Restriction of access to approved sites only or restrict only certain sites.
- Use of chat programs such as mIRC and ICQ.
- Use of streaming audio and video.

There are two types of access control—explicit denial or explicit approval. Explicit approval restricts access to approved sites only and denies all other services by default. This is the most secure method, but is more difficult to implement and maintain. Explicit denial restricts only certain sites and is easier on users, but new services that become available may expose the network to security problems.

The firewall installed should have the following features:

- The firewall should be able to support a 'deny all services except those specifically permitted' design policy, even if that is not the policy used.
- The firewall should support the company's security policy, not impose one.
- The firewall should be flexible; it should be able to accommodate new services and needs if the security policy of the organization changes.
- The firewall should contain advanced authentication measures or should contain the hooks for installing advanced authentication measures.
- The firewall should employ filtering techniques to permit or deny services to specified host systems as needed.
- The IP filtering language should be flexible, user-friendly to program, and should filter on as many attributes as possible, including source and destination IP address, protocol type, source and destination TCP/UDP port, user and inbound and outbound interface.

- The firewall should use proxy services for Internet services such as FTP and TELNET, so that advanced authentication measures can be employed and centralized at the firewall. If services such as NNTP, http, or gopher are required, the firewall should contain the corresponding proxy services.

- The firewall should contain the ability to centralize SMTP access, to reduce direct SMTP connections between site and remote systems. This results in centralized handling of site e-mail.

- The firewall should accommodate public-access to the site, such that public-information servers can be protected by the firewall but can be segregated from site systems that do not require the public access.

- The firewall should contain the ability to concentrate and filter dial-in access.

- The firewall should contain mechanisms for logging traffic and suspicious activity and should contain mechanisms for log reduction so that logs are readable and understandable. Mechanisms for alerting someone when suspicious activity occurs is also important.

- If the firewall requires an operating system such as UNIX, a secured version of the operating system should be part of the firewall, with other security tools as necessary to ensure firewall host integrity. The operating system should have all patches installed.

- The firewall should be developed in a manner that its strength and correctness is verifiable. It should be simple in design so that it can be understood and maintained.

- The firewall and any corresponding operating system should be updated with patches and other bug fixes in a timely manner.

4. Internet Usage

S9.4 INTERNET USE POLICY

The company encourages the use of the Internet and e-mail as a means to make business and communication more effective. However, Internet service and e-mail are valuable and costly corporate resources and their purpose is to facilitate the business of the company. Irresponsible use of these resources reduces their availability for critical business operations, compromises corporate security and network integrity, and leaves the company open to potentially damaging litigation.

> **Comment:**
> **A new problem for employers is an influx of web sites that pay end-users to surf, search and send e-mail. These sites are enticing employees to use their speedy Internet connections at work to earn a little extra cash while on the clock. A survey of at-work Internet usage by Nielsen/ NetRatings found that the 7,000 employees in the survey spent an average of 67 minutes at iWon.com during a one-month period.**

S9.4.1 Tracking Internet Usage

The company will begin tracking all Internet transactions by employees. The purpose of this is simply to enable the company to manage our Internet and e-mail resources in a cost-effective and efficient manner and to plan more efficiently for future technology expansion. Please note that the company does not currently intend to examine the content of communications over the Internet, whether in e-mail, chat, or any other medium. The intention is to monitor the existence of the traffic being generated, much like a telephone bill tracks the calls made, the numbers called, and the time of the calls, but not the content. In this manner the company will be aware of how its resources are being used, where they are needed, where new capacity is required, and other infrastructure management issues. Additionally, because of the vulnerability companies have to litigation over inappropriate conduct in the workplace environment, it is the company's responsibility to ensure that company resources are not being used to support inappropriate activities.

S9.4.2 Internet and E-mail Usage Guidelines

To ensure that all employees understand their responsibilities, the following guidelines have been established for using company e-mail and Internet access. Any improper usage of the Internet or e-mail jeopardizes the company's legal standing and therefore cannot be tolerated.

A. Acceptable uses of company e-mail and Internet access

The company provides Internet and e-mail access for business usage. Every staff member has the responsibility to maintain and enhance the company's public image and to use company e-mail and access to the Internet in a responsible and productive manner that reflects well on the company. The company recognizes that there will be occasional personal use on lunch breaks and during nonworking hours (with the approval of management), but this shall not be excessive or unreasonable.

B. Unacceptable uses of company e-mail and Internet access

The company e-mail and Internet access may not be used for transmitting, retrieving, or storage of any communications of a discriminatory or harassing nature or materials that are obscene or "X-rated." Harassment of any kind is prohibited. No messages with derogatory or inflammatory remarks about an individual's race, age, disability, religion, national origin, physical attributes, or sexual preference shall be transmitted. No excessively abusive, profane, or offensive language is to be transmitted through the company's e-mail or Internet system.

Electronic media also may not be used for any other purpose that is illegal or against company policy or contrary to the company's best interests. Solicitation of noncompany business, or any use of the company e-mail or Internet for personal gain, is prohibited.

C. Communications

Each employee is responsible for the content of all text, audio, or images that he or she places or sends over the company's e-mail and Internet system. No e-mail or other electronic communications may be sent that hides the identity of the sender or represents the sender as someone else or someone from another company. All messages communicated on the company's e-mail and Internet system should contain the employee's name.

Any messages or information sent by an employee to another individual outside the company via an electronic network (e.g., bulletin board, online service, or Internet) are statements that reflect on the company. While some users include personal "disclaimers" in electronic messages, there is still a connection to the company, and the statements may legally be tied to the company. Therefore, the company requires that all communications sent by employees via the company's e-mail and Internet system comply with all company policies and do not disclose any confidential or proprietary company information.

D. Software

To prevent computer viruses from being transmitted through the company's e-mail and Internet system, there will be no unauthorized downloading of any unauthorized software. All software downloaded must be registered to the company. Employees should contact IS if they have any questions.

E. Copyright Issues

Employees on the company's e-mail and Internet system may not transmit copyrighted materials belonging to entities other than the company. Note that nonadherence to this policy puts the company in serious legal jeopardy and opens the company up to significant lawsuits and public embarrassment. All employees obtaining access to other companies' or individuals' materials must respect all copyrights and may not copy, retrieve, modify, or forward copyrighted materials, except with permission. Failure to observe copyright or license agreements may result in disciplinary action up to and including termination. If an employee has questions about any of these legal issues, speak with the person's manager or IS before proceeding.

F. Security

The company routinely monitors usage patterns in its e-mail and Internet communications. The reasons for this monitoring are many, including cost analysis, security, bandwidth allocation, and the general management of the company's gateway to the Internet. All messages created, sent, or retrieved over the company's e-mail and Internet are the property of the company and should be considered public information.

Notwithstanding previous comments regarding the company's current intention not to monitor content, the company must reserve the right to access and monitor the content of all messages and files on the company's e-mail and Internet system at any time in the future with or without notice. Employees should not assume electronic communications are totally private and should transmit highly confidential data in other ways. E-mail messages regarding sensitive matters should warn that such communications are not intended to be secure or confidential. This is just good business sense.

G. Violations

Any employee who abuses the privilege of company-facilitated access to e-mail or the Internet will be subject to corrective action up to and including termination. If necessary, the company also reserves the right to advise appropriate legal officials of any illegal violations.

Comment:

One source of Internet usage monitoring software is Sequel Technology. Their product supports all major Internet platforms. The software reports usage, volume, and protocol information, as well as cost allocation. They can be reached at <u>www.sequeltech.com</u>.

S9.4.3 E-mail Etiquette

As the use of e-mail has not only replaced paper-based communication but has also become a substitute for having a conversation, the proper use of e-mail etiquette has become increasingly important. Communication received in an e-mail does not easily convey the mood and emotions of the communicator. Most messages come across as harsher than what was intended. The following are useful guidelines for communicating by e-mail.

A. Be brief

Your e-mail messages should be concise and to the point. It is helpful to think of your e-mail as a telephone conversation, except you are typing instead of speaking. You should also make your main point as quickly as possible. Many software programs used for reading e-mail allow for a preview mode, where only the first couple of sentences are displayed. Many people receive hundreds of e-mails a day and use this preview mode to determine which e-mails they will read completely.

Comment:

Thank you for sending me a copy of your book—I'll waste no time reading it.
—Moses Hadas (1900–1966), book reviewer

B. Use the subject line wisely

An accurate subject line is also helpful for determining which e-mails merit closer attention by those who receive mountains of e-mail, but be careful not to earn a reputation for overhyping your message in the subject line; your really important messages may not get read.

C. Use grammar and punctuation currently

Poor grammar and punctuation reflect poorly on the sender. Don't overuse exclamation points (sometimes called "bangs") in an attempt to emphasize the importance of what you are saying. If something is important it should be reflected in your text, not in your punctuation.

D. Use special formatting sparingly

Avoid the use of fancy formatting within your message. What might look great using your e-mail client software may look like gibberish to the e-mail client of the recipient. Stick to commonly available fonts, and realize that the spacing as displayed by the recipient may be different from that from which the message was sent, especially when displaying columnar data.

E. Abbreviations

Abbreviation usage is quite rampant with e-mail. In the quest to save keystrokes, users have traded clarity for confusion (unless you understand the abbreviations). Avoid using abbreviations that you would not normally use in a paper-based communication. Some of the more common abbreviations follow.

This:	Means this:
BCNU	be seeing you
BTW	by the way
FAQ	frequently asked questions
FWIW	for what it's worth
FYI	for your information
HTH	hope this helps
IMHO	in my humble opinion
LOL	laughing out loud or lots of luck
OBO	or best offer
ROTFL	rolling on the floor laughing
RTFM	read the funny manual
TNSTAAFL	there's no such thing as a free lunch
TTFN	ta ta for now
TTYL	talk to you later

<G>	grinning
<J>	joking
<L>	laughing
<S>	smiling

F. Smilies or emoticons

Smilies or emoticons (emotional icons) are used to compensate for the inability of written communication to express the emotions, facial expressions, and gestures we would see in a verbal or face-to-face communication. Emoticons can be useful in avoiding misunderstandings of the writer's intentions. Most emoticons are designed to resemble what a person's face would look like if rotated 90 degrees counterclockwise. The most commonly used emoticon is the smiley face :) or :-), which resembles a person smiling. Following are some more examples:

This:	Means this:
: (or :-(	unhappy
;-)	light sarcasm
;->	heavy sarcasm
:-|	indifference
:-/ or :-\	undecided
:-0	surprise
:-p	tongue sticking out
:-S	loss of words

Emoticons are typically found at the end of sentences and will usually refer back to the prior statement. They should be used sparingly, as their meanings are not universal.

G. Salutations

Each situation will be different, but in general, use what you would use in a business letter. Some sort of salutation should be included in every e-mail as a common courtesy.

H. Signatures

Do not rely on your e-mail address to inform the recipient who sent the e-mail. You should sign your e-mail just as you would a business letter. Include your full name, title, company name, and telephone number. You may want to also include your e-mail address, because it can sometimes be difficult to locate your e-mail address within the e-mail. Avoid using quotes or images at the end of your e-mail.

I. Printing e-mail

Avoid printing a paper copy of e-mails you receive unless absolutely necessary. Most e-mail systems will allow you to create folders for storing old e-mails if you need to save a copy.

> **Comment:**
>
> **According to an American Management Association survey published in *The Wall Street Journal*, 27 percent of major corporations surveyed in 1999 monitored employee e-mail; 84 percent of those told employees that their e-mail was being monitored.**

J. Privacy

Remember that e-mails are not private. The company reserves the right to monitor e-mail content to ensure that the e-mail system is being used for appropriate purposes. Also, no security is 100 percent hacker-proof; someone outside the company may be able to intercept and read your e-mail. The routing of e-mail is not without errors; someone other than the intended recipient may receive your e-mail. Do not send anything by e-mail that you would not place on the company bulletin board.

> **Comment:**
>
> **The consequences of what is said in an e-mail were recently highlighted in the Microsoft anti-trust trial, in which the government used e-mails written by Microsoft executives to undermine their credibility. The statements made by the executives in e-mails contradicted their public statements.**

K. Other

Remember that all recipients may not read your e-mail immediately. While your e-mail will usually arrive quickly after it is sent, this is not always the case. E-mail is not designed for immediacy (that's why you have a telephone); it's designed for convenience. Do not use e-mail to schedule a meeting the same day or for anything that requires an immediate response.

Avoid using e-mail to deliver bad news. You cannot answer questions when a person reads the e-mail.

If you receive an e-mail that causes you to have a strong negative re-action, avoid responding immediately by e-mail. Use the telephone to clear up any possible misunderstanding.

Using all capital letters in an e-mail is the equivalent of SHOUTING.

When replying to an e-mail, either leave the old message as part of the new one or clearly reference what you are responding to. Do not assume the reader will know exactly what you're talking about.

S9.4.4 Instant Messaging

Instant Messaging is one of the most popular and most interactive ser-vices on the Internet. Using an instant messaging program such as ICQ or mIRC, you can chat instantly with anyone anywhere in the world. Many companies are finding instant messaging to be a useful tool for communi-cating with coworkers and customers. If you are on the phone, a message can be sent and will pop up instantly on your screen. But the capability to interrupt concentration—such as a ringing telephone—can make instant messaging very disruptive in the office. Many instant messaging programs will not work through a firewall and can be difficult to monitor. The use of external servers to distribute the messages can present a security issue. In-formation systems is responsible for developing policies and procedures for using instant messaging programs within the organization.

Comment:
According to Media Metrix, over 29 million home users and about 7 million business users use instant messaging.

S9.4.5 Training

Training for connecting to the Internet and for using the e-mail system will be provided by the information system's IT training unit. If the site does not have an IT training unit, training material will be made available by the local training unit. If this is not available, the company information systems organization will provide the training material.

Internet connection and e-mail system usage training will be available as individualized training. The material will be loaned to the user and then returned to the unit that provided the material. The training provided will be one of the following forms:

A. Tutorial

The user will learn via a tutorial. The user—at his/her own pace and as time is available—will learn how to connect to the Internet and how to use the e-mail system. The user will be provided with a learning guide with step-by-step instructions that assume basic knowledge of the computer's operating system. After the user has completed all the items in the learning guide, he/she will return the tutorial to the training unit.

B. On-the-Job training

The OJT (on-the-job training) will be provided by an experienced Internet user. The OJT instructor will have a learning guide provided by the information systems organization. The IS organization will provide the user with a copy of the learning guide via the instructor.

The OJT instructor will follow the learning guide when working with the student. They will proceed as time and the student's learning skills permit. A skill test may be provided with the learning guide to ensure the student's mastery of the material.

5. Acceptable Use Agreement

S9.5 ACCEPTABLE USE AGREEMENT

An acceptable use agreement will be put in place to ensure that all employees understand and agree to the company's Internet usage policies. The employee's immediate supervisor should review the policy with the employee to be sure that the employee understands the seriousness of the policy.

S9.5.1 Sample Acceptable Use Agreement

Following is a sample E-mail and Internet user agreement that should be signed by all existing employees and by all new employees at orientation. The employee will receive a copy, and another copy will be placed in the employee's personnel file.

E-MAIL/INTERNET USER AGREEMENT

Employee Agreement:

I have received a copy of XYZ Company's E-Mail and Internet Acceptable Use Policy #_____, dated _____. I recognize and understand that the company's e-mail and Internet systems are to be used for conducting the company's business only. I understand that use of this equipment for private purposes is strictly prohibited.

As part of the XYZ organization and use of XYZ's gateway to the Internet and e-mail system, I understand that this Acceptable Use Policy applies to me. I have read the aforementioned document and agree to follow all policies and procedures that are set forth herein. I further agree to abide by the standards set in the document for the duration of my employment with XYZ Company. I understand that e-mail and Internet usage may be monitored by the company to ensure compliance with the Acceptable Use Policy.

I am aware that violations of this Acceptable Use Policy may subject me to disciplinary action, up to and including discharge from employment. I further understand that my communications on the Internet and e-mail reflect XYZ Company worldwide to our competitors, consumers, customers, and suppliers. Furthermore, I understand that this document can be amended at any time.

_____   _____
Employee's Signature   Date

_____
Employee's Printed Name

_____
Manager's Signature

Chapter 10
MOBILE DEVICES

---

1. Policy

S10.1 MOBILE DEVICE POLICY

The purpose of the mobile device policy is to formalize standards for how Personal Digital Assistants (PDAs), wearable computers, single and two-way pagers, browser-enabled mobile phones, and related portable devices are used and managed within the organization. This policy applies whether the mobile devices are used on or off company property. This policy mandates the endorsement and support by the CEO/head of the organization.

S10.1.1 Scope

The scope of this policy covers all mobile devices not traditionally considered computers, but which are used to store and/or collect information that is in some way connected to the organization. It covers all data and information from the input of raw data to the disposition of output documents and/or data. All raw source material and stored data are company property and must be used only for company-approved activities. Examples of covered items include customer lists, company directories, schedule information, etc.

S10.1.2 Operation Policy

Information systems is responsible for maintaining and enforcing a company-wide operation program for all mobile devices. The head of information systems will assign the responsibility to an IT unit to coordinate usage of mobile devices. An end-user committee will be formed, containing no more than seven or fewer than three end-users. A purchasing department representative should be included on the committee. A representative of the IT unit will chair the committee. The committee will follow management's policy and define it for company-wide policies and procedures.

All user unit heads will comply fully with the policies. There will be procedures in place to enforce these policies. Each unit head will be provided with a policy and procedures manual, which will include a recommended equipment list. The approved equipment list will be referred to for all acquisitions. In cases of mobile needs not on the approved list, a request memo will be sent to the committee chairperson. The committee may grant a waiver.

Personally owned mobile devices and other equipment of any kind are not allowed on company property without special permission from the policy committee.

2. Mobile Device Inventory

S10.2 INVENTORY OF MOBILE DEVICES

The information systems unit head will assign the mobile device inventory responsibility to the IT manager. If there is not an inventory or equipment system in place, the IT asset manager will establish one.

S10.2.1 Tagging Mobile Devices

Before the tagging of equipment begins, there will have to be a coding method devised. Devices are tagged upon receipt by a sequential numbering system. The numbering of mobile devices will employ a two-character preface, followed by a space and a sequential number. The two-character preface will identify the type of mobile device being tagged.

After the inventory system is in place, an agent of the asset manager will do the tagging upon receipt of new devices. The device and packing slip will be compared with a copy of the purchase order to confirm that what was received was what was ordered. Supply items received will be checked with the packing slip and a copy of the purchase order. If the purchase is done by a blanket purchase order, the quantity received each time will be added to the total received to date and the quantity compared with the original blanket-ordered quantity.

It is recommended that a bar-coded tag be used, along with a visually identified number posted on the tag. New mobile devices received will have tags made and attached to the item. After the tag is secured to the device, it will be used as its identification number during inventory checks, when it is moved to a new location, repaired, or disposed of.

S10.2.2 Mobile Device Inventory

A computer inventory system will be maintained by each type of mobile device. The following file-record information will be maintained for each mobile device:

- Tag number, prefix, and sequential number.
- Date of purchase.
- Original cost.
- Manufacturer's code number.
- Vendor from which the device was obtained.
- Purchase, lease, or free-trial code identification.
- Last date of preventive maintenance.
- Last date of repair service.
- Last date of warranty service.
- Maintenance code.

A telephone number will be provided for end-users who may need maintenance. This number can be an IT service unit's number doing preventive or repair maintenance, or the vendor's number.

Annual reports will be run by type of equipment, department assigned, department total, and grand total by type of equipment. The amount of usage will also be reported when such records can be provided. When equipment is acquired, moved, or disposed of, the information will be used to update the information database files.

3. Mobile Device Maintenance

S10.3 MAINTENANCE OF MOBILE DEVICES

The information systems unit head will assign the mobile device maintenance support to the IT service unit. The IT service unit head will compare maintenance service with vendor and in-house service for quality and cost. The service may be a form of hybrid mix of vendors and in-house service. The maintenance service should be reviewed annually because of the changing technology, availability of in-house and vendor service personnel, and the needs of the company.

S10.3.1 In-house Maintenance Control

The IT service unit that performs in-house maintenance will perform whatever mobile device repairs and preventive maintenance it can perform. Cost and in-house availability will be a determining factor as to who will perform what service. A service telephone number will be available for people needing service. This may be called the service desk. The service desk can assist the person, by telephone, with a device problem. If the problem cannot be resolved over the telephone, the service desk will inform the person calling that he or she will be called back. The service-desk person will then contact an in-house service person or the vendor that has the contract to service the device.

The vendor will be contacted for a warranty or repair service call. The service desk will have that information. The person who contacted the service desk will be informed when he or she may expect the service person to arrive.

In smaller operations, the help desk and the service desk may be combined into the same job. These smaller operations may also have the IT PC services unit people perform some of the mobile equipment maintenance. There is also the value of having well-trained power users. It broadens the scope of their job, and it provides for a level of care that will not require a skilled technician's attention. The extra training is well worth the investment. With this, smaller operations may not require a full-time help desk.

S10.3.2 Service Budgeting

The budgeting for in-house maintenance control and the service desk will come from the IT service unit's lump-sum budget. Although the item purchased may come from a department's budget, the IT service support cost may or may not be charged to the department. This charge will depend on the company's accounting policy.

All service maintenance done by the IT service unit will be reported on a daily service log. The completed work log sheets will be turned in daily to the IT service unit's head. The log report will contain the following information:

- Service person's name.
- Machine number serviced.

- Time spent on the service call.
- Type of call: service, preventive maintenance, or operator problem.
- Any replacement parts that were used.

Departments that purchase their own mobile devices with their own budget will require funds with which to obtain their own maintenance service. The departments will have to request funds for this maintenance service in their budgets. Some items that are leased may come with a provided service agreement.

All service performed by the in-house IT service unit or vendor will be reported by the IT service unit. The IT service people will provide their daily report to the IT service unit head. The service desk will record the vendor service. The vendor code number and device number will be reported. The vendor's service document will be turned over to the help desk. Each day the service report is given to the unit head along with the vendor's service document; a copy will be made for the IT unit head and the original copy sent to the department head. A request for vendor service may come in one of the following forms:

- Time and parts.
- Blanket maintenance contract.
- Warranty service call.

S10.3.3 Maintenance Service Report

Vendor maintenance will be reported by the device types each vendor has a contract to repair. The kind of vendor maintenance service reported will be shown as warranty, preventive, or service maintenance. Time and replacement parts service charges will be listed.

The monthly maintenance service reports will list the devices and locations that were serviced. The report will provide the following information:

- What type of device was serviced.
- Who performed the service.
- The estimated cost for the service.
- The kind of in-house service performed.
- The kind of vendor service performed.
- What kind of service was performed.

- What kind of service was performed on the device the last time it received a service call.

- When the last service call date was and what the current service call date is.

- A total monthly expense by device type and a monthly grand total; there will be a year-to-date cost by device type and a year-to-date grand total.

A second report (IT and Vendor Maintenance Cost Report) will be printed with information by vendor and the IT service unit. The report will list who provided what service to which devices. The report lists the subtotal cost for the month. Year-to-date costs will be listed by the service provider and a grand total year-to-date sum.

S10.3.4 Vendor Maintenance Contracting

The IT unit head, the asset manager, and a purchasing department representative will work together to solicit vendor contract bids. The same purchasing department representative should be used from year to year. It would be very beneficial if the same purchasing agent would also be responsible for mobile supplies and computer supplies. After IT has identified what items they cannot do or will not be able to service because of not having the required people, a list will be composed of the devices that will require vendor's maintenance bids. A form letter will be used listing all the items for which bids are requested. Vendors can provide an offer for any one item, any number, or the entire lot of items listed.

The list of vendors to contact can come from the IT service unit's head, the IT asset manager, and the purchasing department. It will be the responsibility of the representative of the purchasing department to check each vendor before the vendor will be sent the letter. The purchasing agent can use information his or her department may already have. Contacts with other firms' purchasing departments may be a source of information along with the firms' D and B rating.

When composing the request-for-bids letter as much information as can be provided will be given. A vendor-company contact person will be provided in the letter. Any site visits will be arranged through the company's contact person. The letter will furnish the name and telephone number of the contact person and the last day the bids will be received. The following information will be furnished in the vendor letter or attachment to the letter:

- A list of unit types that the bid calls for servicing.
- The number of units for each unit type.
- The age and condition of each device.
- Units that are under current warranties and when those warranties expire.

If a particular vendor's bid were selected, would they be willing to provide a help-desk telephone number? This would allow for company employees to contact them for information or for a service call. Will there be a charge for this service if it is available?

Vendor selection will be based on several variables. Each variable will be weighted before the request for bid letters are dispatched. Vendor analysis will be based on this matrix. See Chapter 15–5.3, Vendor Selection, of the main volume, *Information Systems Policies and Procedures Manual,* for information about setting up a weighted matrix. Short-term contracts may be considered for yet unproven vendors. Before any contract is signed, contact the firm's legal representative, who will have the last word before the firm's authorized representative signs it.

4. Mobile Device Operation Procedures

S10.4 OPERATION OF MOBILE DEVICES

Mobile devices cover a wide range of applications and complexities. The total investment in mobile devices can be difficult to track and is not known in most companies. More important, the data that is kept on mobile devices is difficult to track and control.

Meanwhile, most mobile devices operate without a central sense of direction. Without the orchestration and guidance of information systems,

Comment:

According to recent *InformationWeek* Redefining Business study of 600 IT execs on the adoption of wireless technology, more than 40 percent of respondents plan to purchase hand-held computers and other wireless technology in 2000.

their costs will continue to grow while their efficiency will diminish. A major part of controlling mobile devices is the procedures set forth by an IT unit of information systems.

Information systems is responsible for maintaining and enforcing a company-wide software application policy for all mobile devices. The acceptable application software list is maintained in the asset-management software database and should be updated monthly by the information systems software committee. Installation of unauthorized application software is not permitted. Help-desk support will not be provided for unauthorized application software.

S10.4.1 Personal Data Assistants (PDAs)

A PDA is a small hand-held computer used to write notes, track appointments and contacts, and otherwise keep your life in order. Early PDAs required data to be input using a keypad with keys the size of Chiclets, but more recent models (e.g., the Palm Pilot or the Palm PC) use a combination of pen-based input and character-recognition software to accept user input. Many can also be used to send and receive e-mail and browse the Internet. Information in the PDA can be synchronized with data in a PC-based application such as Microsoft Outlook.

Information systems is responsible for maintaining and enforcing a company-wide synchronization policy for all mobile devices. A standard synchronization package should be selected that supports all the different PDAs in use at the company. The applications and data to be synchronized must also be determined. It is desirable to use synchronization software that can be administered from a single server to control what is being transferred to and from the PDA. Other items to consider include:

Filtering of data. Information systems must determine what subset of data records is to be synchronized with the PDA. Filter setting can protect sensitive data that should not be synchronized and can be used to save time by only transferring data that is actually needed.

Comment:

The popularity of these types of devices will prove a headache for corporate IS departments. Palm and Windows CE have long targeted enterprise customers, touting the benefits of employees connecting remotely to corporate

databases of information via their hand-held computers. According to Ken Dulaney, vice president at Gartner Group, the influx of new products, designs, and technologies will add 10 percent in technical support costs.

Field mapping. This is used to map fields from the PC application to the PDA application. Information systems must create standards for which data fields can be synchronized and where they map between the PC and the PDA.

Conflict resolution. Data that is kept on both a PC and on a PDA will have conflicts when the data is changed in one or both places. Policies must be established as to how these conflicts are to be resolved.

Control at the server. Some synchronization products allow settings to be controlled at a central server. This also makes it possible to synchronize over the LAN without being connected to a PC.

The use of PDAs makes good backup procedures even more critical, as there are more opportunities for data to be changed inadvertently. Verified backups before the first synchronization are very important.

PDA users will be notified that the data on the PDA is valuable and sensitive company information and must be protected. All PDAs should be password enabled to prevent unauthorized access to the data if the PDA is lost or stolen.

Comment:

Intellisync from Puma Technology synchronizes data from all Windows-powered PCs, hand-held PCs, and Palm devices with a broad number of PC-based PIM, contact management, and groupware applications using advanced features such as conflict resolution, filtering, and field mapping. Intellisync supports Microsoft Outlook 97/98/2000, Microsoft Schedule+ 7.0/7.0a/7.5, Lotus Notes 4.5/4.6, Lotus Organizer 2.12/97/GS/4.1/5.0, Novell GroupWise 5.2/5.5, Symantec ACT! 3.08/4.0/4.01/4.02, Goldmine 3.2/4.0, Meeting Maker 5.0.3/5.5 and other PC-based PIMs.

S10.4.2 WAP-Enabled Cellular Phones

A WAP-enabled cellular phone allows users to access the Internet using their cellular phone. Information systems is responsible for maintaining and enforcing a company-wide usage policy for all cellular phones. Usage should be monitored periodically to ensure that the phones are used for business related purposes.

Cellular phone users will be notified that the data on the cellular phone is valuable and sensitive company information and must be protected. All cellular phones should be password enabled (if possible) to prevent unauthorized access to the data if the cellular phone is lost or stolen.

Comment:

The market research firm Strategy Analytics predicts that as many as 525 million WAP-enabled devices will ship in the United States and Western Europe by 2003.

S10.4.3 Wearable Computers

A wearable computer is a computer that is used by users who must move around and cannot be tied down to a single location. The system is normally worn on a belt, with optional peripherals that might include a wrist-mounted touch-screen display, a voice-enabled headset, and a head-mounted monitor. Information systems is responsible for maintaining and enforcing a company-wide usage policy for all wearable computers.

Wearable-computer users will be notified that the data on the wearable computer is valuable and sensitive company information and must be protected. All wearable computers should be password enabled to prevent unauthorized access to the data if the wearable computer is lost or stolen.

Information systems will be responsible for setting up processes for backing up data on all wearable computers. Procedures will include standards for use of docking stations, connections to the LAN, and backing up data to a server. A directory on a server that is regularly backed up should be created for storing data and applications from the wearable computer. Instructions for backing up data and applications will be created by information systems and provided to all users of wearable computers.

Comment:

IBM's Almaden Research Center is working on Personal Area Network (PAN) technology, which uses the natural electrical conductivity of the human body to transmit electronic data. In the future, a user of PAN technology will be able to transfer information via touch rather than by issuing typed commands or pressing buttons. For example, your computer might recognize you as you if you simply touch the keyboard. The capability could yield significant benefits in the area of access control and data privacy.

S10.4.4 Power Users

This is a person who uses a particular device on a regular basis (usually daily) and becomes very knowledgeable about the operation of the device. This person usually enjoys sharing information about using the device with others in the organization. Power users should be asked if they could be contacted if a new user needs assistance. If they agree, their names should be listed as power users with the instructions given to new users.

A power user should be able to operate and perform minor device adjustments. He or she will know how to replenish its expendable stock items, and perform standard housekeeping and preventive maintenance procedures. A power user will be able to be walked through some of the malfunctions by the service desk or a maintenance person over the telephone. At the service desk will be a power user's location book with the power user's name, telephone number, and location listed. A second listing will be by location with the power user's name and telephone number listed. This will be used to contact another power user that is close by for assistance when the nearest power user is not available.

S10.4.5 Mobile-Device Operations Procedures

These are the operating procedures furnished to all device users. The operator procedure manuals will be furnished by the IT service unit or the systems and procedures unit. The manuals will provide operator instructions, minor maintenance instruction, backup procedures, and procedures for troubleshooting. Minor preventive maintenance procedures will be provided.

The procedure manuals will contain any manufacturer's furnished material that is helpful to clarify the device's operation. The illustrations used by the manufacturer could be beneficial to the operator. Close-up and wide-view photographs would be helpful if included in the operator procedure manuals.

A prototype manual will be developed and tested before it is placed into service. An unskilled person will be used for the test. This should be done with more than one subject. The brightest person in the area and any experienced operator should be avoided for debugging the procedure manual.

S10.4.6 Supply Requisitions

The standard supply requisitions that the firm has in place will be used. If the form is outdated or there is no form, one will be designed by the IT systems and procedures unit.

A central supply location should be placed to limit the travel time involved. This will prevent unnecessary travel for the person seeking supplies. The supply center could also function as supply-distribution location for the end-user computer operations supplies. Supplies that are not too large can be delivered by interoffice mail. Other items that may require a device to deliver will make a daily run to deliver the items.

A requisition system will be employed to obtain supplies. The unit head will approve the requisition after all the items are listed with their respective quantities. A line will by drawn across the lines not used by the person before signing the requisition. Depending on the company accounting practice, the supplies will be charged to the unit receiving them or come from a lump-sum company budget. Spot checks on usage that are employing a lump-sum budget are recommended. The loss on supply items can be costly to a company. The supply area will be locked when unattended. Supplies stored in operating units will be locked at the end of the day or locked at all times if the view to the area is not seen.

S10.4.7 Service Desk Assistance

Help desks, along with service desks, cannot solve all user problems. It will require other assistance to cover the users' special needs. Some operations such as mobile phones will be better off with a vendor-supplied service. Vendor help and service desks for special systems can provide much better service than an in-house service. If the company is willing to provide for an in-house service desk and support it, there are still vendor services that can provide better assistance. They will do it better, and the equipment will be up and running faster.

The asset manager will publish an approved mobile device acquisition list for new mobile device purchases. This will cover what is in-house, currently operating and found on the mobile device inventory property list, but not on the approved mobile device acquisition list. Mobile device inventory property list is company property, identified and tagged. The approved mobile device acquisition list is a list of items that the IT service unit can repair or for which the service desk has a vendor contact. The service desk will also have the mobile device inventory property list and the source of service for each item. Some items were company property before the service desk assistance program was established.

Some devices either have long life spans and never need to be replaced, or the device is no longer manufactured—it can be replaced only with used equipment. The help desk will have a special number to call to have the item serviced. In cases of this kind, it is in the best interest of the company to have a power user trained to do most of the repairs and preventive maintenance. The vendor service person will be contacted only if the problem is beyond the scope of a power user or if one is not available. Some of the items may not use the English measuring system and may require special tools to repair the equipment, or the manufacturer may be the only one that makes the tool.

The service desk does not have to be covered at the company site any more than the help desk does. This is why so many vendor help desks are not found at company sites. This may make it more difficult having the vendor provide full-service desk coverage. If coverage is needed other than during normal working hours, service-desk personnel can be on call at their homes for specific time periods. This can also apply to help-desk personnel. In smaller firms these two jobs can be combined into one. There would be one number to call in the event of a problem. There is also the possibility that the problem may be related to both the help-desk and the service desk. The help- and service-desk person should be able to have at home the current information that he/she has at his or her desk at work. It would be desirable to have it installed in a notebook computer.

5. Training

S10.5 USER AND IT SUPPORT TRAINING

The provision for training will cover a wide area of needs. The technology skill levels required for each mobile device will be one or more levels. Vendor-contracted mobile-device service will not require as many levels of skills as an in-house service program. The service desk will have the levels of skill that are available for each device listed in the mobile device inventory property list. Depending on the nature of the problem, a skill level will be determined to resolve the problem. The item listed will have posted to it the persons who can perform a given level of skill. A person with a higher level of skill can perform a lower level of skill task. But a lower-level skilled person should not perform a higher-level skill task. The training will certify a level at which the service person can perform a task.

The training provided will be for certain skill levels. This training will be for vendor-serviced and company-serviced equipment.

S10.5.1 User Training

The user should learn the basic operation of the device to produce the desired results. The more complex the device, the more there will be to learn. The job of changing batteries would be considered a task level that would be expected of a user. The job of loading applications into a PDA is much more complex, but it also is a user's job. User training will be provided in more than one form:

A. New user training

When a new mobile device is to be used by users, the training will be conducted in class. The vendor or a power user will conduct the classes. The vendor should provide any of its handouts. The company instructor will provide any handouts that may be needed. A video or slide presentation would be helpful along with any hands-on training.

A list of the people attending the meeting will be taken. Anyone missing the class will be notified that they missed it and should attend the next class offered. If the classes are over, they will take the individual training provided to new employees later.

B. New employee training

Anyone missing the class will take the self-paced individual training. New employees who have no experience with the device will receive the self-paced individual training. They will be credited with receiving the instruction for the new device. Part of the instruction will be provided to the user as OJT instruction.

S10.5.2 Power User Training

The power user training will be given for all users desiring to be recognized as power users. The training can be from more than one source. The IT service unit will hold classes for power users or OJT instruction for the devices they maintain. The power users will receive manuals from the IT service unit.

Vendor-training programs will be provided at the company site or at the vendor's place of instruction. The vendors will provide manuals. The IT unit will also provide power-user procedure manuals. Some sort of certificate will be provided by the vendor showing the person is now a certified power user for the given mobile device.

The power user should be able to provide OJT to new device users. They should be able to operate the device, make adjustments to its operation, and perform some light preventive maintenance. They will be the key contact person in the area for users, service desk, vendor service people, and the IT service personnel.

S10.5.3 IT Service Unit Training

Each IT service person will have a list of devices that he or she can service for his or her own records, along with the service desk and the IT unit head.

Training will come from one of the following sources:

- OJT.
- A self-paced learning program provided by the vendor.
- Attending vendor's classes.
- Passing a qualifying exam for the equipment.
- Taking a correspondence course from the vendor or a private correspondence program.

S10.5.4 Service Desk Training

Effective service desk people are often individuals who have some experience as an IT service person. Their training can come from the areas where the IT service person receives his or her training—as a power user and from operator training. It would help a new service desk operator to work with an experienced worker, which would be a form of OJT learning. On days when there is not a heavy load, they may try their skills at manning the service desk.

Service-desk personnel can be expected to work overtime and to be on call at their homes. The unit will have one or two laptop computers that service people can take home with them when they are on call. They are expected to have no less knowledge than a power user about each device and a general knowledge about vendor-maintained devices. They should have enough knowledge to assist a user and communicate with a service person who works for the company or vendor. They should be able to assign service people to be used most effectively and best serve the company's needs. They can reduce maintenance costs with the proper assignments and the ability to walk users through problems.

6. Mobile-Device Acquisition Procedures

S10.6 MOBILE-DEVICE ACQUISITION PROCEDURES

The budgeting can come from a corporate lump-sum budget or department budgets or both.

S10.6.1 Budgeting Procedures

Each department will submit its expected needs for the following year's budget. This will be based on the last year's budget plus any inflation, replacement of old equipment, and new needs. It is supported by the utilization of the current equipment and forecasted usage for the next budget year.

Budgets will be needed for the department's use of supplies and replacement of current equipment. Departments that have their own hardware for their one-of-a-kind use will require a budget for the maintenance of the equipment.

The information systems IT service unit will need a budget for their operation. They will need a budget for capital expenses that benefit the whole company plus a replacement-parts budget. Also, a vendor-service budget will be required.

S10.6.2 Requisition Procedures

Items that have been budgeted can have a requisition issued. The requisition will go to the IT asset manager to confirm that it meets standards or will require a standards waiver.

The requisition will be approved and sent on to the budget department so they can adjust their records and then send it on to the purchasing department.

S10.6.3 Purchasing Procedures

Purchasing will receive the approved purchase requisition. If needed, they will take care of the competitive bids for the item. After the purchase order has been sent to the vendor, a copy will be sent to the receiving department and to accounts payable.

S10.6.4 Receiving Procedures

The agent for the asset manager or a special-order item representative will inspect the item for their approval. After it is approved, a receiving notice will be sent to accounts payable.

The asset manager's agent will affix a tag to the device and record the information. The information will be sent to the asset manager.

Chapter 11

APPLICATION SERVICE PROVIDERS

1. Policy

S11.1 USE OF APPLICATION SERVICE PROVIDERS

The purpose of the Application Service Provider (ASP) policy is to formalize standards for how ASPs are used and managed within the organization. With the increasing shortage of skilled workers to operate systems in-house, more companies are turning to ASPs to manage and maintain their system's infrastructure. It is critical that the Information Systems group manage the selection and use of ASPs to ensure that the company is receiving the value for which the ASP was hired to provide. This policy mandates the endorsement and support by the CEO/head of the organization.

S11.1.1 Scope

The scope of this policy covers all applications that reside on a remote server and are run remotely, either over a direct connection, frame relay, or over the Internet.

S11.1.2 Definition

An ASP is a supplier who makes applications available on a subscription basis. The ASP model works very similarly to the time-sharing systems used in the sixties and seventies. ASPs typically provide access to the following types of applications:

- Supply Chain Management
- Accounting
- E-Purchasing

- Human Resources
- Recruiting
- E-mail
- Document and Workflow Management
- Customer Relationship Management
- Group Scheduling
- Help Desk
- Secure Collaboration Communities

An ASP combines service offerings that are traditionally not offered by one company. The four primary ingredients are the following:

1. Packaged software applications. Licenses to products developed by ISVs are sold for a sizeable up-front fee or on a per-use basis.

2. Data centers and connectivity. Data-center services are offered by hosting companies (e.g., Level3), hardware companies (e.g., IBM), and telecom providers (e.g., MCI/UUNet). Telecom and business Internet service providers (ISPs) provide connectivity.

3. Application monitoring and ongoing support. Firms such as AmQUEST, Digex, and Data Return typically offer application monitoring. Ongoing support is typically offered at the first level by firms such as Support Technologies. SIs or ISVs typically provide second-level support.

4. Systems implementation and integration. Systems integrators (SIs) or the service arms of ISVs traditionally offer these services.

Comment:
Over one third of information technology and development managers at large corporations expect to rent applications from application service providers (ASP) in the year 2000, according to a study conducted by Evans Marketing Services (EMS).

The ASP can be used to provide access to a single application or can be used to replace the entire user desktop.

S11.1.3 Application Outsourcing Policies

Corporate and IS management must have a clear set of long-term goals and objectives for the outsourcing of applications. ASPs should be used:

- For operations that are difficult to manage and staff. ASP can reduce headcount needs.
- To avoid hardware and software obsolescence.
- To improve focus on core competencies. Most companies do not include IT as part of their core competency.
- To supply talent and/or resources not available in the organization.
- To reduce internal operation costs.
- To make applications available to a mobile, distributed workforce.
- For their ability to scale rapidly.
- To make IT cost more predictable.
- For turnkey solutions. The role of general technology contractor shifts from the company to the ASP.
- To free resources for other efforts.
- To bring systems up and running faster. ASPs can generally deliver software to a customer more rapidly than in-house resources or an external software developer.

The areas for which an ASP will be used will be budgeted for annually. ASP contracts that will expire within the next budget year will require a new contract proposal three months before the cutoff for budget consideration. If the current ASP's performance or new proposal is not satisfactory, and RFP will be sent to no fewer than two other vendors.

2. VENDOR SELECTION

S11.2 SELECTION PROCESS

Selecting a vendor to provide application services requires the use of stringent evaluation procedures. Not only must the applications themselves be evaluated, but hosting facilities, bandwidth, and support capabilities must also be carefully considered. The relative newness of the ASP market and the volatility of the stock market upon which they rely for funding make the selection of the right ASP extremely important. Betting your organization's technology infrastructure on a company that may experience a sharp drop in their stock price may cause you trouble. If their stock price drops, they may not have the money to invest in research and development, which may impact your ability to service your customers.

In addition to technical considerations, you should constantly reevaluate with whom you are doing business. Have a company-wide agreement on the criteria for choosing a technology vendor. Get involved in a professional network of CTOs that you can talk to on a regular basis about technology providers' performance. Bet your infrastructure on a combination of established and newer companies. The best dot-com companies, and the ones most likely to stay in business, are those that have formed a technology and business alliance with an established company such as IBM, Microsoft, or Oracle. These more established companies have done their own evaluation of the technology provider and have found them a credible partner. A small sample of ASPs is listed here:

ASP	Product	Web Site
eALITY	eALITY eXPress	www.eality.com
eOnline Inc.	SAP R/3	www.eonlineinc.com
FutureLink, Inc.	Microsoft, Great Plains	www.futurelink.com
Great Plains Software	eEnterprise	www.greatplains.com/hosting
Smart Online, Inc.	Small business	www.smartonline.com
TeleComputing	Microsoft BackOffice	www.telecomputing.net
USIS Health	Medical apps	www.usishealth.com

S11.2.1 Request for Proposal

When IS management is ready to receive vendor proposals, a formal request for proposal (RFP) letter will be sent to all possible candidates. The RFP will define the format of the proposal to ensure that a responding vendor can be evaluated and compared easily with others. The RFP should cover the following items:

- Type of applications to be outsourced.
- Minimum performance requirements and evaluation criteria.
- Reliability level required.
- Level of integration with other systems required.
- Any required reporting capabilities.
- Service volume expandability.
- Vendor contact person.
- IS contact person.
- Vendor maintenance, training, and operation support.
- Current users of the ASP's systems.

This request for proposal is for an ongoing service contract, with a given time limit. The service will be billed monthly at a flat rate or prorated by transaction or user volume.

All items in the contract with the ASP are negotiable. A three- to five-year contract is typical. Standard support is usually 12x5 (twelve hours a day, five days a week) with 24x7 support available at an additional cost. Systems with a small number of users are typically placed on a shared server with other customers of the ASP. Dedicated servers are available for an additional cost. The base fee per user normally covers the infrastructure at the ASP (but not the cost to connect) and any software licenses required. A fixed amount of hard-disk storage space is usually included, with 100 MB per user typical. It is critical to carefully evaluate what your users will need and try to make sure that as much as possible is covered in the standard agreement. As with any major purchase, the add-ons can significantly add to the cost of the service.

The method by which you will connect to the ASP is also an important consideration. A dedicated frame relay connection to the ASP is the most secure and reliable, but is usually much more expensive than connecting over the Internet. A connection over the Internet can be much less reliable, as overall Internet traffic can impact your performance. Using a dedicated frame connection, a good rule of thumb is 10 users for a 64K line, 20 users on a 128K line, and 50 to 60 users on a full T1 connection. For the same connection over the Internet, about one half to two thirds as many users can be supported as on the frame connection.

For each vendor selected to receive a copy of the RFP, an internal IS person will be assigned the task of being the liaison between that vendor and the company. That person's job will be to manage the communication between the vendor and the company and to encourage the vendor to provide their best response to the RFP. The vendor should be encouraged to put the maximum effort into their response, especially if the vendor suspects that another vendor may have an advantage. Even if another vendor is selected, any attractive items in the losing vendors' proposals can be used as negotiating points with the vendor ultimately selected.

S11.2.2 Evaluating Vendors' Proposals

All proposals received should be analyzed using a predetermined set of criteria. The elements to be compared should be in the same sequence on each proposal. Copies will be given to each evaluator, and a date and time will be selected to meet and discuss them.

Vendors who provide clear and complete information that was asked for in the RFP and who meet preliminary evaluation standards are selected for more detailed analysis. Those that do not or that indicate pushy vendors will be removed from further consideration.

The vendors' proposals should address the specification elements noted in the RFP. Clear statements should be made by the vendor to address the following items:

- Credentials of the firm.
- Former and current customer references.
- Documentation clarity and completeness.
- User-training and implementation resources available.
- Process to ensure data security and availability.
- Reliability of service.
- Scalability of service.
- Availability of support.
- Quality of support (credentials of staff, average length of service, etc.)
- Security of connection.
- Physical security of the data center.
- Next expected release of the software.
- Types of reports issued detailing application access and usage statistics.
- Management of the software-upgrade process.
- Dedicated or shared server.
- Storage space available per user and cost.

- Backup and redundancy resources available.
- Customization options available, if any.

Current and former customers should be contacted to discuss their experiences with the vendor. The following questions are helpful for obtaining useful information:

1. Would you go with the same vendor again? If so, why? What has been the major problem with the vendor? Do you know of other users of the vendor's product? Are they generally happy? If so, why so? Who are the other users? What are their names and telephone numbers?

2. How long does it take for the vendor to respond to problems? Are the people who respond knowledgeable and friendly? Has the vendor ever lied? Has the vendor had the resources to resolve your problem(s)?

3. Does the application satisfy your needs? Follow up with questions about how long they have had the system and how often it has gone down. Ask about its expandability and upgrading possibilities.

4. Do the users like the service? Ask to talk to users and confirm this. Ask users what they liked and disliked about the service and why.

5. Ask how long it took to put the application into operation. Did they receive adequate training? Are the user manuals easy to understand and follow?

6. Is the service they are being provided better than what they could do themselves, and why? Is the service worth the cost?

7. Were there any unexpected or hidden costs? What was the nature of these costs? Were the costs reasonable? Was the vendor confronted about this? If so, what was the reaction?

8. Were the vendor's employees easy to work with? Did their salesperson follow up after the sale was made? Does the vendor seem to have a genuine interest in the success of service?

9. If they were starting all over, what would they do differently?

S11.2.3 Vendor Selection

The final selection of a vendor is based on more than one factor. To make the process more objective, a weighted matrix can be set up to compare vendors by selection factors, with the weight of any one factor a percentage of the whole. An example may be seen in Exhibit 11–1. The nature

Exhibit 11–1. Vendor Selection Matrix 1

Factor	Weight	Vendor A	Vendor B	Vendor C
Suitability of application	.25			
Availability of extensions	.20			
Level of integration	.15			
Reporting capabilities	.10			
Availability of support	.15			
References	.10			
Cost	.05			
Total	1.00			

of the item being requested by an RFP will determine the factors and their weights. The factors should be determined and the matrix parameters prepared before the request for proposal is mailed out to avoid a subjectively weighted matrix.

The compilation of the weighted factors is best done using the Delphi method. Have seven to nine people who are familiar with the proposal needs, on their own with no discussion, list those factors and their corresponding weights that each considers important for the vendor to possess. Send the lists to a person not involved with the selection to compile. This person will make a list of all the factors and return this new list to the participants. They will once more go through these factors, choosing and weighting their choices. Again, the papers will be sent to the person not involved with the selection, who will group together the factors (together with their weights) that are the most prevalent. He or she will discard the ones that have been assigned low weight values or that have been mentioned only once. The possible combinations are then placed on one sheet of paper and copies are distributed to all contributors for reselection. This process is repeated until a general consensus is reached.

The vendors that have passed the preliminary selection process are rated from one to ten by the same seven- to nine-person panel or by a new panel. An example of this rating system is shown in Exhibit 11–2. Each rating (from one to ten) is then multiplied by its weighted factor to get a vendor-rating value. These values are then totaled by vendor. The one with the highest total is rated first, as shown in Exhibit 11–3.

Exhibit 11–2. Vendor Selection Matrix 2

Factor	Weight	Vendor A	Vendor B	Vendor C
Suitability of application	.25	8	6	5
Availability of extensions	.20	4	7	3
Level of integration	.15	1	8	5
Reporting capabilities	.10	5	2	4
Availability of support	.15	8	7	3
References	.10	4	9	5
Cost	.05	3	7	9
Total	1.00			

Exhibit 11–3. Vendor Selection Matrix 3

Factor	Weight	Vendor A	Score	Vendor B	Score	Vendor C	Score
Suitability of application	.25	8	2.00	6	1.50	5	1.25
Availability of extensions	.20	4	0.80	7	1.40	3	0.60
Level of integration	.15	1	0.15	8	1.20	5	0.75
Reporting capabilities	.10	5	0.50	2	0.20	4	0.40
Availability of support	.15	8	1.20	7	1.05	3	0.45
References	.10	4	0.40	9	0.90	5	0.50
Cost	.05	3	0.15	7	0.35	9	0.45
Total Score	1.00		5.20		6.60		4.40
Vendor Ranking		2		1		3	

Weight X Rating = Score

The vendor rated number one is chosen to receive the contract and will then submit, usually, a standard contract that will, of course, be in his or her favor. So, the vendor's representative will be invited to discuss this offered contract in the information systems head's office.

The contract terms will be negotiated by the vendor's representative and IS management. Training, documentation, conversion, performance, and acceptance are all included in the bargaining process. Some items in general to consider are:

- Delivery or start dates.
- Finish or completion dates.
- Vendor vs. customer responsibilities.
- How and when vendor will bill.
- Removing vendor's disclaimers.
- Provisions for equipment, software, and personnel backup.
- Emergency and preventive maintenance.
- Provision for detailed specifications for hardware, software, or service performance.
- Contract for outsourcing on a job-by-job basis.
- Realistic launch dates for implementations.
- Avoid long-term contracts with new or unproven vendors.
- Local support options.

Comment:

A recent report from Deloitte Consulting estimates the entire United States market for ASPs, Web hosting, and application outsourcing at close to $10 billion. It is projected to grow to more than $50 billion by 2003.

Any contract should include performance clauses and penalties for nonperformance or late delivery times. After the negotiation the legal representative of the company must examine the final contract before it is signed.

3. VENDOR MANAGEMENT

S11.3 VENDOR MANAGEMENT

Managing a long-term ASP project is not an easy task. Some of the reasons for difficulty include:

- Pricing and service levels established at the beginning of the contact do not contain meaningful methods for measurement and improvement of service.

- Expectations and assumptions of both parties change over time. Most contracts cannot anticipate changes in technology, personnel, business processes, etc.

- Cultural differences between the two companies can cause misunderstandings and mistrust.

- Differences in the goals and objectives of the two companies can cause problems.

- Lack of management oversight my cause priorities to become out of sync with the reasons for entering into the contract in the first place.

S11.3.1 Service Level Agreement

Information services and the affected business units must work together to determine what the service level requirements are for the applications that are outsourced to the ASP. These service levels are determined at the outset of the agreement, and they are used to measure and monitor the supplier's performance. The services levels are written in a contract called a Service Level Agreement (SLA). The SLA defines the consequences for failing to meet one or more service levels.

The SLA should include the following sections:

- A precise definition of key terms.
- Specific service levels for all key categories (system availability, help-desk responsiveness, security administration, change management, etc.).
- Frequency of service-level measurement (usually monthly).
- Weighting by importance of key service levels.
- Calculation of credits for missing service levels.
- Calculation of credits for frequency of missing service levels. Increased frequency of missed service levels might increase the service credit by some predetermined factor.

The performance factors specified in the SLA not only provide an objective measure of the vendor's performance, but can also serve as a basis for termination of the service if threshold service levels cannot be met. Other "nonkey" performance levels can also be specified to add to the case for termination if warranted.

Typical credit for failure to meet routine services levels range from 5 to 15 percent, with penalties for severe service failures reaching 20 to 25 percent. *Force majeure* clauses excuse a party's failure to perform if the failure resulted from an act of nature such as an earthquake or other natural disaster beyond the party's control. The ASP vendor will attempt to include as much as possible in this category; this should be kept as narrowly defined as possible. Under no circumstances should a *force majeure* absolve the vendor completely from their responsibilities.

The SLA might also include provisions for rewarding the vendor for extra value-added services that might be provided. Make sure that these services will really add value before agreeing to payment for these items.

Negotiating and designing an SLA is difficult and time consuming, but a fair and comprehensive SLA is critical for a successful ASP relationship. During the negotiation, both parties will learn a lot about how their future partner will approach the various aspects of their relationship.

Chapter 12
GLOSSARY OF IT TERMS

S12.1 GLOSSARY

ABORT To cancel, or terminate, a program, command, or operation while in process.

ACCESS To retrieve data or program instructions from secondary storage or another online computer device.

ACCESS CODE An identification code or password used to gain access to a computer system.

ADDRESS A unique identifier associated with a station, line, path, or unit. In LANs, addresses are assigned by local or universal administration.

AFTERMARKET The market for peripherals or software that is created by the sale of large numbers of a specific computer brand.

ALGORITHM A specific set of mathematical and logical procedures which a computer can follow to solve a problem.

ALPHA-NUMERIC CHARACTERS Any mixture of character letters (A to Z) and numbers (0 to 9), punctuation, and special symbols.

ALTERNATE A secondary communications path used to reach a destination.

ANALOG A continuously varying electrical signal with an infinite number of amplitudes.

ANCILLARY EQUIPMENT Office equipment that is not part of a computer system but supports information processing. A sample would be a multi-function machine that can act as a copier, Fax, scanner, and computer printer.

ANSI SCREEN CONTROL A set of standards developed by ANSI to control the information display of computer CRT screens.

APPLICATION A term used to refer to a software program that accomplishes as certain task.

APPROVED COMPUTER SOFTWARE LIST This is a list of computer software that may be acquired by end-users. This is software the IT asset manager has approved and will be supported by the help desk.

APPROVED COMPUTER HARDWARE LIST This is computer hardware that has been approved by IT management; the list is released by the IT asset manager that allows the hardware to be acquired by end-users.

APPROVED PURCHASING SUPPLY LIST A list that is provided to purchasing and end-users of computer and ancillary equipment that allows its purchase.

ARCHIVAL BACKUP A backup procedure for secondary storage of files to be copied onto another secondary storage device.

ARTWORK Material prepared from copy and/or a layout sheet that is ready to be photographed (camera ready).

ASCII American Standard Code for Information Interchange. A standard for encoding characters (including the upper- and lower-case alphabet, numerals, punctuation, and control characters) using seven bits. The standard is 128 characters; IBM expanded the set to 256 bky, adding an eighth bit to each existing character. The expanded set provides graphic character, Greek, scientific, financial, and foreign language characters.

ASP Application Service Provider. An ASP deploys, hosts, and manages access to a packaged application to multiple parties from a centrally managed facility. The applications are delivered over networks on a subscription basis. This delivery model speeds implementation, minimizes the expenses and risks incurred across the application life cycle, and overcomes the chronic shortage of qualified technical personnel available in-house.

AUDIT GUIDE MANUAL A manual provided by the auditors for the design of systems and software with built-in audit trails and check points.

AUDIT TRAIL A process of locating the origin of specific data that appears on final reports.

BACKUP A copy of a file, directory, or volume on another storage device for the purpose of retrieval in case the original is accidentally erased, damaged, or destroyed.

BACKGROUND PROCESS A multi-tasking operating system that has operations occurring in the background while it runs a second operation in the foreground.

BAR CODE A printed pattern of vertical lines used to represent numerical codes in a scramble reading form.

BATCH PROCESSING Grouping like transactions into a single batch for processing.

BENCHMARK A standard measurement used to test the performance of hardware or software.

BETA TESTING Using and testing software for software producer that has not yet been put on the market by the vendor.

BINDER A paper envelope with an attachable flap that can fit into a file cabinet to store group of sheets of printed paper and documents.

BIT A binary digit; must be either a zero (on) or a one (off). The smallest possible unit of information in a digital system.

BLANKET MAINTENANCE A vendor contract to repair more than one kind of computer and/or ancillary equipment.

BLANKET PO One purchase order for given quantity of goods, but to be delivered in part shipments as requested.

BODY TYPE Type used for the main body or text of a job.

BOLDFACE Heavy-face type in contrast to light-face type. Used for emphasis in headings, subheadings, titles, etc.

BOILER-PLATING The use of parts of texts stored on disk for word processing or desk-top publishing. This saves the time and effort of repeatedly entering the same data.

BOND PAPER A grade of writing or printing paper where strength, durability, and permanence are essential requirements. Used for letterheads, business forms, etc.

BOOTLEG FORM An unauthorized form outside the jurisdiction of the forms control program within an organization where such a program exists.

BOOTLEGGED SOFTWARE Unauthorized software that end-users have obtained or written. This is not pirated software.

BORDER RULE Heavy rules at top or bottom, or completely around the printed form.

BOTTLENECK A factor that restricts the flow of data through a system. When a bottleneck exists, performance is restricted by this factor.

BRIDGE A device used to connect LANs by forwarding packets across connections at the media access control sublayer of the data link layer of the OSI model.

BROWNOUT A period when there is low-voltage electric power because of increased demands.

BUG A programming error that causes a program or a computer system not to perform as expected.

BUNDLED SOFTWARE Software that is included with hardware for a total price as a system.

BYTE Eight continuous bits that represent a character in memory.

BURSTER Machine used to separate continuous forms into single-part forms or sets.

CAD/CAM Computer-aided design/computer-aided manufacturing.

CALENDAR TIME This time is the actual duration of a project, from the date it starts until it is completed. It includes work and non-work days.

CAMERA-READY COPY Any material ready to be photographed for reproduction without further change. May be type-written copy, reproduction proofs, artwork, or previously printed material.

CAPTURED DATA Data that is in machine readable form.

CD A compact optical disk with over six hundred million characters of storage.

CD READ/WRITE DRIVE A CD read- and write-only-once device employing compact optical disks.

CD/ROM DRIVE A read-only optical storage device employing compact optical disks.

CE Customer engineer, or the hardware vendor's engineer.

CEO Chief executive officer—the firm's highest operating officer.

CFO Chief financial officer.

CIO Chief information officer. This places the head of information systems at the level of a company's officer.

CHARACTER Number, letter, or other symbol that is one unit of a font or type array.

CHARACTER READING Machine reading of printed characters by optical means.

CHIP A miniature electronic circuit which is mass produced on chips or silicon wafers.

CLIENT A computer that accesses the resources of a server. See client/server.

CLIENT/SERVER A network system design in which a processor or computer designated as a server such as a file server or database server provides services to clients' workstations or microcomputers. The type of system employed by end-user work groups.

CLIP ART A collection of graphic images available for use with desk-top publishing.

COAXIAL CABLE A commonly used cable type that is relatively insensitive to noise interferences, consisting of one or two insulating layers and two conductors. A central conductor wire is surrounded by the first layer of insulation. An outer shielding conductor is laid over the first layer of insulation. Usually, it is then covered with the second layer of insulation.

COLLATING Gathering sheets or computer records in proper preidentified order.

COLOR CODING Use of different colored stock, tinting, or printed marks on individual parts of a set to aid in identification and distribution.

COLUMN HEAD A heading that identifies a series of entries to be made in columnar sequence below.

COMMUNICATIONS PROTOCOL A list of communications parameters and standards that govern communications between computers employing telecommunications.

COMPILER A program that reads high-level program coding statements (source code) and translates the statements into machine executable instructions (object code).

COMPOSITION Typographic material that has been set and/or assembled. The process of preparing it for printing.

COMPRESSED SPEECH COMPUTER SYSTEM A computer audio system that will allow speech, on tape, to be compressed to reduce the listening time. It does this by reducing the time span between spoken words and slicing small parts of each spoken word.

COMPUTER STORE This is an IT support unit of information systems that provides company employees with the opportunity to view and try out approved hardware and software.

COMPUTER SYSTEM A complete computer installation with all the required peripherals to work with each other as one unit.

CONSOLE A computer display terminal consisting of a monitor and keyboard.

CONTRAST The tonal gradation between highlights and dark areas on a monitor screen.

COPY Any material furnished (typewritten manuscript, pictures, artwork, etc.) to be used in the production of printing.

COPY MACHINE A freestanding machine that copies onto paper from a flat scanning source.

COPY PREPARATION Directions as to desired size and other details for illustrations, and the arrangement into proper position of various parts of the page to be photographed for reproduction.

COPY PROTECTION The inclusion of a program of hidden instructions intended to prevent unauthorized copying of software.

COST-BENEFIT ANALYSIS A projection of the costs incurred and benefits derived for installing a proposed system, hardware or software.

COVER PAPER A great variety of papers used for the outside covers of catalogs, brochures, booklets, and similar pieces.

CPM (CRITICAL-PATH METHOD) A process used in project management for the planning and timing of tasks that relies on the identification of a critical path. The series of tasks along the critical path determines the total project completion time. Most PERT operations are really CPM.

CUSTOM FORM Form manufactured to unique order specifications by a vendor.

DATA Units of information stored on some type of magnetic media that can be called into a computer program for use. Can also be called captured data.

DATA COMMUNICATIONS The transfer of information from one computer to another.

DATA DICTIONARY A list of data elements used in database management programs. The information of each data element has its: use, size, characteristics, who can use it, who can alter it, who can remove it, and who can view it only.

DATA ELEMENT A field of data for an element of information used in records found in database management systems. Examples include: FICA number, name, part number, etc.

DATA INDEPENDENCE The storage of data so that users can gain access to data in a database system without knowing where the data is located.

DATA MANAGER A person responsible for the management of all corporate data. The database manager may report directly or indirectly to this person.

DATA PROCESSING The preparing, storing, or manipulation of information within a computer system.

DATA RECORD A complete addressable unit of related data elements expressed in identified data fields used in files and database systems.

DATA REDUNDANCY When the same data are stored in more than one location.

DATABASE A collection of related information in an organized manner, in random access secondary storage, made up of related data records. There can be more than one database in a computer system.

DATABASE MANAGEMENT PROGRAM A data application program that provides for the retrieval, modification, deletion, or insertion of data elements. Database systems tend to reduce data redundancy (the storage of the same data in more than one location).

DATABASE MANAGER The person responsible for managing the corporate IS database. This person reports to the head of corporate information systems, but can also report, for policy guidance, to the corporate data manager/director.

DATABASE SERVER A database server is the back-end processor that manages the database and fulfills database requests in a client/server database system.

DATABASE MANAGEMENT SYSTEM The operating software system that provides for the access and storage of data. The acronym for this system is DBMS.

DATAFLOW DIAGRAMS A method of showing dataflows all on one page. It starts at the lowest detail level, which is the system level. Corresponding processes parts are all shown in more detail, each on its own page. Dataflow diagrams have their own flowcharting symbols.

DDOS Distributed denial of service. Denial-of-service attacks are attacks in which a hacker floods a network server with data in an attempt to crash the system. A distributed denial-of-service attack uses multiple computers all attacking at the same time.

DEBUGGING The procedure of locating and correcting program errors.

DEDICATED FILE SERVER A file server that cannot be operated as a user's server workstation. See file server.

DE FACTO STANDARD A standard based on board usage and support.

DEFAULT A value or option that is chosen automatically when no other value is specified.

DESK CHECKING Checking for errors in a program listing or on a computer monitor screen.

DESK-TOP PUBLISHING The use of a microcomputer to generate camera-ready copy for printing. The computer will require one of the available desk-top publishing software programs.

DIGITAL PHOTO EDITING The process of editing a photo displayed on a monitor. The process is done with the use of photo editing software.

DIRECT COST These are costs that are measurable and accounted for in a given process.

DIRECTORY An index to the files stored on a disk that can be displayed on the monitor.

DISK DRIVE The unit in a computer that reads and writes information to and from disks.

DISK DUPLEXING A method of safeguarding data in which the data are copied simultaneously onto two hard disks on separate channels. If one channel fails, the data on the other channel remain unharmed. With data duplexing, read requests are sent to whichever disk in the pair can respond faster, increasing the file server's efficiency.

DISK MIRRORING A method of safeguarding data in which the same data are copied onto two hard disks on the same channel. If one of the disks fails, the data on the other disk are safe. Because the two disks are on the same channel, mirroring provides only limited data protection; a failure anywhere along the channel could shut down both disks and data would be lost. See also disk duplexing.

DISTRIBUTED PROCESSING A computer system designed for multiple users with fully functional computer access.

DOCUMENTATION The instructions and references that provide users with the necessary information to use computer programs and systems or to alter it at a later date.

DOCUMENT FLOWCHART A flowchart constructed all on one page showing the flow of documents used in a given system. It shows the documents traveling from left to right across a page from one user to another, each user is in its own vertical column.

DOMAIN NAME-SERVICE HIJACKING A hack in which inquiries seeking one domain are routed to another domain without the user's knowledge.

Such attacks on the Internet's control structures could make packets of information undeliverable, quickly snarling traffic on the network.

DOT-MATRIX PRINTER An impact printer that employs ends of pins against a ribbon for printing text.

DOWN-LOADABLE FONTS Printing fonts that are stored on a hard disk and transferred into printer memory prior to printing.

DOWN-LOADING The reception and storage of data from one computer to another; often via data communications.

DSL Digital Subscriber Line. DSL is a modem technology that transforms ordinary phone lines (also known as "twisted copper pairs") into high-speed digital lines for ultra-fast Internet access.

DUMP The transfer of the contents of computer main memory to a printer or a secondary storage device.

EEOC The Equal Employment Opportunity Commission.

ELECTRONIC MAIL (E-MAIL) A network service that enables users to send and receive messages via computer from any place in the world.

EMULATOR A computer program that makes a programmable device imitate another computer, producing the same results.

ENCRYPTION The scrambling of information for transmission over public communication systems. The receiver will require the same technology key to unscramble the coded information.

END-USER A person who benefits, directly or indirectly, from a computer system.

ERGONOMICS The science of human and machine interaction factors for designing work tools and providing a working environment for people to perform their duties better.

ERROR MESSAGE A display of information that states that a computer program is unable to perform as programmed.

EXPENDABLE SUPPLIES Supplies consumed with the process of a service or product. The supply items can be direct costs or indirect cost in the products consumption. It most often is considered as a indirect cost item.

EXPERT SYSTEM A computer program containing the knowledge used by an expert in a given area that assists non-experts when attempting to perform the duties of the expert.

FACSIMILE The exact reproduction of a letter, document, or signature. Sometimes abbreviated as "fax."

FAX The transmission and reception of documents between two locations via telecommunications.

FAX SERVER A network device or service that provides a LAN workstation access to incoming or outgoing faxes across the LAN.

FEASIBILITY STUDY A study to determine the possibility of undertaking a systems project.

FILE A name given to a collection of information stored in a secondary storage medium such as a tape or disk.

FILE ALLOCATION TABLE A table on a disk that records the disk location of all the file parts.

FILE SERVER A computer that provides network stations with controlled access to shareable resources. The network operating system is loaded on the file server and most shareable devices, such as disk subsystems and printers, are all attached. The file server controls system security. It also monitors station-to-station communications. A dedicated file server can be used online as a file server while it is on the network. A non-dedicated file server can be used simultaneously as a file server and workstation.

FILE RECORD A data storage record that contains information fields of data. The record is addressable on tape by its record identification. On disk systems the access is not direct. To find the record more than one system is used.

FILE SHARING The ability for multiple users to share files. Concurrent file sharing is controlled by application software, workstation operating system, and/or file server/database server operating system.

FLOPPY DISK A removable secondary storage medium that uses a magnetically sensitive, flexible or firm disk. The 5¼″ floppy disk is enclosed in an envelope. Sizes are 3½″ and 5¼″ and are available in high and low density. The 5¼″ is seldom found in operation today.

FLOWCHART Analysis tool consisting of a diagrammatic representation of a system process or abstract relationship, normally made up of labeled blocks or keyed symbols connected by lines.

FONT It consists of all characters and spacing material of different size and shapes. Computer-generated fonts come in two forms, hard and soft fonts. Soft fonts are software fonts stored in memory, and down-loaded to the printer. Hard fonts come in the form of cartridge hardware fonts, which plug into the printer.

FOOT Bottom edge, or area at bottom, of the form, held as it is normally read or used. The finger grip area of unit sets is normally at the foot of the form.

FORM A preprinted document available as a flat or continuous pin feed document. Forms can be stored in disk memory and retrieved as needed as in boiler-plating.

FORMAT The size, style, type page, margins, printing requirements, etc. of a printed piece.

FORMS DESIGN The art or science of devising a form to efficiently fill a given function or systems need; includes selection of materials, construction, and layout.

GANTT CHART A project scheduling tool using graphic representations of a project showing start, elapsed times, and completion time of each task within a given project. It can also show the planned "schedule" time and the actual "completed" time. At any point, the Gantt chart indicates the status of a given project. A Gantt chart employing dollars can also illustrate money budgeting for given tasks versus money spent. Gantt chart monitor screen displays are available with some project management software. This allows for online reference of the status of projects that can be networked. Gantt charts are also drawn on varies size sheets of paper. The 8½″ by 11″ size is inserted in binders for project progress recording. Larger size sheets of paper can be used for displaying Gantt charts in the project team work areas.

GANTT CHART

PROJECT: _____

PROJECT TASKS	S C	JAN	FEB	MAR	APR	MAY	JUNE
ANALYSIS							
DESIGN							
PROGRAMMING							
TESTING							
CONVERSION							

GATEWAY A device that provides routing and protocol conversion among physically dissimilar networks and/or computer for example: LAN-to-HOST, LAN-to-LAN, X.25, or SNA gateways.

GIGABYTE (GB, BYTE) A unit of measure for memory or disk storage capacity; two to the thirtieth power (1,073,741,824 bytes).

HACKER A technically knowledgeable computer enthusiast who enjoys programming, not usually employed as a programmer.

HALFTONE An illustration in which the gradation of tone in a photograph is reproduced by a graduated system of dots of varying size, usually nearly invisible to the unaided eye, produced by interposing a cross-ruled screen directly in front of the sensitized plate or negative. Now photographs, negatives, or slides can be read into a desk-top publishing system and produce camera-ready copy with halftone illustrations included in the page layout.

HANDSHAKE A predetermined exchange between two entities in order to establish communication.

HARD COPY Printed output from a computer printer, microfilm, or typewriter.

HARDWARE Electronic components, computers, and peripherals that make up a computer system.

HARDWARE INVENTORY FILE This file contains all the computer devices that are owned by the company. All hardware items purchased and their locations will be listed on this file. Not all hardware found on the hardware inventory file will be on the approved hardware list. Hardware removed from the approved hardware list may still be retained by the firm.

IMPACT PRINTER A printer that forms an image by pressing a physical representation of the character against the paper to make an impression. The most common impact printer is the dot-matrix printer. Most impact printers utilize an inked ribbon to transfer the image, and is required for multiple carbon copy output.

INDIRECT COST Sometimes called burden costs or overhead. These costs are prorated to direct costs to determine the total cost of a product or service. Part of the indirect cost samples would be company grounds keeping, building maintenance, heat, electricity, water, etc.

INFORMAL UNIT ORGANIZATION This is the unofficial unit organization structure and culture. It also identifies the undercurrent of power within the unit.

INFORMATION SYSTEMS This is the department within a company that is responsible for computer information systems processing and the storage of all centralized data.

INFORMATION TECHNOLOGY These are the different techiques required to perform the task of information systems processing. These technology units within the information systems organization are required to be orchestrated by the information systems head.

IN-HOUSE Denotes that the task is done within the company.

INPUT DEVICE Peripheral hardware that inputs data into a computer system.

INTERFACE A shared boundary between two systems such as data communications (terminating) equipment and data terminal equipment (DTE). Also a boundary between adjacent layers of the ISO model.

INTERNET The largest network in the world. Successor to ARPANET, the Internet includes other large inter-networks. The Internet uses the TCP/IP protocol suite and connects universities, government agencies, businesses, and individuals around the world.

INVOICE A hard copy document sent in form of a bill for a given purchase order number.

I/O An acronym for input/output of data or information.

IS AUDITOR An information systems auditor. Usually working for a CPA firm as an auditor of information systems processing and storage of data.

ISO The International Standards Organization. ISO developed the milestone Open Systems Interconnection (OSI) model.

IT ASSET MANAGER The person responsible for the inventory and record keeping of all company hardware and software.

ITEMIZED BUDGET An annual unit budget based on a line item amount of money.

IT HARDWARE PERSON The person receiving shipments of computer hardware. The person will confirm that the item received is what was stated on the purchase order. The shipment will have a packing slip enclosed with the hardware which will identify the item(s) and the purchase order number that was used to place the order. This person will notify the asset manager and the party receiving the hardware that it has been received. After the hardware is confirmed to be in working order, the IT hardware person will notify accounts payable that the invoice can now be paid.

INTERNAL IT AUDITOR A person representing the company with internal information technology auditing. He/she will follow the guidelines provided by the CPA firm's auditors. They are concerned with computer systems audit trails and the security of the hardware, software and data.

ISP Internet Service Provider. An ISP is used as your local connection to the Internet. They provide other companies or individuals with access to, or presence on, the Internet.

JAZ DRIVES Jaz drives employ secondary storage cartridge that hold one or more gigabytes.

KEY CODE Copy coded by means of symbols, usually letters; insertions are sometimes "keyed" in.

KEYBOARDING The mechanism used to manually record data onto a microcomputer or terminal.

LEASED LINE A full-time link between two or more locations leased from a local or inter-exchange carrier.

LASER PRINTER A high-resolution printer that uses electrostatic reproduction technology, as do electrostatic copy machines, to fuse text or graphic images onto plain paper.

LAYOUT The drawing or sketch of a proposed printed piece; a reference to the imposition of a printed piece.

LAYOUT SHEET Form with guidelines or scales along the margins to assist the forms designer in forms layout.

LETTERPRESS A method of printing from a raised surface, such as type or metal, rubber, or plastic plates. This can be the final form of desk-top publishing output.

LIBRARY A collection of programs and data files for a computer system's offline storage.

LINE COPY Any copy suitable for reproduction without using a halftone screen. This can be a output of desk-top publishing without halftone illustrations.

LOCAL AREA NETWORK (LAN) The linkage of computers within a limited area, enabling users to exchange information and share peripherals. This can be wired or wireless.

LUMP-SUM BUDGET A unit's budget that allows the budgeted money to be spent in any fashion the unit head desires.

MAINFRAME A large computer, generally with high-level and multiprocessing power and the capacity to support many users at once.

MARGIN The blank area along any edge of a sheet that must be kept free of printing due to production considerations.

MEGABYTE (MG, M-BYTE) A unit of measure for memory or disk storage capacity. Two to the twentieth power (1,048,576 bytes).

MICROCOMPUTER Smaller computers that employ microprocessor chip technology. These can be identified as: palm type, mini-notebooks, notebooks, lap-tops, transportable, desk-top, workstations, and PCs (personal computers).

MICROCOMPUTER COORDINATOR This is an end-user person responsible for the coordination and operation of an end-user microcomputer operation. The person can have full- or part-time responsibility for this duty. The person can be hourly or salaried, and he/she can be a union or a non-union worker.

MICROCOMPUTER MANAGER A person who has the responsibility for managing and providing support and training to users of microcomputers. This person reports to IS management and most often is a full-time responsibility. It is advisable that this person be a salaried worker.

MILESTONES Used with Gantt, CPM, and PERT charting, to know when measurable units of task(s) have been completed. With Gantt charts the actual milestones can be drawn on the charts. This writer, installed one of the only two electrical/mechanical Gantt chart display systems that was "online" to 20 operations with real time displays ever installed in the USA.

MINICOMPUTER A multi-user computer, generally with more power than a personal computer yet not as large as a mainframe.

MODELING An analytical process based on mathematical network behavior formulas called models to predict the performance of product designs. The first program modeling was done for electric motor performance modeling and artificial intelligence programs for General Electric Company.

MODEM A device that converts digital to analog and analog to digital signals between computers via telephone transmission.

MODULAR PROGRAMMING A style of programming that requires that program functions be broken into self-contained units. It is a form of program segmentation and is now the prefered way to write program codes. Quick BASIC and Visual BASIC programming requires this type of program coding. This is also a good way to write a reusable coded module.

MULTIFUNCTION MACHINE A machine that can do the work of more than one online computer-attached machine. An example would be a combination of copier, fax, scanner, and printer.

MONITOR Viewing screen for computer output. It also has been called CRT(s).

NETWORK A series of points connected by communications channels. Public networks can be used by anyone; private networks are closed to outsiders.

NON-LINEAR VIDEO EDITING A system of video editing at a professional level of quality in a digital form employing a microcomputer system.

OBJECT CODE The machine readable instructions created by a computer or assembler from a source code.

OFFSET LITHOGRAPHY An adaption of stone lithography in which the design is drawn or photographically reproduced on a thin, flexible metal plate or other medium from which the design is transferred.

ONLINE A peripheral device is externally attached to a computer.

OPERATION MANUAL Operating instructions for the benefit of those who may run a given program including any restart procedures in case of program failure. Most often used by computer operators.

PACKING SLIP A document listing the contents of the shipment. It most often does not contain any pricing information, but does contain the purchase order number.

PAPER MASTER A paper printing plate used on an offset duplicator. The image is made by hand drawing, typewriter, or laser printer.

PASSWORD A security identification used to authorize users of a computer system or given program.

PDA Personal Data Assistant. A small hand-held computer used to write notes, track appointments, and otherwise keep your life in order. Early PDAs required data to be input using a keypad with keys the size of Chiclets, but more recent models (e.g., the Palm Pilot) use a combination of pen-based input and character-recognition software to accept user input. Many can also be used to send and receive e-mail and browse the Internet.

PERIPHERAL A physical device (e.g., such as a printer or disk sub-system) that is externally attached to a workstation or directly to the network.

PERT Programmed Evaluation Review Technique is a planning and control tool for defining and controlling the tasks necessary to complete a given project. The PERT chart and CPM charts are one and the same. The difference with PERT is the computing of the task time. The task is computed as the longest possible time, the shortest possible time, and four times the "normal" expected time totaled and divided by six for the expected time.

PIRATED SOFTWARE Software that has been stolen; its possession is illegal.

PLASTIC BINDING A solid-back comb rolled to make a cylinder of any thickness and inserted through slots punched along the binding side. Used for project proposals, procedures, instruction manuals, etc.

PO See purchase order.

POTS Plain old telephone service.

PRINT SERVER A device and/or program that manages shared printers as would be found in end-user work groups. Print service is often provided by the file server but can also be provided from a separate LAN microcomputer or device.

PROCEDURE FLOWCHART A flowcharting method that was originally developed for documenting manual procedures.

PROJECT SLIPPAGE This is when a project becomes late with the completion of a critical path milestone finish date. The critical path of a PERT or CPM chart determines the project completion time. Projects that are not using a PERT or CPM technology can also have project slippage. A project slippage is first known when the project finish date will be later than the planned.

REAM A package of five hundred sheets of paper.

ROM Read-only memory that is found on CDs and permanent microcomputer main memory.

PURCHASE ORDER A document sent to a vendor to place an order for a product or service. When the company has an approved D and B rating the item will be provided.

PURCHASE REQUISITION A document sent to purchasing to issue a purchase order. The purchase requisition will be required to provide information of the budget source account number.

SCANNER A microcomputer input device that copies documents into computer memory. Scanners can be page or line scanners.

SCHEMA Schema and sub schema are the defining tools used to define the structure of a database.

SERVER A network device that provides services to client stations. Servers include file servers, disk servers, and print servers.

SHIELDED TWISTED-PAIR CABLE Twisted-pair wire surrounded by a foil or mesh shield to reduce susceptibility to outside interference and noise during network transmission.

SIMULATE A technique for evaluating the performance of a network before downloading it. Simulation employs timers and sequences as opposed to mathematical models to produce network behavior.

SIGN-OFF APPROVAL The receiver of software or system has signed the approval for receiving it. IT meets his/her approval.

SITE LICENSING Procedure in which software is licensed to be used only at a particular location.

SOFT FONTS These are software fonts that are available with word processing and desk-top publishing software. There are also soft-font software packages available that can be down-loaded to word processing and desk-top publishing software. These are fonts that are available in styles and are scalable to required sizes.

SOFTWARE SITE LICENSE The software firm has sold a license for a given number of locations that the software can be used.

SOURCE CODE The written code before the program has been compiled into machine instructions.

STRUCTURED PROGRAMMING A standard that requires programs to be written in modular forms without the use of GO TO statements. Structured and modular programming have replaced "spaghetti" coding of programs.

SURGE PROTECTOR An electrical device that prevents high-voltage surges from reaching the computer system.

SYSTEMS FLOWCHART A one-page illustration depicting a system with easy to follow lines and symbols.

TAG A type of identification label attached to company-owned hardware.

TERMINAL A keyboard and display screen through which users can access a host computer.

TEXT The body matter of a page, feasibility study, or book.

THIRD-PARTY VENDOR A firm that markets hardware for manufacturers.

TIME WINDOW The time that is open from the start time to the closing time that an event may occur.

TROJAN HORSES OR LOGIC BOMBS Malicious pieces of code that lie dormant on networks or systems until they are detonated at an appointed time.

TURN-KEY SYSTEM A system in which the vendor takes full responsibility for complete system design, and provides the required hardware, software, operations manual, and user training.

TWISTED-PAIR CABLE A cable with four wires, found with telephone systems used in local area networks.

UPLOAD The transfer of data to a file, database, or file server computer.

USER FRIENDLY A computer system that is easy for persons with no computer experience to use without being frustrated or upset.

UPS Uninterrupted power source. This is a device that provides electric backup power to a computer system or other devices when the normal electric power fails. It does it so fast that the devices that depend on electricity are uninterrupted in their operation.

VISUAL BASIC A more advanced form of programming than Quick BASIC and available from Microsoft. The program operation is screen driven, which makes the program operation user friendly. It is modular programmed.

WAN Wide area network. A network extending more than a few miles. It can employ more than one form of message carrying.

WALKTHROUGH A technical review of a newly designed program or system. The review is conducted by interested parties such as programmers, systems analysts, users, and/or auditors. Program walkthroughs are conducted by peer programmers to detect program errors. A walkthrough is a situation in which people play the role of the "devil's advocate" in reviewing another person's/team's effort. It is sometimes called the "egoless" walkthrough to play down the fears of the person whose efforts are being reviewed.

WAP Wireless Application Protocol. A standard used by mobile phones and other hand-held devices to access the Internet.

WIRELESS NETWORKS A LAN system that does not require physical connections—information is transmitted through the air.

WORK SAMPLING Consists of a large number of random observations of predetermined tasks an employee or group of employees may perform. The tasks are predefined categories and the categories represent the percent of time spent for each defined category of observation.

WORKSTATION A highly intelligent terminal often found on a LAN or client/server system. Some workstations do not require floppy disk drives, because data and/or programs are down-loaded from a computer server.

WORM ATTACK A worm is a program that replicates itself over and over. A worm capable of penetrating networks could quickly overload the Internet.

ZIP DRIVE Drives that employ zip disks that carry 100 megabytes of data.

INDEX

A

Abbreviations and e-mail etiquette, 9-12–9-13
Absenteeism, 8-17, 8-31
Acceptable use agreement, 9-16–9-17
Access issues, security and:
  external access, 7-2–7-3
  Internet and e-mail, the, 9-6
  programmer's database access, 7-16
  room access, 3-20
  See also access to the Internet *under*
    Internet and e-mail, the; external
    access *under* Security
Activity log, 4-45
Administrator, systems, 5-18–5-19
Advertising:
  blind, 8-11
  classified ads, 8-11–8-12
  staff, recruiting software support, 3-66
AliMed, 3-10
Almaden Research Center, 10-11
American Express, 1-23, 1-26
American Management Association, 4-14, 8-40
Analysis and failed projects, 4-15
Ancillary support systems:
  device acquisitions, 6-25–6-26
  inventory, equipment, 6-2–6-4
    file record information, 6-3–6-4
    tagging, 6-2–6-3
  machine operations, 6-10–6-13
    key machine operator, 6-11
    posted, 6-10
    procedures, 6-11
    service desk assistance, 6-12–6-13
    supply requisitions, 6-11–6-12
  maintenance, equipment, 6-4–6-9
    budgeting, service, 6-5–6-6, 6-25
    contracting, vendor, 6-7–6-8
    in-house control, 6-4–6-5

    outsourcing legal ramifications, 6-8–6-9
    reports, service, 6-4, 6-6–6-7
  micrographics, 6-13–6-22
    archiving, document, 6-13–6-14
    forms of, 6-14–6-16
    operation procedure, 6-21–6-22
    procedure methods, 6-16–6-20
    system selection, 6-20–6-21
    training, 6-22
  policy, 6-1–6-2
    corporate position, 6-1
    objectives, 6-2
    scope, 6-1–6-2
  training, 6-22–6-24
    key operator, 6-23–6-24
    operator, 6-23
    overview, 6-22
    service desk, 6-24
    service unit, IT, 6-24
Antivirus procedures, 2-26
Aperture card, 6-15–6-16
Application controls, 8-14
  See also application controls *under* Auditing
    controls, IT
Application form, IT, 8-13
Application service providers (ASPs):
  matrixes used to compare vendors, 11-7–11-9
  policy, 11-1–11-3
    definition, 11-1–11-2
    goals/objectives for outsourcing of
      applications, 11-3
    scope, 11-1
  sample of, 11-4
  service level agreement, 11-11–11-12
  service offerings, 11-2
  vendor management, 11-11–11-12
  vendor selection, 11-3–11-10
    evaluating vendors' proposals, 11-6–11-7
    final selection process, 11-7–11-10